Dangerous Weather

FLOODS

Revised Edition

Michael Allaby

ILLUSTRATIONS by Richard Garratt

Facts On File, Inc.

For Ailsa
—M.A.

To my late wife, Jen, who gave me inspiration
and support for almost 30 years
—R.G.

Floods, Revised Edition

Copyright © 2003, 1998 by Michael Allaby

Facts On File, Inc.
132 West 31st Street
New York NY 10001

Library of Congress Cataloging-in-Publication Data

Allaby, Michael.
　　Floods / Michael Allaby; illustrations by Richard Garratt.—Rev. ed.
　　　　p.　cm. — (Dangerous weather)
　　Includes bibliographical references (p. 180).
　　　　ISBN 0-8160-4794-4
　　1. Floods—Juvenile literature. I. Title.
GB1399.A45 2003
551.48′9—dc21   2002153845

Facts On File books are available at special discounts when purchased in bulk quantities for businesses, associations, institutions, or sales promotions. Please call our Special Sales Department in New York at (212) 967-8800 or (800) 322-8755.

You can find Facts On File on the World Wide Web at
http://www.factsonfile.com

Text design by Erika K. Arroyo
Cover design by Nora Wertz
Illustrations by Richard Garratt

Printed in the United States of America

VB Hermitage 10　9　8　7　6　5　4　3　2　1

This book is printed on acid-free paper.

Contents

Preface: What is a flood?   vii

Introduction   xi

HOW WATER MOVES   1

Where floods happen   1
El Niño   7
Evaporation, precipitation, and transpiration   9
Partial pressure and vapor pressure   14
Humidity   16
How the land drains   17
Rivers   24
Why it rains more on mountainsides   25
Kinetic energy   28
Floodplains and meanders   31
The Bernoulli effect   35
Flash floods   37

RAINSTORMS   43

Storms and cloudbursts   43
Lapse rates and stability   44
Latent heat and dewpoint   46
Thunder and lightning   50
Charge separation   53

WHEN THE SEA RISES   58

Tsunamis   58
Tsunami Warning System   65

Tides   65
   Laws of motion   66
   The Coriolis effect   71
Tidal surges   73
   Air pressure—highs and lows   74

COPING WITH FLOODS   78

Monsoons   78
   Intertropical convergence and the equatorial trough   79
Aquifers, springs, and wells   84
Vegetation and natural drainage   91

FLOODS AND AGRICULTURE   98

The Nile floods and the Aswân Dams   98
Wet rice farming   106

THE COST OF FLOODS   112

Coastal erosion   112
   Glacioisostasy   113
   Isle of the Dead   114
Saltwater infiltration   120
   Osmosis   120
Flood damage   125
Floods and soil erosion   131
   Soil erosion   134
Floods of the past   137

PREVENTION, WARNING, AND SURVIVAL   145

Land drainage   145
Wetlands   150
Levees   155
Dams   161

Canalization 168

Flood prediction 171

Safety 175

Appendixes

SI units and conversions 180

Prefixes and SI units 181

Bibliography and further reading 182

Index 189

Preface

What is a flood?

It had been raining for days on end throughout most of October, and the citizens of Florence, Italy, were longing for the weather to improve. They began to hope that it might when November began with two fine days, but on November 3, the rains returned with a vengeance. In just 48 hours, 19 inches (483 mm) of rain fell on the city. It also fell in the Appenines, the mountain range that runs like a spine down the center of Italy. Water flowing off these mountains is carried away by rivers that eventually join the Arno, the river that flows 150 miles (240 km) from the mountains to the Mediterranean, passing through Florence along its way. The year was 1966.

Often, the Arno carries so little water it is almost dry, but the river is treacherous. Over the centuries it has overflowed its banks countless times, whenever heavy rain has sent water cascading down the mountain slopes, across bare, impermeable clay. On the night of November 3–4, 1966, the reservoir behind a hydroelectric dam was filling rapidly, and in order to protect the dam, workers suddenly released a great surge of water. This arrived at a second hydroelectric dam further downstream, and at about 9 P.M. on November 3, the excess water was released from the second dam into the Arno.

Down in Florence, many people had gone to bed early, so they did not see the rate at which the river level was rising. The river flooded the sewers, driving back sewage that rose up through manholes and onto the streets, then burst through walls. All the power supplies failed, and at 7:26 A.M. every electric main–powered electric clock stopped. Oil storage tanks burst open under the battering from the waters, releasing oil to mix with the mud that had been swept down from the hills. By dawn on November 4, floodwaters were flowing through the city, and they continued to flow for several hours.

The torrential rain, meanwhile, continued to fall. In some places, the dirty water was 20 feet (6 m) deep, and 100,000 people were trapped on the upper floors of buildings. Inmates at the Santa Teresa prison were taken to the roof, where they overpowered their guards although imprisoned by the swirling waters on all sides. Every road and rail line into the city was blocked. When a party sent by the government in Rome managed to enter the city at about 6 P.M., one of them described the main square, the Piazza San Marco, as a "storm-tossed lake."

When at last the waters subsided, Florence lay beneath a thick layer of mud mixed with oil. The city was renowned for its beautiful churches, museums, and galleries, which together housed some of the world's most important art treasures, and it was also the site of Italy's largest library, the Biblioteca Nazionale Centrale. All were flooded. Books and manuscripts were soaked, paintings covered in oily mud. A huge international effort was mounted to recover as much as possible from the tragedy. Eventually much of the damage was repaired.

This was one of the most serious floods of modern times but famous only because it struck at such an important cultural center. (Florence has suffered no flood since then.) Fortunately, considering the flood's magnitude, only 35 people died. But had no art treasures been at risk, the disaster would have been quickly forgotten. All floods leave behind a thick carpet of mud and slime to add to the damage caused by the water itself, but in most cases the victims are ordinary people, whose treasured possessions have little cash value. And many floods claim far more lives than the one that devastated Florence in 1966.

Mozambique and China

In late January 2000, southern Africa suffered its worst floods in 40 years. Water streamed from the sodden ground into the rivers that drain the highlands, principally the Limpopo, Changane, and Zambezi. As these great rivers made their slow way across the low-lying plains of Mozambique, where the ground could absorb no more water, they overflowed their banks, inundating vast areas. Then, on February 22, Cyclone Eline arrived, with winds of 162 mph (260 km/h) and more torrential rain. The waters destroyed about 200,000 homes and more than 500 people lost their lives.

As though that were not bad enough, the floods struck again one year later. By March 2001, more than 80,000 additional people had been made homeless and more than 50 others had died. It is not only homes that the floods destroy; they also ruin farm crops and are often followed by famine. Mozambique lost some 54,000 acres (22,000 hectares) of crops in the 2001 floods.

China has suffered severe floods throughout its long history. In 1996, for example, more than 1,500 people died in floods that were locally 20 feet (6 m) deep and that destroyed at least 2.5 million acres (1 million ha) of crops. The summer monsoon season brought more rain than usual in 1998, causing the Yangtze (Chang) River to overflow. All the valleys along the river and its tributaries were under 13–14 feet (4–4.3 m) of water. The floods covered about 53 million acres (21.5 million ha) of farmland and destroyed or damaged more than 17 million homes. More than 2,000 people may have died.

Chinese scientists blame forest clearance and poor land management for having disrupted the natural drainage patterns and increased the risk of flooding. The government has launched a major tree-planting program in order to repair the damage, but it will be some years before the rivers are brought under control. Meanwhile, the floods continue. The Yangtze overflowed again in the summer of 2002. Thousands of people were driven from their homes, and by the end of August more than 1,500 had lost their lives.

Tropical cyclones and tsunamis

The rains never arrive alone. The fierce storms that cause heavy rain also bring strong winds, and the experience of Mozambique is not unusual. Tropical cyclones—known specifically as hurricanes in the Atlantic and Caribbean, typhoons in Asia, and cyclones in the Bay of Bengal—are the most ferocious of all storms and also bring the heaviest rain, 20 inches (500 mm) in 48 hours being fairly common. A typhoon once brought more than 60 inches (1,525 mm) of rain to the Philippines.

Rain is freshwater, but the sea can also inundate coastal areas. Tropical cyclones form over the ocean, and if they cross a coast, they usually cause a storm surge, in which the low pressure makes the sea level rise and hurricane-force onshore winds produce huge waves. The most terrifying of all sea waves, however, is the tsunami, or "harbor wave," often known incorrectly (because it has nothing to do with the tide) as a "tidal wave." This arrives suddenly, traveling with immense speed, as a series of solid walls of water that demolish everything in their path.

Historically, floods have caused more damage and killed more people than any other kind of natural disaster. During the 1990s, natural disasters affected almost 2 billion people across the world. Floods and droughts between them accounted for 86 percent of these and affected 1.7 billion people. Floods may be less sensational than hurricanes and less horrifying than tornadoes, but they are far more frequent than either and are confined to no particular regions of the world. They can, and do, happen anywhere.

Introduction

Several years have passed since the first edition of this book was published. Much has happened during those years, and the decision to update the book for a second edition gives me a welcome opportunity to report at least some of the events of recent years. In doing so, I have substantially altered, expanded, and in some places rewritten the original text.

There have been more floods, of course. In July 2002, floods in eastern and central Texas were so severe, for example, that many counties were declared disaster areas and eight people lost their lives. Tragic though it was, however, it was far from unusual. There are floods somewhere in the world every year. The rising water is never far away, and no matter how the climates of the world may change in years to come, there is little chance that floods will cease to ruin homes and claim lives. Indeed, they could become worse if climate change brings heavier rain.

Climate research has also intensified in recent years. Concern over the possibility that we may be altering the global climate has stimulated funding agencies to increase the resources available for evaluating the likelihood of global warming and its consequences. If we are to understand the extent of this threat—if it is a threat—scientists need to learn much more about the ways the Sun, atmosphere, and oceans interact to produce our day-to-day weather. New discoveries are now being made at an unprecedented rate, and although there is still a long way to go before the global climate is fully understood, we are learning more about it almost every day. This new edition takes into account the most recent, relevant findings.

Updating the text has also given me the opportunity to expand the text and explanations of subjects. I have added three new chapters in which I explain storms and cloudbursts, thunder and lightning, and monsoons in more detail.

I have retained the use of sidebars to provide further discussion of a topic or information about items of interest without interrupting the main flow of the text. This edition contains many more sidebars than there were in the first edition. They explain concepts from atmospheric science, such as partial pressure and vapor pressure, charge separation in storm clouds, and glacioisostasy to why it rains more on mountainsides than it does in valleys.

Measurements are given in familiar units, such as pounds, feet, miles, and degrees Fahrenheit, throughout the book, but in each case I have added the metric or scientific equivalent. All scientists now use standard international units of measurement, but these may be unfamiliar, so I have added them, with their conversions, as appendixes.

Also new to this edition is suggested further reading for the book's main topics. All the sources appear as a complete list at the end of the book. The sources include a number of books that you may find useful but a much larger number of web addresses. If you have access to a computer, these sites will allow you to learn more about floods and about climate in general quickly and free of charge.

Furthermore, photographs from the first edition have been omitted so as to increase the number of diagrams and maps. These provide more useful information than any photograph of a swirling river or a sea of mud. My friend and colleague Richard Garratt has drawn all of the illustrations. As always, I am deeply grateful to him for his skill in translating my crude drawings into such accomplished artwork.

I am grateful, too, to Frank K. Darmstadt, my editor at Facts On File, for his hard work, cheerful encouragement, and patience.

If this "new, improved" edition of *Floods* encourages you to pursue your study of the weather further, it will have achieved its aim and fulfilled my highest hopes for it. I hope you enjoy reading the book as much as I have enjoyed writing it for you.

—Michael Allaby
Tighnabruaich
Argyll, Scotland
www.michaelallaby.com

HOW WATER MOVES

Where floods happen

The town of Bourke, in New South Wales, Australia, receives a little more than 13 inches (330 mm) of rain in an average year. The climate is dry, and Bourke is located more than 400 miles (644 km) from the sea. People in Alice Springs, a town in the Northern Territory of Australia, expect about 10 inches (250 mm) of rain a year. Over much of Australia, and especially in the interior of the country, water is a valuable resource that is used with care. But very occasionally, there is too much of it.

In the summer of 1973–74, for example, the weather was unusual: it rained heavily and persistently. Rivers rose and overflowed their banks; thousands of sheep drowned; and floodwaters covered large areas of New South Wales, Queensland, and even the vast deserts of the interior. Nothing like it had ever been known, although there had been extensive floods in southeastern Australia in the past. In 1955, for example, 40,000 people from 40 New South Wales towns were made homeless when the Macquarie, Castlereagh, Namoi, Hunter, and Gwydir Rivers overflowed. The following year, floods inundated an area 40 miles (64 km) wide, also in New South Wales, between the towns of Hay and Balranald, both on the Murrumbidgee River.

Ulaanbaatar, the capital of Mongolia, is 4,347 feet (1,326 m) above sea level and about as far from the sea as it is possible to be. It also has a dry climate, with an average of only 8.2 inches (208 mm) of rain a year, making it drier even than Alice Springs. Yet it was flooded in August 1996 when two rivers overflowed.

The 1973–74 Australian and 1996 Mongolian floods were very rare events. Although these were the kind of floods that might be expected only once in several centuries, they reiterated the fact that if a desert can be flooded, clearly floods can happen anywhere.

How floods are rated

Hydrologists, or the scientists who study the movement of water, rate the severity of floods by the probability of their occurrence. Before the Aswân High Dam was built in Egypt, the Nile overflowed its banks every year, inundating land to either side throughout much of the country (see pages 98–106). The Nile flood happened regularly, therefore hydrologists rated it a "one-year flood," meaning that people should expect this amount of flooding to happen once a year. Similarly, high tides (see pages 65–73) flood beaches regularly—usually twice a day—and are not really counted as floods, but every so often an especially high tide, driven by onshore winds, may carry water higher up the shore. If this happens fairly often, it may count as a one-year flood. If it happens less often, it may be designated a 10-year or 100-year flood. As the diagram illustrates, a one-year coastal flood may carry water some distance into the shore vegetation. A one-year flood is such a frequent event, however, that the shore vegetation comprises wetland plants that are not harmed by it. A 100-year flood, on the other hand, carries it much higher, into vegetation that is not adapted to inundation by seawater and is therefore likely to be harmed.

A flood that happens on average once a year causes little harm. Plants can cope with it, and if it affects a town or village, its frequency makes it economical to build defenses against it to protect homes and businesses, because it is cheaper to build and maintain the defenses than to bear the cost of the flood damage. Even the scale of flooding that is likely to happen only once in a century warrants measures to protect property.

The assessment is purely statistical and not a prediction. Scientists study past records and calculate the probability of a flood extending to a particular area in any one year as one chance in so many. If they reckon there is a one in 10 chance, it is called a "10-year flood." It does not mean floods of this scale will occur at 10-year intervals. The Mississippi overflowed to produce a 10-year flood in 1943 and did the same thing again in 1944, 1947, and 1953. There were further Mississippi floods in 1973, 1982, 1997 (affecting mainly the Red River and causing severe damage at Grand Forks, North Dakota), and 2001.

Shore zones. Each one faces a different flood risk.

There are other floods, however, that are expected to occur much less frequently than this. It is difficult, perhaps impossible, to provide adequate

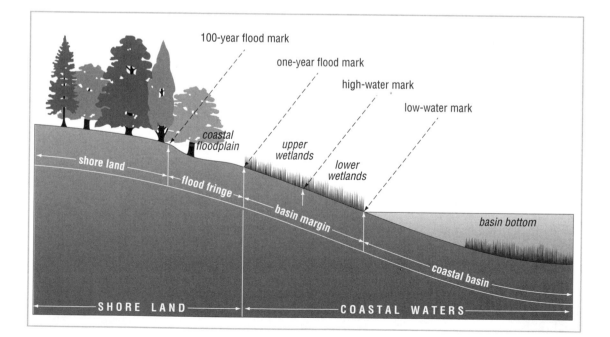

protection against an event that can be expected only once in a thousand years, or even less frequently than that. The flood that devastated the small English village of Lynmouth in 1952 (see pages 37–43) was rated a 50,000-year flood. This is not to say a similar flood occurred there 50,000 years ago (during the last ice age!), but only that the 1952 flood was an exceedingly rare event. These very rare floods cause the most damage because they are so unexpected. In 1993, the Mississippi overflowed to produce "the Great Flood," rated by some experts as a 100-year flood and by others as between a 500-year and 1,000-year flood. In January 1999, the Mary River in southeastern Queensland, Australia, flooded following what were described as the heaviest rains for a century. Houses in some parts of the town of Maryborough were submerged up to their roofs by a 100-year flood. Eastern New South Wales suffered in November 2000 from the worst floods for 40 years—a 40-year flood.

When the tide keeps rising

Unless sea walls are built to keep out the water, floods are almost bound to happen occasionally in low-lying coastal regions when seawater sweeps inland. Unfortunately, coastal areas are popular places to live, so large numbers of people live under this threat. Land along most of the Atlantic coast of the United States lies close to sea level. The map shows the extent of the low-lying coastal plain where there is a risk of flooding. Miami, for example, is only 25 feet (7.6 m) above sea level; Norfolk, Virginia, 11 feet (3.4 m); and Charleston, South Carolina, only 9 feet (2.7 m). Sea level is measured as the halfway point between the lines marking high and low tides. The tidal range, the difference in height between high and low tides, averages about 4 feet (1.2 m) along most of the southeastern coast of the United States. This means that Charleston is only about 7 feet (2 m) above the sea at average high tide; therefore, it would not take an unimaginably large rise in the tide (see pages 73–78) for the streets to be underwater.

Along much of the Atlantic coastal plain the coastline itself is sandy. People enjoy walking and playing on sandy beaches, and naturally enough, these are favorite places to build homes. Building there is unwise, however, because sandy coasts are also the most vulnerable. Sand is often unstable. Dunes move, slowly but perceptibly, and the sand barrier, called a beach berm, standing between homes and the shore may vanish. Some years ago, at Bude, a popular resort with a sandy beach in southwestern England, a storm lowered the beach by 6 feet (1.8 m) in a single night. The doors of beach chalets from which vacationers used to be able to step directly onto the sand were perched precariously, high above the beach. It is storms that build beach sand into berms, but the storms that build them can just as easily demolish them.

To add to the risk, the U.S. Atlantic and Gulf coasts lie on the track of hurricanes—tropical cyclones that develop over the tropical Atlantic, cross the Caribbean, then swing northward as they approach the American coast. Whether they cross the coast is a matter of chance, but many do and

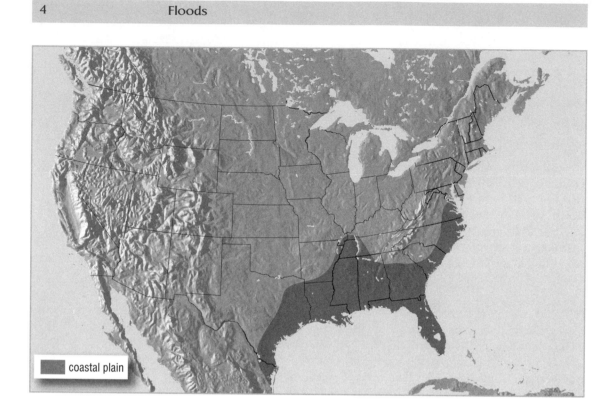

U.S. coastal plain. The low-lying land in the southeastern United States is especially at risk from flooding.

those that miss, although remaining out at sea, may still generate large waves that can cause storm surges (see pages 73–78) capable of causing flooding for a considerable distance inland.

Polders and floodplains

Low-lying coastal plains are not confined to North America, of course. They are found on all continents and such areas are always prone to flooding, even in latitudes that are too high to experience tropical cyclones. In northwestern Europe, for example, there are extensive coastal areas lying very close to sea level. The northern part of Flanders, in Belgium, is almost at sea level. In the Netherlands, 2,500 square miles (6,475, km²), amounting to 19 percent of the total land area, is really land reclaimed from the sea that forms level fields, or "polders," protected by dikes, which must be maintained constantly. At one time, the maintenance of the dikes was the responsibility of the farmers who owned the polders and knew that a breach at any point would cause widespread flooding.

The best-known story about the Dutch dikes concerns Pieter, the lock-keeper's son who sealed a hole in a dike by sticking his finger into it, thereby saving his community. In fact, "The Boy Who Saved Holland" was one of the tales in *Hans Brinker, or the Silver Skates* (1865), written by the American author Mary Mapes Dodge, who wished to teach her readers how to behave responsibly. Pieter became so famous that eventually two statues of him were erected in Holland, at Spaarndam and Harlingen. Obviously, it would take more than a finger to secure a dike that was close to breaking. The story is entirely fictitious—and American, not Dutch.

Away from coasts, the level land along the floodplain of a large river is also liable to flood, not by the migration of the meander system (see pages 31–37), but because heavy rain or melting snow far upstream loads the river with more water than its banks can hold. The Mississippi, meandering south toward the Gulf of Mexico, has overflowed many times. Rains that began in August 1926 caused it and its tributaries to inundate more than 25,000 square miles (64,750, km²) in seven states. In places, the floods were 80 miles (129 km) across and 18 feet (5.5 m) deep, and they did not recede until July of the following year. In January 1937, the river flooded again, destroying 13,000 homes, and at the end of April 1973, it inundated nearly 1,000 square miles (2,600, km²). In the summer of 1993, the overflowing Mississippi caused damage costing $12 billion in nine states, and it burst its banks yet again in April 2001. The 2001 floods affected Minnesota, Wisconsin, Iowa, and Illinois.

The Mississippi is not unique, of course, and its floods are not the worst in the world. Several Asian rivers must share that notoriety. One is the Yellow (Huang) River in China. When it flooded in 1887, the Yellow River inundated at least 1,500 towns and villages. Estimates of the number of people killed in that flood range from 900,000 to 2.5 million. In 1931, another of its floods left 80 million people homeless.

Another great Chinese river, the Yangtze (Chang), which flows 3,400 miles (5,470 km) from the Himalayas to the East China Sea, also floods. The map shows its location. Ordinarily, the Yangtze discharges less than 6 million gallons (23 million liters) of water per second, but at times this can double, causing the river to inundate a plain on either side covering 70,000 square miles (181,300 km²). This plain is home to some 250 million people, and the land there is fertile, producing a substantial proportion of the nation's grain crop. In 1931, the same year that the Yellow River overflowed, heavy rain caused the Yangtze to rise 97 feet (30 m) above its normal level. The resulting flood destroyed crops, leading to famine, disease, and a death toll of more than 3.7 million people. In the summer of 1996, the Yangtze, its tributaries, and other rivers further south caused widespread flooding in which more than 2,000 people died. Heavy rain during the 1998 and 1999 summer monsoons caused the Yangtze to flood yet again. The 1998 flood cost 4,100 lives, and more than 700 people died in 1999. Since these disasters, the authorities have allocated $16 billion for flood control and have evacuated settlements in the most vulnerable areas. Other protective measures against flooding in China include banning tree-felling and urging farmers to plant more trees. Chinese authorities have also established special army units to work on schemes to prevent flooding along major rivers and are pressing ahead with the Three Gorges Dam project to control the flow of water along the Yangtze.

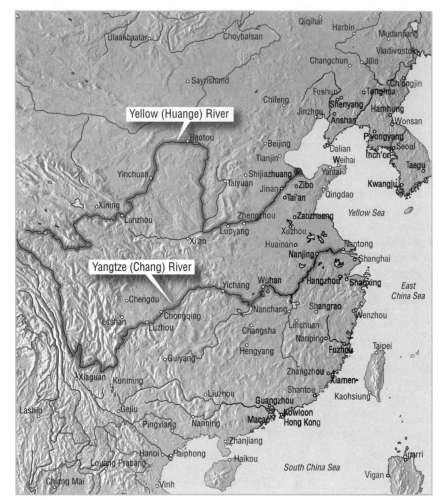

Yangtze (Chang) River. The Yangtze is China's longest river. The Yellow (Huang) River is to the north.

Deltas

Some Asian countries suffer both from rivers and the sea. Vietnam, for example, has two large, fertile river deltas. In the north, the Red (Hong) River flows into the Gulf of Tonkin, and in the south, the Mekong flows into the South China Sea. The climate is affected by the summer monsoon. Da Nang, only 10 feet (3 m) above sea level, receives almost 38 inches (965 mm) of rain in September and October. Both deltas lie close to the tracks of typhoons, the tropical cyclones that occur in the western Pacific and China Sea. In July and August 1996, the country suffered a succession of tropical storms, verging on typhoons. Hanoi was flooded when the Red River burst its banks. About 480 people, most of them children, died during floods in the Mekong Delta in 2000, and more than 250 people lost their lives when the river overflowed again in the fall of 2001.

Korea likewise suffers. In July 2001, South Korea experienced the heaviest rain in 37 years, following months of drought. The rain caused floods and triggered landslides in which at least 40 people died. At one point, a bridge over the Han River in Seoul had to be closed because the river was above the roadway. Later the same year, on October 9 and 10, heavy rain caused extensive flooding in Kangwon, the southeastern coastal province of North Korea. On October 10, 4.5 inches (114 mm) of rain fell in just two hours. It sank ships and destroyed factories.

Vietnam and Korea are often flooded, but Bangladesh is the country most severely affected in the region. All but about 10 percent of the country lies in the deltas of the Ganges and Brahmaputra Rivers, known in Bangladesh as the Padma and Jamuna, respectively. These discharge into the Bay of Bengal, a sea area where cyclones (the local name for tropical cyclones) form and move north. When the monsoon rains swell the two rivers, they merge. Consequently, floods are commonplace and many homes are built on stilts to keep them clear of the water. It is not at all unusual, and not especially serious, for houses to be isolated when the water rises around them, provided that is all that happens. All too often, however, the water washes away mud embankments that surround fields, destroying crops and drowning livestock.

Despite their protection, every year people die in floods and storms, even when the rains are no heavier than normal. If the monsoon is heavier than usual, or a cyclone causes a storm surge, the stilts are not enough protection, and the resulting disaster is often severe because the country is very densely populated. The total population is about 111 million (according to the 1991 census), and people live at an average density of more than 2,200 per square mile (850 per km²). The 1996 monsoon was heavy, and flooding began in early July. Both the Padma and Jamuna overflowed. At least a half million people were forced to leave their homes, and more than 120 died.

Low-lying coastal plains and level river valleys are where floods are most likely. Where both occur in the same place, as they do along the deltas of major rivers, it is inevitable that land will be flooded from time to time.

El Niño

At intervals of between two and seven years, the weather changes across much of the Tropics and especially in southern Asia and western South America. The weather becomes drier than usual in Indonesia, Papua New Guinea, eastern Australia, northeastern South America, the Horn of Africa, East Africa and Madagascar, and the northern part of the Indian subcontinent. It becomes wetter than usual over the central and eastern tropical Pacific, parts of California and the southeastern United States, eastern Argentina, central Africa, southern India, and Sri Lanka. The phenomenon has been occurring for at least 5,000 years.

The change is greatest at Christmastime—mid-summer in the Southern Hemisphere. That is how the weather phenomenon earned its name of

(continues)

(*continued*)

El Niño, "the Christ child," in Peru, where its effects are most dramatic. Ordinarily, the western coastal regions of South America have one of the driest climates in the world, but El Niño brings heavy rain. Farm crops flourish, but many communities rely on fishing, and the fish disappear.

Most of the time, the prevailing low-level winds on either side of the equator are the trade winds, blowing from the northeast in the Northern Hemisphere and from the southeast in the Southern Hemisphere. At high level, the winds flow in the opposite direction, from west to east. This is known as the Walker circulation, in memory of Sir Gilbert Walker (1868–1958), who discovered it in 1923. Walker also discovered that air pressure is usually low over the western side of the Pacific, near Indonesia, and high on the eastern side, near South America. This pressure distribution helps drive the trade winds, and the trade winds drive the Equatorial Current that flows from east to west, carrying warm, surface water toward Indonesia. The warm water accumulates around Indonesia, in a "warm pool."

In some years, however, the pressure distribution changes. Pressure rises over the western Pacific and weakens in the east. The trade winds then slacken. They may cease to blow altogether or even reverse direction, so they blow from west to east instead of east to west. This causes the Equatorial Current to weaken or reverse direction. Water then begins

El Niño. A reversal of pressure distribution allows warm water to flow eastward.

to flow out of the warm pool, moving eastward, and the depth of warm water increases off the South American coast. This suppresses upwelling cold water in the Peru current and deprives fish and other marine life of the nutrients brought close to the surface in the cold water of the upwellings. Air moving toward South America is warmed and carries a great deal of moisture. This brings heavy rain to the coastal region. This is El Niño.

In other years, the low pressure deepens in the west and the high pressure in the east rises. This accelerates the trade winds and Equatorial Current, increasing the rainfall over southern Asia and the dry conditions along the South American coast. This is La Niña, El Niño's counterpart.

The periodical change in pressure distribution is known as the Southern Oscillation, and the complete cycle is called the El Niño–Southern Oscillation (ENSO) event. The diagram illustrates how this happens.

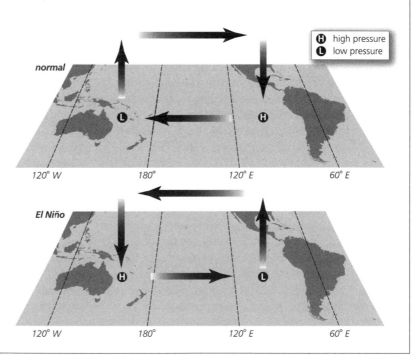

H high pressure
L low pressure

normal

120° W   180°   120° E   60° E

El Niño

120° W   180°   120° E   60° E

Evaporation, precipitation, and transpiration

Whether salt or fresh, all the water on Earth comes from the sea and returns to it in an endless cycle called the hydrologic, or water, cycle. When the floodwaters sweep through streets and homes, they may come from a river that has burst its banks, but ultimately the water that fills the river, and the rain that supplies it, come from the ocean.

The oceans are the reservoir of the planet. They cover almost 71 percent of the surface of the Earth to an average depth of a little more than 2 miles (3.2 km), and they contain nearly 330 million cubic miles (1.37 billion km^3) of water. This is all salt water, of course. In addition, the polar icecaps and glaciers contain about 10 million cubic miles (42 million km^3) of freshwater, but it remains permanently frozen, so it cannot form part of the supply that we use for drinking, washing, and many industrial processes. It is not available to plants, either. We, as well as plants, must rely on the water that is present in lakes and rivers and below the surface of dry land instead. Together, these contain a total of about 3.5 million cubic miles (14.6 million km^3), or about 1 percent of all the water on the planet, and at any one time, the atmosphere contains about 1.2 million cubic miles (5 million km^3) of water vapor and cloud droplets. Clouds are often large, but all the clouds in the world, and all the invisible water vapor in the air, together amount to no more than about 0.3 percent of all the water on Earth.

Airborne water vapor accounts for only about 4 percent of the volume (or 3 percent of the weight) of air at low level over the tropical oceans, and even less elsewhere. The water vapor content of average air below about 33,000 feet (10 km) is 1 percent by volume, and above that altitude, there are only 3–6 parts of water vapor to every million parts of air. Even when the air is at its most humid, water is only a very minor constituent.

The hydrologic cycle

As the diagram shows, water is constantly moving from the land and sea surface to the air and back again. This movement constitutes the hydrologic cycle, but the length of time an individual water molecule remains in one part of the cycle varies widely. When it enters the air, it remains there for an average of nine or 10 days before it falls as rain or snow. When it falls, it may evaporate again almost immediately, but if it falls on dry land, it may soak into the ground and enter an aquifer (see pages 87–91). It may spend only a few days there if the aquifer is not far below the surface and is made of a substance such as gravel, through which water flows easily, but there are some deep aquifers in which water can spend millions of years. A water molecule may remain in a river for only a few days, but if the river carries it into a big lake it may stay there for tens of

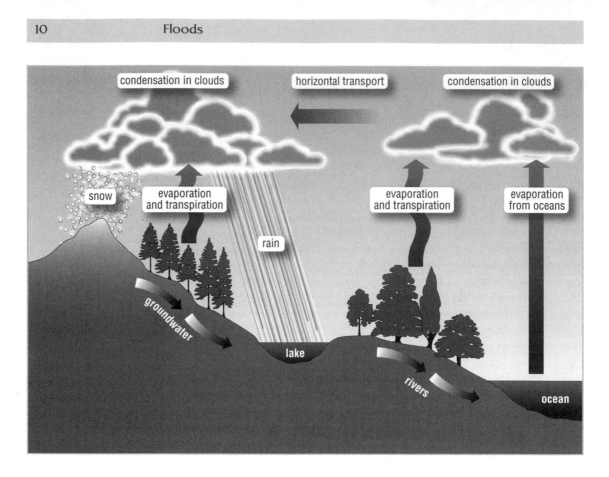

The hydrologic cycle.

years. Water that falls as snow may form part of an ice sheet or glacier. On one of the polar ice sheets, a molecule may be trapped for hundreds of thousands of years, but a small glacier will retain it for only a few tens of years. Once the molecule enters the ocean, it is likely to remain there for up to 3,000 years.

The average time a water molecule spends in one part of the cycle is called its "residence time." Except for water that is trapped in aquifers deep below ground, the residence time is proportional to the amount of water present in each stage of the cycle. The air contains little water, so molecules remain there only briefly. Ice sheets and the oceans contain much more water, so water remains in them for a long time.

The amount of water at each stage in the cycle is not completely constant. During ice ages, the ice sheets and glaciers expand to cover a much larger area than they do today. Because they then contain much more water, the residence time of water molecules in them is greater than that for the smaller amount of liquid freshwater that is carried by rivers and aquifers. Water accumulates in the ice sheets, and the amount held in the oceans decreases. Sea levels fall as water moves from one major reservoir to another. When an ice age ends and the ice sheets melt, their water returns to the oceans and sea levels rise again.

Most of the time, however, the cycle is in balance. Water evaporates. Once it is in the air the water vapor condenses to form clouds, and water returns to the surface as rain or snow. Rivers carry back to the sea the same amount of water as fell over land from clouds that formed from water evaporated over the sea. A small amount of water is lost into space from the top of the atmosphere, where solar energy breaks molecules of H_2O into hydrogen (H) and oxygen (O) and the hydrogen escapes the gravitational pull of the Earth. This loss is balanced by "juvenile water" released from volcanoes.

Precipitation is the term meteorologists use to describe water falling from the sky, regardless of whether it is liquid or solid or the size of its flakes or drops. Rain, drizzle, sleet, snow, hail, frost, dew, and fog are all types of precipitation. Most precipitation falls into the oceans, as oceans cover a much larger area than land, and it is from the oceans that most water evaporates. On average, about 210 cubic miles (875 km^3) of water (85 percent of the total evaporation) evaporate from the oceans every day, and about 38 cubic miles (158 km^3) of water (15 percent) enter the air from land by evaporation and transpiration. About 186 cubic miles (775 km^3) of this (75 percent of total precipitation) fall as precipitation over the oceans, and 24 cubic miles (100 km^3) are carried over land by the air from the oceans. About 62 cubic miles (258 km^3) of airborne water (25 percent) fall as precipitation over land. The 24 cubic miles (100 km^3) that are carried from the sea to land return to the sea through rivers.

Life on a dry planet

Obviously, no plant or animal that lives on Earth could survive without liquid water. Water is essential to all life on our planet. This does not mean that nothing at all could live on a completely dry planet, but only that anything that did live there would be very different from the living things on Earth.

We could visit such a planet, though (as long as we brought water with us), and if we did, we would find its climate was also different from any climate on Earth. There would be no clouds or rain or snow, and without them there would be no lakes, rivers, or glaciers. It would not be long before we began to notice other differences. At night the temperature would fall very low, and during the day it would rise very high. In middle latitudes the summers would be very hot and the winters extremely cold. The difference in temperature between air at the equator and air at the poles would be much greater than it is on Earth.

These differences are entirely due to the presence or absence of water. Water has a much higher specific heat capacity than rock and sand. This means that water absorbs much more heat than dry land for a given rise in its temperature—in fact, about five times more. Consequently, water warms much more slowly than dry land during the day and during summer. This affects the temperature of the air that crosses the ocean and in this way the water helps keep the land cooler than it would otherwise be. For the same reason, water also cools more slowly than land. Air crossing the relatively warm water helps keep the land warmer than it would otherwise be at night and during the winter.

When water evaporates or condenses, freezes or thaws, it either absorbs or releases heat, called "latent heat" (see page 46). This provides a mean whereby water carries warmth from the equator and into high latitudes. Evaporation at the equator absorbs heat, cooling the surface from which it evaporated. The moist air then moves away from the equator. When the vapor condenses to form clouds, heat is released, warming the air. The amount of heat that is released by condensation is equal to the amount absorbed by evaporation, so this represents the transport of heat from the equator to higher latitudes.

A dry planet would also be much windier than Earth. The huge differences in temperature between one place and another would produce equally large differences in pressure, because warm air would expand and rise, reducing surface pressure, and cold air would contract and subside, raising surface pressure. Air, as wind, moves around centers of high and low pressure at speeds proportional to the rate of change of pressure, or pressure gradient. The big temperature differences on a dry planet would produce much steeper pressure gradients than usually occur on Earth, so although the top wind speeds would probably be no higher, gales and hurricane-force winds would be much more common than they are here.

We would find conditions on a dry planet extremely uncomfortable, even if we carried with us enough water for all our needs. There would be no floods, but instead there would be huge extremes of temperature and fierce winds.

Changing phase

At the temperatures and atmospheric pressure prevailing over the surface of the Earth, water can exist in all three of its phases—as a solid, liquid, or gas. Quite often, all three are present in the same place at the same time. Over a partly frozen lake or at the edge of the polar sea ice, the solid (ice) floats on top of the liquid (water), and the air above them contains the gas (water vapor). Our weather results from the constant changes of phase, between solid, liquid, and gas, and the transport of liquid water by rivers and ocean currents and of water vapor by air movements.

Earth is the only planet in the solar system where water can exist on the surface as a liquid. Water is abundant on some of the outer planets and their satellites, such as the moons of Jupiter, but only as ice. Europa (also called Jupiter II) and Ganymede (Jupiter III) are covered in ice. Astronomers suspect that beneath the ice covering the entire surface of Europa, there may be an ocean of liquid water that might conceivably support simple forms of life, such as bacteria. Titan (Saturn VI), the largest of Saturn's satellites, has a thick, opaque atmosphere (with a surface pressure of about 1.5 bar—50 percent higher than that on Earth), but about half the mass of the satellite consists of water ice (the other half is rock). Titan's atmosphere is very dry, however, because its surface temperature, about –290°F (–179°C), is too low for water to exist in the atmosphere as vapor. Triton (Neptune I) is the largest of Neptune's satellites and 25 percent of its mass is water ice. Triton is unusual in having ice volcanoes that erupt what scientists believe to be liquid nitrogen, dust, or compounds containing methane.

Mars has water, but it is beneath the surface, and the atmospheric pressure is so low that any ice that melted would vaporize instantly—although it is likely that there were times in the past when the pressure was high enough for liquid water to exist at the surface. Venus is much too hot for water to exist except as a gas, and its atmosphere contains very little water vapor.

Boiling

If you heat pure water to about 212°F (100°C), it will vaporize rapidly. We call this "boiling," and it occurs at this precise temperature only if the atmospheric pressure is at the sea level average of 1,013.25 millibars (which is the same as 100 kPa, 29.5 inches [75 cm] of mercury or 14.5 pounds per square inch; 1,000 millibars [mb] = 1 bar). Water boils at a lower temperature at any pressure lower than this: Tibetans like to drink their tea while it is boiling hot, and they live more than 12,000 feet (3,660 m), where the average air pressure is around 660 mb. Water in Tibet boils at about 190°F (88°C). Conversely, if the atmospheric pressure increases, the boiling temperature rises.

Even at sea level pressure, it is only pure water that boils at 212°F (100°C). If any other substance is dissolved in the water, its boiling temperature rises. Water is such a powerful solvent that it never occurs naturally in a pure state. Consequently, if you boil ordinary domestic water and measure its temperature accurately, you will find the temperature is a little higher than "boiling." Seawater, for example, boils at 213°F (100.56°C).

Evaporation, condensation, melting, freezing, sublimation, and deposition

Water molecules enter the air at any temperature. The water does not need to be boiling. If you leave a bowl of water uncovered and sheltered from the rain, the water will gradually disappear from it. When a shower of rain makes the streets wet, it does not take long for them to dry again. The water in the bowl and on the street does not boil; it just evaporates. Evaporation, or vaporization, is the change of phase from liquid to gas. In order for water to evaporate, energy is needed to break the bonds that hold the molecules together. This is absorbed as latent heat.

At the surface between water and air, water molecules are constantly escaping into the air and airborne molecules are entering into the body of water. This produces a very thin layer, called a "boundary layer," of water vapor mixed with air that lies immediately above the surface (see sidebar). Whether molecules can escape from this layer into the air beyond depends partly on the force with which the air presses down on the water surface. The air pressure over a particular area, such as 1 square inch (6.5 cm²), is the weight of all the air above that area. At sea level this pressure averages 14.5 pounds per square inch (2.6 kg cm⁻²). The lower the pressure, the more readily water molecules escape into the air.

The ease with which water molecules can escape also depends on the concentration of water vapor already present in the air, because there is a limit to the amount of water vapor that air can hold. When this limit is reached, the boundary layer above the water surface is saturated, and no more water molecules can enter it unless a similar number leave. If the number of water molecules leaving the water surface precisely balances the number entering it, the boundary layer is saturated. If more molecules leave the water surface than enter it, the boundary layer is unsaturated and the liquid water is evaporating. If the number of water molecules exceeds the limit for saturation, some of the vapor condenses into liquid. Condensation is the change of phase from gas to liquid. This process releases energy.

Partial pressure and vapor pressure

The atmosphere exerts a pressure on the surface of the land and sea, as determined by the weight of the air. Air is a mixture of gases, so the pressure it exerts is the sum of the pressures exerted by each of those constituent gases. Suppose you were carrying a sack containing groceries. The total weight you were carrying would be equal to the weight of each of the grocery items plus the weight of the sack itself. In the same way, the weight, or pressure, of the atmosphere is equal to the weight of each of the gases it contains.

Air is approximately 78 percent nitrogen and 21 percent oxygen. Of the total pressure it exerts, 78 percent is accounted for by nitrogen and 21 percent is accounted for by oxygen. If the pressure is 1,000 mb (= 100 kPa, 14.5 lb. in.⁻², or 29.5 inches of mercury [Hg]), then nitrogen exerts a pressure of 780 mb (78 kPa, 11.3 lb. in.⁻², 23 in. Hg) and oxygen exerts 210 mb (21 kPa, 3 lb. in.⁻², 6 in. Hg). These are known as the partial pressures for each of the gases. Similarly, any gas that is held inside a con-tainer exerts a pressure on the walls of the container. If that gas is a mixture of other gases, then each of the constituent gases exerts a partial pressure equal to the proportion of the total mass that it represents.

Water vapor is a gas, too. As a constituent of the air, therefore, it exerts a partial pressure. In the case of water vapor, however, the partial pressure is known as the vapor pressure. Water molecules are constantly escaping into the air from an open surface of water or ice. These molecules add to those already present in the air, thus increasing the vapor pressure. Vapor pressure also drives water molecules to merge with the exposed surface. Consequently, there is a two-way motion of molecules leaving and entering the air. If the rates at which molecules are leaving and entering the air are equal, there is no net gain or loss of water vapor, and it is impossible for the density of the water vapor to increase. The water vapor is then "saturated," although we usually say the air is saturated.

Water vapor does not always condense immediately from saturated air. It condenses most readily if there are minute particles, called "cloud condensation nuclei" (CCN), onto which the vapor can turn into liquid. If suitable CCN are present, water vapor will condense before the air is saturated. In their absence, however, the air may contain slightly more water vapor than is needed to saturate it. This condition constitutes supersaturation. It is common in clouds, but seldom exceeds by more than 1 percent the amount of water vapor needed for saturation.

When the temperature falls to 32°F (0°C), liquid water solidifies to form ice; in other words, it *freezes*. It freezes at this temperature only if the water is pure, however. Substances dissolved in the water lower its freezing temperature. Seawater freezes at 28.6°F (–1.91°C), for example.

This rule applies to large bodies of water, such as the sea, lakes, and puddles, but it does not always hold true for very small water droplets. If a cloud droplet falls very slowly through very cold air, its temperature can fall to well below freezing without the droplet turning to ice. It is then termed *supercooled*. When its temperature falls to between about 5°F (–15°C) and –13°F (–25°C) a cloud droplet will freeze, but only if there is a particle, a freezing nucleus, onto which ice crystals can form. Under laboratory conditions, where air can be purified until it contains no freezing nuclei at all, water droplets can be cooled to –40°F (–40°C) before they start to freeze spontaneously.

Water can also change directly between the solid and gaseous phases without passing through the liquid phase. This is what happens when ice cubes are left too long in the freezer. The cubes grow smaller and smaller because water molecules have broken free from the ice surface and escaped into the air. The process is called "sublimation"; the reverse process is called "deposition." The latter occurs when moist air encounters a very cold surface. As water vapor comes into contact with the surface, it turns directly into ice. This is how hoar frost forms.

The amount of water vapor air can hold varies according to the air temperature. Warm air can hold more than cool air. The amount of water present in air as a proportion of the amount needed to saturate the air is called the "relative humidity" (RH) of the air. It is given as a percentage and varies with temperature. The amount of water vapor needed to saturate air (100 percent RH) at 40°F (4°C), for example, produces an RH of only 24 percent in air at 60°F (15°C). (See sidebar.) Provided the air is not saturated, water will evaporate into it from all exposed water surfaces. It evaporates from the oceans and lakes and also from the ground when this is wet.

Transpiration

Water also evaporates from plant leaves, even when they are dry. Plants absorb water through their roots and use it partly to transport the mineral nutrients they need from the ground to their living cells. These nutrients serve both as a source of hydrogen, which is used to make carbohydrates

Humidity

The amount of water vapor air can hold varies according to the temperature. Warm air can hold more than cold air. The amount of water vapor present in the air is called the "humidity" of the air. This is measured in several ways.

The absolute humidity is the mass of water vapor present in a unit volume of air, measured in grams per cubic meter ($1 g m^{-3}$ = 0.046 ounces per cubic yard). Changes in the temperature and pressure alter the volume of air, however, and this changes the amount of water vapor in a unit volume without actually adding or removing any moisture. The concept of absolute humidity takes no account of this, so it is not very useful and is seldom used.

The mixing ratio is more useful. This is a measure of the amount of water vapor in a unit mass of dry air, that is, air with the water vapor removed. Specific humidity is similar to mixing ratio, but measures the amount of water vapor in a unit mass of air including the moisture. Both are reported in grams per kilogram. Since the amount of water vapor is always very small, seldom accounting for more than 4 percent of the mass of the air, specific humidity and mixing ratio are almost the same thing.

The most familiar measurement is relative humidity. This is the figure you read from hygrometers, either directly or after referring to tables, and it is the one you hear in weather forecasts. Relative humidity (RH) is the amount of water vapor in the air expressed as a percentage of the amount needed to saturate the air at that temperature. When the air is saturated the RH is 100 percent (the *percent* is often omitted).

by the process of photosynthesis, and to make their cells and tissues rigid. This water flows through the plants constantly, and when it reaches the leaves, it evaporates through pores, called "stomata" on the surface. This process is transpiration, and it adds to the water evaporating into the air.

Although the rate of evaporation of water from the ground or an open water surface is easy to measure, the rate of plant transpiration is much more difficult to measure. It is almost impossible, however, to measure them separately in the open air; consequently, the two processes are usually considered together and called "evapotranspiration."

Clouds

When water vapor mixes with the air, it moves with it. Air over the ocean may drift across land, taking its moisture with it, and dry air over land may drift over the ocean, where water evaporates into it. Some of the water vapor is carried upward. Air temperature decreases with height, so, assuming the amount of water vapor in a given volume of air remains the same, RH increases with height. If the air contains enough water vapor, it will condense into droplets and form clouds at a certain height known as the lifting condensation level. The cloud base is found at the height where water vapor starts to condense in rising air.

Cloud droplets are so small that they fall only slowly, and those that are heavy enough to fall from the bottom of the cloud evaporate again in the drier air below the cloud base. Droplets move up as well as down, carried in vertical air currents. Most of them reach heights at which the temperature is below freezing and become ice crystals. These tend to cling to one another, forming snowflakes, but as they descend again they may enter warmer air where they melt. Most rain is snow that has melted on its way down, even in the middle of summer. As they fall, droplets collide and this can cause them to join together, like the drops that run down a windowpane, until they are large enough to fall all the way to the ground before they evaporate completely. If the air temperature throughout the cloud and beneath it is below freezing, of course, the snowflakes will not melt.

How the land drains

If you watch rain falling onto the ground, you will see that the water soon disappears. Puddles may form and little rivulets may run down slopes, but these seldom last long. When the rain stops, the ground soon dries. Where does the water go?

Some of it evaporates almost immediately, so it returns to the atmosphere as water vapor. How much of the water evaporates depends on the relative humidity of the air (see page 16), which in turn depends on the air temperature. More of the rain evaporates in warm weather than in cold weather, and water evaporates faster in windy weather than when the air is still. This is because the wind brings a constant supply of dry air that replaces moist air near the surface. Puddles that form above rock or other impermeable surfaces lose their water by evaporation.

Rainwater also flows across the surface. How much travels this way depends on the intensity of the rainfall and how long it continues, the slope of the ground, and the condition of the surface. Buildings and city streets have hard, impermeable surfaces. All water falling on them runs off them and down into drains below the streets that carry it away. This is known as storm water (even if the shower that delivered it fell far short of a storm), and the storm drains discharge it either into a treatment plant, where it mixes with sewage, or directly into the nearest river or the sea. Under certain conditions water will also run over the surface of soil. This will happen when rain falls faster than water can soak into the soil and when heavy rain batters the surface of the soil so tiny soil particles fill all the open spaces, forming a cap that water cannot penetrate. Under these conditions, the water finds the lowest parts of the surface, forming small rivulets that merge into larger ones and eventually find their way into a river.

When a river carries much more water than usual it is said to be "in spate," a term of uncertain origin but that may be derived from the Dutch verb *spuiten*, meaning "to flood." When a river is in spate, its water flows fast and turbulently, with many swirls and eddies. The water is also opaque and muddy brown in color, because of the soil it carries.

As rainwater flows over the surface of soil, it dislodges soil particles and carries them with it. By the time the water reaches the river it has gathered a considerable amount of soil, enough to color the water (see pages 131–137).

How hard does the rain fall?

Plants protect the soil surface. Much of the rain that falls on them evaporates directly from their leaves and stems and does not reach the ground. After a shower, the ground beneath shrubs is often as dry as it was before the rain, while beyond the sheltered area the ground is sodden. Water that does fall from plants falls slowly, dripping gently from leaves or running down their stems, rather than striking the surface directly.

This makes a great difference. Really heavy rain, during a thunderstorm, for example, falls with considerable force; many of the droplets are traveling at about 20 miles per hour (32 km/h). If the storm delivers 2 inches (50 mm) of rain in an hour, that rain will hit the ground with a force of about 6 million foot-pounds for every acre of surface (20 MJ per ha). (A foot-pound [ft lb] is a unit of work equal to the force needed to move a mass of 1 pound [0.454 kg] a distance of 1 foot [30 cm]; 1 ft lb = 1.356 joules [J]; 1 MJ = 1 million joules.) The droplets break clods of soil into individual particles, which can be splashed to a height of 2 feet (60 cm) and land 5 feet (1.5 m) away.

Water rarely flows across the surface of ground covered by vegetation, but it often flows across bare ground. Heavy rain on a bare hillside is likely to flow immediately into the valley below, carrying a large amount of soil with it. The clearing of plants, often trees, from hillsides has led to many floods, as well as being a cause of serious soil erosion (see pages 92–97).

Soil water

Ordinarily, the rain soaks into the ground. Soil is made of particles derived originally from rock, mixed with decaying plant and animal material. Dead leaves and twigs, the roots of dead plants, animal wastes, and the bodies of animals that have died all contribute to this material and form part of the soil, along with the vast numbers of small animals, fungi, and bacteria that feed on it.

Particles pack together closely, but there are always spaces between them. How many there are and their size depend on the size and shape of the particles. Clay particles pack together very tightly, with few spaces between them, because the particles are flat, stack one on top of another in overlapping patterns, and are very small—less than 4 micrometers (μm) in diameter (1 μm = 0.001 mm = 0.00004 in.). It would take, in other words, 5,000 clay particles, laid side by side, to measure one inch. Sand grains, in comparison, are 62.5–2,000 μm (0.002–0.08 inch) across, and their shape is irregular. Being much bigger than clay particles, there is more space between them. When soil is dry, the spaces between particles

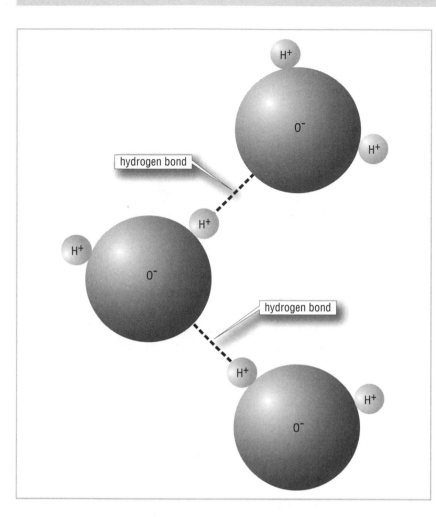

The hydrogen bond. Attraction between the positive charge on the hydrogen atoms and the negative charge on oxygen atoms forms bonds that link water molecules.

are filled with air. As water soaks downward, sinking under the force of gravity, it flows through these spaces, which fill with water.

Water molecules are polar: the two hydrogen atoms are both on the same side of the oxygen atom. Two lines drawn from the center of each hydrogen atom meet at the center of the oxygen atom at an angle of 104.5°. This arrangement leaves the molecule with a slight positive charge on the side with the two hydrogen atoms and a slight negative charge on the opposite side. The charges balance, so the molecule is neutral overall, but it has two poles. As the figure shows, this results in an attractive force between the oxygen side of one molecule and the hydrogen side of another. The attraction, known as a hydrogen bond, links water molecules to each other while the water remains in the liquid or solid phase (in the gaseous phase, water molecules move independently of each other).

Hydrogen bonds are weak, however, and if water comes into contact with other charged molecules, its hydrogen bonds will break and the water

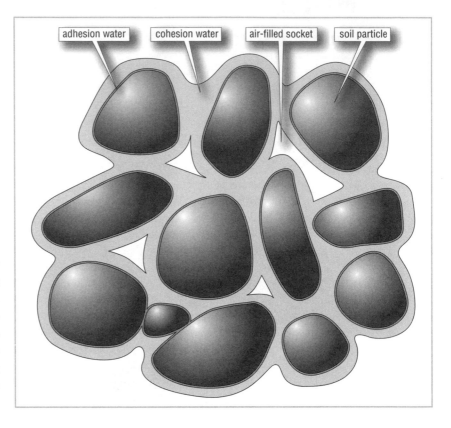

adhesion water   cohesion water   air-filled socket   soil particle

Soil water. Adhesion water forms a layer a few molecules thick that clings tightly to soil particles. Cohesion water is held together by the hydrogen bonds between water molecules; it moves more freely through the soil.

molecules will bond much more strongly to the charged molecules. Soil mineral particles have charged molecules on their surfaces. Consequently, when water enters extremely dry soil, a film of water just a few molecules thick will spread rapidly across the surfaces of all the particles it encounters. The water is adsorbed onto the surface of the particles and is then known as adhesion water. Adhesion water is very reluctant to move. It is bound firmly to the soil particles, and plant roots cannot absorb it. The only way to remove it is to heat the soil either by exposing it to hot sunlight for a long time or by placing it in an oven. When the water is adsorbed it loses energy, some of it in the form of heat. If you place some oven-dried soil in the palm of your hand and then add water to it, you can feel the warmth as its temperature rises.

Outside the layer of adhesion water, water molecules between the soil particles remain linked by their hydrogen bonds. This is called cohesion water, because the molecules stick, or cohere, to each other. Cohesion water moves fairly easily through the soil. The illustration shows how adhesion and cohesion water partly fill the spaces between soil particles but leave small pockets of air in soil that is not waterlogged.

As the drawing shows, however, soils are not always composed of particles of the same type and size. Diagram A shows a soil composed of large particles with large spaces, through which water flows rapidly. In diagram B, most of the spaces between the large particles are filled by much smaller particles, which impede the flow of water. The particles in diagram C, on the other hand, are large and also porous, so they absorb water into themselves. Water would flow easily through a soil of this kind once the particles are saturated, and because the particles retain the water they absorb, the soil would remain moist. Only after the water had drained from the spaces between particles, would the particles start to release the water they had absorbed. This would provide a continuing supply of water to plant roots.

Groundwater and the water table

Eventually all the spaces between particles will fill with water. The soil is then said to be at its "field capacity." It can hold no more water, but drainage continues as water continues to arrive from above. Still moving under gravity, the water flows down further and continues to do so until it reaches a layer of impermeable material. This may be the solid rock lying beneath the soil, or a bed of tightly compacted clay. Water cannot penetrate it, so it accumulates above it.

Above the impermeable layer is now a layer of soil that is completely saturated with water. Water fills all the spaces between its particles. Such a layer lies below all soils, even in deserts, although there it may be far below the surface. The water it contains is known as groundwater. Layers of rock or other impermeable material are rarely horizontal, so the groundwater flows downhill. It flows very slowly, because it is moving between and around soil particles. Its speed depends on the structure of the soil through which it moves. Fast-flowing groundwater might travel a few feet in a day, but through denser material or down a shallower gradient, it might move only a few feet in a month.

The soil above the saturated layer is not permanently saturated, and the boundary between the two layers is called the "water table." It marks the upper surface of the groundwater, but it is not like the surface of a river or lake, because all the water is held between soil particles, so the surface is not sharply defined.

As the diagram of underground water illustrates (see page 20), when it rains, water moves downward through the upper soil and continues to do so until this layer reaches its field capacity. Then water drains further and joins the groundwater in the saturated layer. If the rain continues, more and more water will accumulate in the saturated layer. The horizontal flow of groundwater is slow and cannot remove water fast enough to prevent the water table from rising as the saturated layer thickens. As the water table nears the surface, the upper soil layer becomes waterlogged. Eventually, surface depressions fill with water that cannot drain away, and before long there is water lying on the surface of level ground. This is one type of flooding.

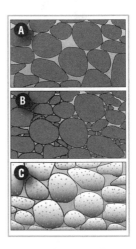

Soil particle size and drainage. A) Large particles. Water passes easily and quickly. B) Large particles with small particles among them. Water flows more slowly. C) Large particles that are porous. Water is absorbed by the particles, but surplus water passes easily and quickly.

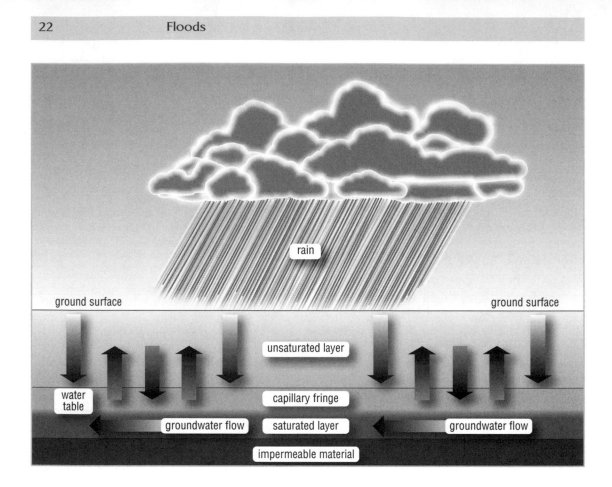

Water below ground. Rainwater drains downward through the soil, eventually reaching the groundwater. Groundwater flows horizontally, but if the rain continues, it cannot remove water fast enough, and the water table rises.

Capillarity

After the rain stops, the soil starts to dry. Water evaporates from the wet soil at the surface. This draws more water from below to fill the spaces between particles, and this water also evaporates. Eventually, the upper soil layer is fairly dry (unsaturated), and many of the spaces between particles are filled with air. Then water starts moving upward from the water table, through the capillary fringe, a layer just a few inches thick.

Capillarity, or capillary motion, is the movement of water through a very narrow passage. It is what happens when blotting paper soaks up spilled ink. In liquid water, the molecules are attracted to one another, and each individual molecule is attracted to others all around it, so the attractive force is equal in all directions. Molecules at the surface are not attracted equally in all directions, however, because there are no molecules above them. The force on them holds them to the molecules on either side and below them. This causes a surface tension, with the surface molecules held so firmly in place that they will support the weight of some insects, such as pond skaters (also known as water striders).

An undisturbed large body of water, such as a puddle or pond, has a flat surface, because gravity is the strongest force acting on it. In a small volume, however, such as a single drop, surface tension pulls the water surface into the shape that requires the least energy to maintain it. This is a sphere, the shape that has the smallest surface area in relation to its volume.

There is also another attractive force. This acts between the electric charge on water molecules (positive at the hydrogen end of the molecule and negative at the oxygen end) and the opposite charge on molecules at the surface of a solid. The figure's four diagrams illustrate the consequence of these two forces for water in a very narrow tube. Molecules are attracted to the sides of the tube and some of them are drawn up it. This gives the surface a concave shape (diagram A). Surface tension then restores the more economical spherical shape (diagram B), making the surface bulge upward (convexly). Now water molecules can move higher up the sides of the tube (diagram C), making the surface concave once more, and surface tension restores the convex shape (diagram D). Water will climb up a narrow tube in this way until it reaches a height where the weight of the column of water exceeds the attractive force between water molecules and the surface of the tube. This prevents it climbing higher. In soil, the tiny spaces between particles are like narrow tubes, but they are not all vertical. Water climbs up them by capillarity but can travel further, because where the "tube" is not vertical it supports part of the weight of the water.

Until more rain falls, water continues to be drawn upward from the saturated layer into the capillary fringe and from there into the unsaturated layer, where it rises close to the surface and evaporates. The removal of water from the saturated layer makes that layer thinner, and the water table moves downward. Below the capillary fringe, the groundwater continues to flow slowly downhill. The movement of water through the soil carries away the rain, but the soil can perform this function efficiently only provided there are plants to protect its surface and make channels below ground with their roots. On bare ground, continuous heavy rain may overwhelm its drainage capacity.

Capillarity.

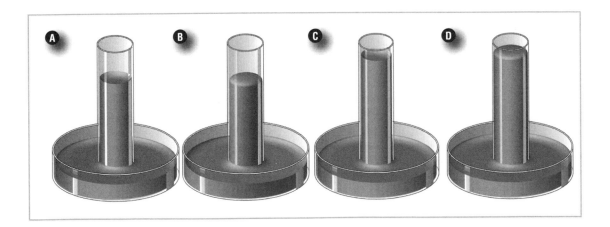

Rivers

Deep below ground, water that has drained from the surface moves slowly downhill. Hills have tops and bottoms, so there is a level at which the downward flow begins and another at which it ends. All continents and islands stand above sea level, although some areas within them may be below it, which means water flowing downhill must eventually reach this lowest possible level. Gravity ensures that water drains from the land into rivers that carry it into lakes and eventually to the sea.

Beyond the top of the hill, where the downward flow, the slope lies in another direction. Water drains in one direction down one side and in another direction down the other side. The hill down which the water is flowing is usually one of a range of hills or mountains, and the tops of these hills or mountains mark a boundary for the water draining from them, rather like the ridge of a roof. This boundary is called a "divide," because it is where the flow of water divides, some going one way and some the other. (In Britain, a divide is often called a "watershed," because it is the place from which water is shed.)

Drainage basins

Rain does not fall only on the divide, of course. As groundwater flows down from the divide, more joins it from the side of the slope. Eventually, the water reaches low ground, but beyond that more hills may rise, and water also drains from them. The entire area from which all the water drains into a particular low-lying area forms a drainage basin. This is often referred to as a watershed in the United States and in Britain as a catchment.

As water flows down the side of the watershed, with more joining it all the time, the volume of groundwater (see pages 17–23) increases and the water table rises until in some places it reaches the surface. After that, the water flows over the surface, finding its way around boulders and other obstructions along the lowest ground. It has become a stream, small at first but growing larger as more water drains into it down the sides of the channel that it makes for itself by washing away soft rock, small stones, and loose soil. Near the bottom of the watershed many small rivers combine into a single, larger river that continues eventually to the sea.

Adjacent drainage basins meet at divides on the high ground separating them, and together a system of drainage basins carries away water from an entire continent. Most of the coterminous United States, for example, is drained by the river basins of the Columbia, Colorado, Pecos, Arkansas, Platte, Red, Ohio, Missouri-Mississippi, and Rio Grande. The first map illustrates how this network covers the entire country.

Drainage basins can be very large, and their rivers, very long. In the United States, the Mississippi and Missouri Rivers, which join and form a

Why it rains more on mountainsides

When air rises, its temperature falls. Warm air can hold more water vapor than cold air can, so reducing the temperature of the air raises its relative humidity (RH), which is the amount of water vapor present in the air as a percentage of the amount needed to saturate the air at that temperature.

There is an altitude at which the RH in rising air reaches 100 percent, and the air becomes saturated. This is called the "lifting condensation level." When air rises above the lifting condensation level, its water vapor starts condensing to form clouds. When the clouds are big enough, their droplets or ice crystals merge until they are heavy enough to fall as rain or snow. No cloud forms or precipitation falls from air in which the RH is below 100 percent. This is the situation shown by diagram A in the illustration. People living on the low ground adjacent to the mountain are enjoying fine weather.

As air approaches the mountain it is forced to rise in order to cross the high ground. This is called "orographic lifting" (from the Greek words *oros*, meaning "mountain," and *graphos*, meaning "writing" or "written"). The air is dry until it is lifted above the lifting condensation level (diagram B), when cloud starts to form and precipitation begins to fall on the mountainside. The air continues to rise (diagram C) and more cloud forms. This intensifies the precipitation, but only on the mountainside; fine weather continues over the low ground.

When the rising air reaches the top of the mountain, it may continue to rise or may subside down the opposite (lee) side of the mountain (diagram D). If it continues rising, eventually it will lose enough water for precipitation to end, although cloud may extend some distance on the lee side. If the air subsides, it will sink below the lifting condensation level once more. Precipitation will then cease, and the cloud will dissipate as its droplets evaporate. The overall result is that mountainsides receive more precipitation than the low ground surrounding the mountain does.

Mountainsides receive more precipitation than the ground below does.

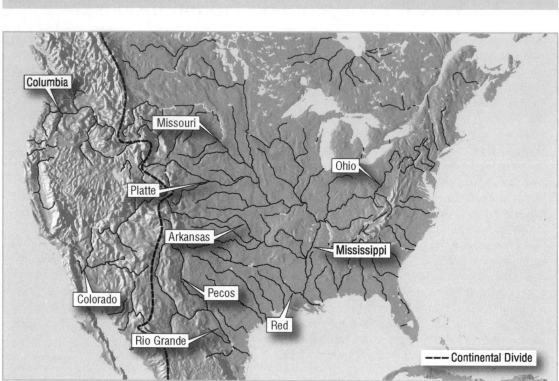

Mississippi-Missouri River basin. Together, the two rivers drain approximately the shaded area.

single river system, drain a basin of 1,243,700 square miles (3,221,183 km²). The basin extends from the Rockies in the west to Pennsylvania in the east (via the Ohio River) and the Canadian border in the north. The second map shows its approximate boundaries and location.

The combined length of the Mississippi and Missouri is 3,860 miles (6,210 km) and constitutes the third largest drainage basin in the world: averaged over the year, it discharges 620,000 cubic feet (17,546 m³) of water per second into the Gulf of Mexico. The largest drainage basin is that of the Amazon, covering 2,722,000 square miles (7,049,980 km²); the river, 4,000 miles (6,440 km) long, discharges 4,200,000 cubic feet (118,860 m²) of water into the Atlantic Ocean every second. The Congo, 2,716 miles (4,370 km) long, drains 1,425,000 square miles (3,690,750 km³) and discharges 1,400,000 cubic feet (39,620 m³) of water per second into the Atlantic. Every continent has rivers of comparable length, the longest of all being the Nile, 4,157 miles from its source to its mouth on the southern shore of the Mediterranean Sea.

The energy of a river

Always following the steepest gradient, rivers, over thousands of years, carry away material from their sides and bed, carving permanent channels. It is the force of gravity that makes rivers flow, and the steeper the slope the faster their waters move, but water is slowed by friction with the riverbed. The deeper the river, the faster it can flow, because the effect of friction is reduced in the water moving well clear of the bed, but no river can flow faster than about 20 miles per hour (32 km/h). Even so, the force of moving water is considerable. Kinetic energy, the energy possessed by a body in motion, is proportional to the mass of the body and the square of its speed (see sidebar). One gallon (3.8 liters) of (pure) water weighs 8.3 pounds (0.45 kg). Imagine standing waist deep in water flowing at 10 miles per hour (16 km/h). The water will push against you with a force of about 275 pounds (125 kg), and if the speed of the river increased slightly to 12 miles per hour (19 km/h), that force would increase to 396 pounds (180 kg). A force of this magnitude would sweep you off your feet unless you were able to hold onto something very tightly. Remember, too, that a human body is weightless when immersed in water (it has neutral buoyancy because its density is approximately equal to that of water), so if half your body is immersed, your weight is effectively halved.

As long as the flow remains constant, rivers cope well enough with the water they transport, but the flow does not always remain constant. Where the upper parts of the watershed lie in mountains above the winter snow-line, the spring thaw sends a surge of water into the drainage system. If the snowfall was heavier than usual, that surge can be big enough to make

Drainage patterns in the United States.

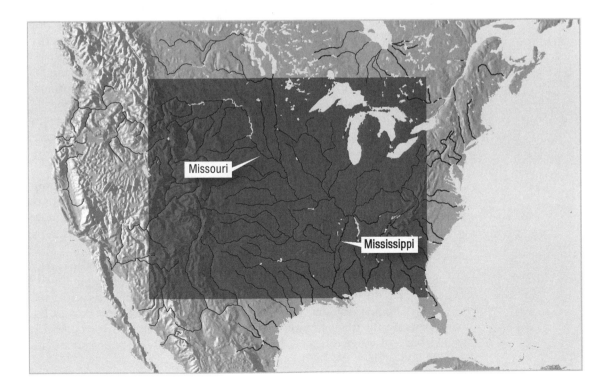

Kinetic energy

Kinetic energy (KE), the energy of motion, is equal to half the mass of a moving body multiplied by the square of its velocity, or speed. Expressed algebraically, it is $KE = \frac{1}{2}\, mv^2$.

This formula gives a result in joules if m is in kilograms and v is in meters per second. To calculate the force in pounds exerted by a mass measured in pounds moving in miles per hour, the formula must be modified slightly to $KE = mv^2 \div 2g$, in which v is converted to feet per second (ft. per second = MPH $\times$ 5,280 $\div$ 3,600) and g is 32 (the acceleration due to gravity in feet per second).

rivers overflow their banks down in the valleys, far from the mountains. This effect can be predicted by calculating the snow coefficient. This is the average depth of snow throughout the watershed, measured as a depth of liquid water (roughly one-tenth of the snow thickness) divided by the total annual precipitation.

Continental and maritime climates

Seasonal fluctuations in rainfall also alter the amount of water carried by rivers. Whether the flow increases in winter or summer depends on the type of climate in the drainage basin. Heavier summer rainfall is typical of continental climates, and heavier winter rainfall, of maritime climates. You can tell which is which by separating the total annual rainfall into two parts, for the summer (April to September in the Northern Hemisphere) and winter (October to March) periods, and dividing the summer rainfall by the winter rainfall. If the result is more than 1, the climate is continental; if it is less than 1, it is maritime; and if it is between 1 and 1.5, the climate is transitional. For Kansas City the value is 2.2, indicating a strongly continental climate, whereas Seattle is 0.3, indicating a maritime climate; New York City, meanwhile, comes to 1.0, indicating a climate that is transitional between the two.

This affects river flow. Dry summers are also warm summers. Consequently, not only is there less rain to feed the rivers, but the rate of evaporation is also higher, so less of the rain reaches the rivers. If more precipitation falls in winter than in summer, the river flow remains more constant.

The seasonal variation in flow increases greatly if the river also carries meltwater. In the Missouri, meltwater from the Rockies, beginning in spring on the lower slopes and continuing into summer as the thaw reaches higher altitudes, joins summer rainwater as the river crosses the prairies. At the time of its lowest flow, the Missouri carries 4,200 cubic feet (119 m³) of water a second, but at the time of its highest flow, it carries 900,000 cubic feet (25,470 m³) per second.

Monsoon floods

Monsoons bring the most extreme seasonal changes. Parts of Africa and North America experience monsoons, but they are most marked in southern Asia. There are two monsoons: the winter monsoon brings hot, dry winds, and the summer monsoon brings winds from the opposite direction and heavy rain. (*Monsoon* is from the Arabic for "season.") Chiang Mai, capital of Phetchabun Province in northern Thailand, receives an average 43 inches (1,092 mm) of rain a year, of which 39 inches (991 mm) fall during the summer monsoon between May and October. The 2001 monsoon caused widespread flooding throughout eight northern and northeastern Thai provinces, including Phetchabun. Despite warnings, villagers refused to evacuate their homes, and more than 110 died.

Seoul, South Korea, has an average annual rainfall of 49.2 inches (1,250 mm), of which 25.3 inches (643 mm) fall in July and August, the two peak monsoon months; flooding is likely if the rains are unusually heavy, which they often are. (See pages 78–84.) The 1999 summer monsoon, for example, caused severe flooding in both South and North Korea, as well as in Cambodia, Thailand, Vietnam, the Philippines, Nepal, India, Bangladesh, and China. A total of more than 1,500 people are believed to have died in those floods.

In August 1998, 25 inches (620 mm) of rain that fell in the course of a single night caused flooding in Seoul in which more than 130 people died. In July 1996, when 21 inches (533 mm) of rain fell in just three days along the border between North and South Korea, two towns, Yonchon and Munsan, were almost completely submerged, sending 50,000 people fleeing onto higher ground; mudslides triggered by the rains killed more than 40 people. The same monsoon rains also caused the Ganges and Brahmaputra Rivers to overflow, damaging or destroying the homes of nearly 5 million people in Bangladesh. By mid-July, 60 villages had been inundated in the state of Assam in India, and 120 camps had to be set up to accommodate 1.5 million people displaced from their homes.

In China, flooding due to the 1996 monsoon started in late June, and by July 8, the floodwaters were 20 feet (6 m) deep in parts of the provinces of Zhejiang, south of Shanghai, and Hunan, in southeastern China. Those floods killed more than 1,500 people, injured or damaged the property of 20 million people, and destroyed at least 2.5 million acres (1 million ha) of crops. In the region of 8 million, soldiers and civilians were mobilized in rescue operations and to strengthen the dikes and flood walls along the banks of the Yangtze. The Chinese government estimated the damage caused by the floods at about $12 billion.

When a large river is severely overloaded, the effects are felt in its tributaries. Water flows as best it can, and with great force. That force is sometimes sufficient to push back the water flowing in tributaries, causing them to overflow as well.

Ice dams and rainstorms

It is not only monsoon climates that make rivers burst their banks. The Lena River flows northward through eastern Siberia, from Lake Baikal to the Laptev Sea. The map shows its location. In winter, the Lena freezes over. The winter of 2000–01 was unusually cold over much of the Northern Hemisphere and especially in Siberia, where during a cold spell that lasted several weeks, temperatures fell as low as –58°F (–50°C), and the river froze solid. In spring, melting snow in the south always increases the amount of water carried by the river, but in May 2001, this water became trapped behind huge blocks of ice that formed a dam. Almost the whole of the town of Lensk (population 27,000) was inundated, and although many people were evacuated, others were trapped on rooftops. The floods next

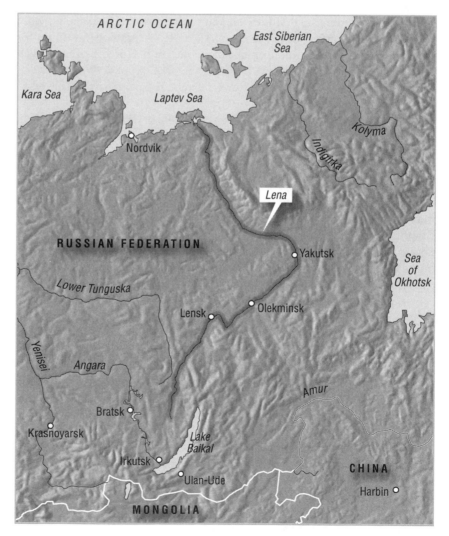

Lena River, Siberia.

threatened the city of Yakutsk (population 200,000), 525 miles (845 km) to the northeast of Lensk. Russian warplanes bombed the ice to break up the dam and allow the water to escape, but then fog settled over the area, grounding the bombers and helicopters. Floods covered nearly half of the city, but the bombing finally prevented the situation from becoming even worse. As well as Lensk and Yakutsk, the 2001 floods also affected the Siberian cities of Kirensk, which was completely submerged, and Ust-Kut, where 80 percent of the buildings were under water. Lensk had previously been flooded in 1998, but the 2001 floods were the worst in a century.

Heavy storms can cause flooding anywhere. While Asia suffered torrential monsoon rains, 11 inches (279 mm) of rain fell in southern Quebec in two days in July 1996, and about 200 miles (322 km) north of Montreal, the Saguenay River and its tributaries burst their banks. Tents had to be used as emergency shelters for about 3,000 of the 12,000 people evacuated from La Baie area for fear that dams might burst, inundating towns. (Two tents were also provided for cats and dogs.) Italy also suffered, when storms caused flooding in the area around Lake Maggiore on July 7 and 8.

Water flows along the easiest route, wearing away soft material and skirting harder rocks. That is how river channels form, and their size is determined by the volume of water they usually carry. A sudden, large increase in that volume causes flooding, but the underlying principle holds firm. Water flows downhill, along the easiest route, even if that route sometimes takes it across fields, along streets, and through homes. Floods are entirely natural, but no less destructive for that.

Floodplains and meanders

Water always flows downhill. The steeper the hill, the faster it flows, and the faster the water flows, the more energy it possesses. In fact, it possesses this energy even before it starts moving. The water that is held behind the dam wall in a high-level reservoir possesses energy, even before the sluice gates are opened, when the surface may be still except where it is rippled by the merest breath of wind. It is potential energy, energy that is waiting to be applied. The potential energy of water held at a high level is called the "hydraulic head" of the river into which it flows (it is also known as the elevation potential energy). The hydraulic head is proportional to the mass of the water and its height above some lower level, such as a valley floor or sea level.

Potential energy is the energy that a body possesses by virtue of its location. Any object has potential energy if it is raised above a surface to which it may later fall. A book on a shelf has potential energy. If someone knocks it down, it will fall to the floor. Its motion, from shelf to floor, converts its potential energy into kinetic energy (energy of motion), and its kinetic energy is transferred to the floor when it lands (see page 000). The floor absorbs the energy and becomes warmer, but by an amount too small to measure.

Rivers, unlike books dropping from shelves, do not fall directly. Their journey is more akin to the one you experience when you ride downhill on a bike. You may start at the top, with just enough push to set you rolling, but by the time you reach the bottom, your speed depends on how long and steep the hill is. In the same way, if you want to know how fast a river will flow, you need one more item of information in addition to the mass of the water. You need to know how far the water travels horizontally while it descends vertically. In fact, you need to know the gradient of the riverbed.

River gradients

High in the mountains, where most rivers begin, gradients are usually steep, because near the summit the mountainsides are steep. The water falls a long way down the mountainside while traveling only a short distance horizontally. Consequently, the water has a great deal of energy. There is not much water, however, and mountains are made from rocks that are not easily worn away, so although the river may be a torrent, it is a torrent that cuts only a narrow channel between hard rocks.

By the time it reaches the plains, far from the mountains, the river carries much more water because of the many smaller rivers that have joined it as tributaries along its route and the groundwater that has entered it below the ground. Here, though, the gradient is much shallower. The river travels a long way horizontally for only a small vertical drop. It slows, and because of its additional volume of water, its channel widens.

Where the gradient is very shallow, the water hardly descends at all as it moves forward, and the river is not contained between banks made from hard rock, eddies may influence its course. Small irregularities in the bank or bed start water swirling, so it does not flow smoothly. Watch any river and you will see eddies and even little whirlpools. This type of flow is said to be "turbulent," and a smooth flow in which all the water is flowing in the same direction at the same speed is called "laminar."

The Büyük Menderes River

Turbulent flow can cause a slow-moving river to follow a very curvy path. The Büyük Menderes River in western Turkey, for example, twists and turns many times as it approaches the Aegean Sea, into which it discharges its waters. In some places, its curves are so extreme that the river actually turns back on itself and almost forms a circle. The map shows just how much it winds. Büyük Menderes, or simply Menderes, is its modern name, but the ancient Greeks knew it as the Maeander. The word *meander* in English derives from the Latin *maeander*, which the Romans adopted from Greek to describe this kind of twisting and turning river course.

A meandering river flows over soil rather than hard rock. It also carries soil, the silt and particles of various sizes that have washed into it and its tributaries further upstream. Because it flows slowly, the water has less energy than it had when it flowed over steeper gradients. When a river

Büyük Menderes River, Turkey. Called the Maeander in ancient times, this river gave us the word meander.

loses energy, it also loses its capacity for transporting solid particles, so some of this suspended material falls to its bed. Accumulating steadily over thousands of years, this raises the bed, making the river shallower and therefore wider.

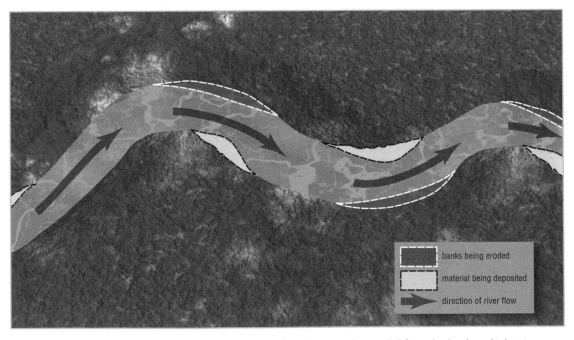

	banks being eroded
	material being deposited
	direction of river flow

How meanders form a floodplain. At the outside of each bend, material is eroded from the banks, which is in turn deposited on the inside of each bend.

How a river builds its floodplain

When flowing water follows a curved path, however, not all the water flows at the same speed. The water on the outside of the curve has further to travel than water on the inside of the curve, but it has only the same amount of time in which to do so because all the water must emerge from the bend together. Consequently, the water on the outer part of the curve flows faster. Flowing faster, it has more energy and therefore is able to carry more suspended material. It erodes the bank against which it flows, but not by battering it. Battering would pack the soil particles closer together and strengthen the bank. Rather, it pulls particles out from the bank—as though sucking them out—and then carries them downstream. This is typical behavior of any liquid or gas flowing through a constriction, as discovered more than two centuries ago by the Swiss mathematician and scientist Daniel Bernoulli (see sidebar).

Under the Bernoulli effect, material is eroded from the bank on the outside of each bend, so the bend itself moves outward. At the same time, because the water on the inside of the bend moves more slowly and has less energy, some of the suspended material it carries is deposited there. As the diagram shows, the bends tend to become more extreme. As a result, there is a second effect: once the pattern of meanders is established, the continuing erosion on one side and the depositing of sediment on the other moves the entire system of meanders forward. The pattern remains more or less the same, but it advances. The land over which it advances is then a floodplain, bounded by the extreme limits of the widest meander.

Types of floodplain

The floodplain is covered with fine-grained soil deposited by the river and through which the river continues to cut its channel. Soil transported by rivers is called "alluvium," and on floodplains the upper layers of soil are alluvial. Ordinarily, soil is composed of mineral particles derived from the underlying rock, but alluvial soils are unrelated to the rock beneath them, because they have been carried to their present location. Alluvial soils are often very fertile, as they accumulate plant nutrients that have drained into the river over its entire length. This fact, combined with the level surface of the area, makes floodplains attractive to farmers and builders. Floodplains are often intensively farmed and densely populated.

Unfortunately, a floodplain is a dangerous place to live. Although the meander system advances only slowly and leaves plenty of time to adjust to the changing position of the river, the rivers are shallow, because of the large amount of material they deposit on their beds, and a sudden surge of water from upstream will make them overflow their banks. Floodplains can and frequently do experience sudden floods that destroy crops and

The Bernoulli effect

In 1738, the Swiss mathematician Daniel Bernoulli (1700–82) published a book entitled *Hydrodynamica*. In it he showed that when the speed of the flow of a fluid (liquid or gas) increases, the pressure within the flow decreases. He reached this conclusion while studying the flow of water through a pipe from one tank where the water level was high to another where it was lower. In the end, of course, the water level is the same in both tanks, but while the water is moving, Bernoulli found the pressure within the flowing stream is related to the speed with which it flows. This is summarized as $p + \frac{1}{2}rV^2$ = a constant, where p is the pressure, r the density of the fluid, and V its velocity (speed). Because the expression $p + \frac{1}{2}rV^2$ is a constant, if

one of the terms in the expression changes one or more of the other terms must also change to compensate; however, the density (r) of a moving fluid is unlikely to change, so pressure (p) is directly related to speed (V). If the pressure increases, the velocity must decrease and vice versa.

If, for example, the fluid flows through a tube with a constriction in it—assuming the fluid is not compressed, which would increase its density—one might logically assume that the rate of flow must increase at the constriction, because the same volume of fluid must pass there in a given time. According to Bernoulli's equation, however, the pressure must *decrease* at the constriction, which is indeed exactly what happens.

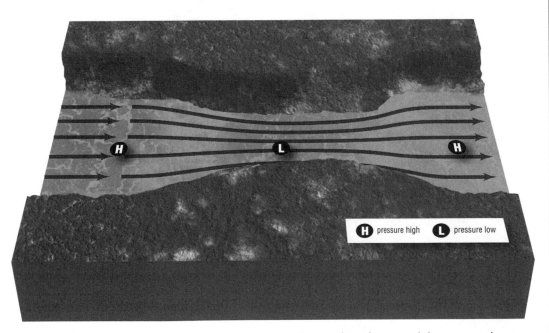

H pressure high   L pressure low

The Bernoulli effect. When a fluid flows past a constriction, the speed accelerates and the pressure drops.

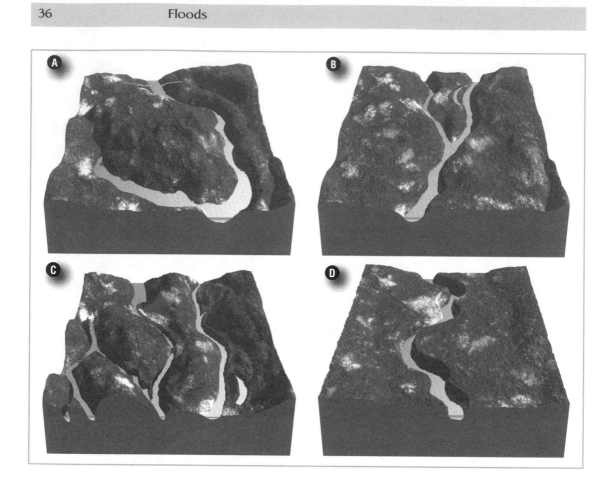

River meanders. The diagrams show the types of floodplains that meandering rivers develop on four different landscapes.

homes. In Bangladesh, where most of the country is low lying, such flooding is common and usually catastrophic.

Drawing A in the illustration shows a floodplain of this type. The main river flows across a level valley with high ground to either side. Smaller rivers flowing along channels cut through the high ground join it as tributaries and some of these have produced smaller floodplains of their own. As you see, the width of the floodplain is determined by the widest meanders.

This is but one kind of floodplain; there are others. Drawing B shows a river much like the Mississippi. It meanders so slowly across such a wide plain that some sections of meanders have become isolated from the main flow. When a meander becomes so extreme that there is only a short distance between the two sides of the loop, the river may cut a new channel across the narrowest part of the meander. This creates a new, straighter channel and leaves what had been the loop in the meander isolated as a curved, sometimes horseshoe-shaped stretch of water known as an oxbow lake. The river may also divide into two or more channels that diverge and rejoin in a braided pattern.

In some places, the ground may be very broken, with many humps. This kind of landscape, shown in drawing C, is most often found where glaciers have retreated, leaving behind a moraine of boulders and gravel, heaped up in mounds. Here, the river divides repeatedly, weaving around the humps with many channels, each of which produces its own small floodplain.

Although meander patterns often remain fairly constant for a long time, they can also change dramatically. This can result in a river with meanders that are apparently much too small for the floodplain they have made, as illustrated in drawing D. In fact, though, the changing course of the river has carried the meanders first to one side of the plain and then the other.

Living on the floodplain

Regardless of its precise pattern, a meandering river is not to be trusted. The fertile soil it deposits across the even surface of its floodplain tempts farming communities, but the river may overflow its banks with little warning, inundating fields and homes. Such flooding is entirely natural. It allows the river to release excess water onto surrounding land, from which it can drain. This makes it difficult, and sometimes hazardous, to prevent flooding on floodplains (see pages 155–161).

It is possible to contain a river by enclosing it between banks that are so high and so solid the river can neither overflow nor breach them. This makes life safe for the dwellers on the floodplain, but there is a price to pay for such security. Water must go somewhere and when a river carries much more water than usual—due to very heavy rain or melting snow in the mountains, for example—it will naturally overflow onto low-lying land. Floodplains serve as "sponges" to absorb floods, and by absorbing them, they prevent them from happening elsewhere. If the river is confined so as to prevent flooding on the floodplain, the additional water inevitably raises the height of the river upstream. Protecting the people living on the floodplain, therefore, simply increases the risk to which people living upstream are exposed. Many scientists believe the only way to prevent this type of flood damage is to advise people not to settle on floodplains.

Flash floods

Lynmouth and Lynton are twin coastal villages in Devon, southwestern England. Lynton lies to the west and Lynmouth to the east of Lyn Mouth, where the Lyn River meets the sea (see map). The Lyn is a single river for only a very short distance. It is formed, a short distance inland of the two villages, by the meeting of two smaller rivers, the East Lyn and

West Lyn. Between them, these rivers drain about 38 square miles (98 km²) of Exmoor, an upland moor and present-day national park. Exmoor is fairly high, and on its northern side it forms a plateau, called the Chains. From there, the two Lyns fall through narrow, wooded valleys 1,500 feet in only 4 miles (458 m in 6.4 km) before joining and then plunging further to the sea.

The villages attract many tourists, as do the sandy beach, the moorland behind the villages, and the beauty of the steep valleys. This is Lorna Doone country, the setting of the romantic novel written by R. D. Blackmore in 1869, a literary association that adds to the area's popularity. In the first two weeks of August 1952, however, vacationers were not having a good time. The weather was miserable. The rain was not constant but was often heavy, and thoroughly soaked the ground up on the moor. On Friday, August 15, the rain was persistent, and the sky so dark that the lights were on in many of the houses. That evening, the rain intensified. In the course of 24 hours, 9.11 inches (231.4 mm) of rain were recorded at one place and 7.58 inches (192.5 mm) at another. Most of the rain fell between eight in the evening and one in the morning on August 16. It was estimated later that by then approximately 3.4 billion tons (3.1 billion

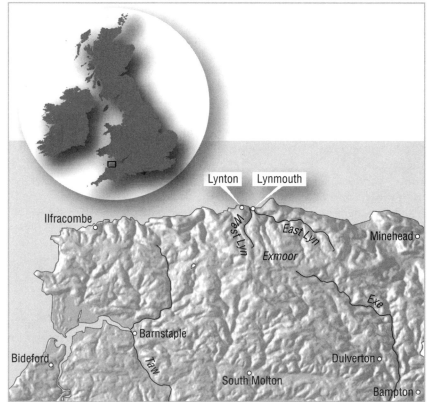

Lynton and Lynmouth on either side of the Lyn River.

metric tons) of rain, equal to 815 billion gallons (3,087 billion liters), had fallen onto the area drained by the two rivers.

At 7:30 P.M. on August 15, the hydroelectric plant supplying power to the area was overwhelmed when the canal feeding water to it turned into a raging torrent. At 9 P.M., the diesel emergency system also failed. Lynmouth and Lynton were in darkness, while the two rivers were carrying so much water that on occasion it built into waves 30 feet (9 m) high. Such a force of water—at times amounting to 23,000 cubic feet (651 m^3), or 575 tons (522 metric tons), per second—falling down a very steep incline dislodged huge boulders, then rolled them forward. In all, about 200,000 cubic yards (153,000 m^3) of boulders, soil, and other debris were washed downstream. For a time, the valley of the West Lyn was blocked by fallen trees, but water pressure built up behind the dam and finally burst through it, sweeping the trees downstream. That was when most of the damage occurred, as the surging water destroyed stone bridges and demolished houses.

The following morning, when the villagers emerged to inspect the scene, boulders weighing up to 15 tons (13.6 metric tons) each covered the beach and about 40,000 tons (36,320 metric tons) of them were piled up in Lynmouth itself. Altogether, 93 houses had been damaged beyond repair or swept out to sea, 132 cars had been washed into the sea, and debris littered the beaches for miles on either side of Lyn Mouth. The flash flood had killed 34 people. It was rated a 50,000-year flood (see page 6–8), although the Lyn had never been known to behave that way before, so there was no previous flood with which to compare it. Nor has it flooded since. Lynmouth has now been rebuilt and is once more an attractive and popular resort.

Taken by surprise

Flash floods always happen suddenly, and it is the element of surprise, combined with the violence they can sometimes attain, that makes them so dangerous. It is easy to understand why they happen but very difficult to predict them. In the case of the Lynmouth flash flood, prolonged rain over the drainage basin of the two rivers had delivered water faster than they could carry it away. The water table had risen, and the land was thoroughly sodden. The rivers were flowing strongly, their levels high, but at this stage they showed no indication of being about to overflow their banks. Then, a single rainstorm dumped yet more water and tipped the balance. The mechanism is simple. What was difficult was predicting the storm that triggered the flood. It was very local and lasted for only a few hours. Had it delivered its rain only a mile or two away it would have fallen over the sea or over a larger drainage basin, and there would have been no flash flood.

Southern West Virginia suffered a similar fate in July 2001. Heavy rains had fallen sporadically for two months, saturating the ground, and there had been several flash floods in the area and across the state border in northern Kentucky. Then, on Sunday, July 8, nearly 8 inches (203 mm) of rain fell in a series of storms. The Guyandotte River is ordinarily 6 inches (15 cm) deep at Corinne, but the storm water increased the depth to 20 feet (6 m). Elsewhere, the river rose to equally alarming levels. Drivers were stranded on mountain roads, and police had to block access to the town of Mullen, where red mud had filled the roads and poured into buildings. A school bus was completely immersed in water, and some mobile homes floated downstream. When the rain ceased, the small town of Kimball was left with shop fronts wrecked and caked with mud. Altogether, approximately 3,500 homes in West Virginia had been damaged by water or mud. Bridges had been demolished and roads left covered with mud. Amazingly, only one person died in West Virginia and three in Kentucky.

The flood stage is the river depth or rate of flow over a particular stretch at which the National Weather Service issues a flood warning. The maximum amount of water a river can carry without overflowing is known as its bankfull flow. When the river is carrying its bankfull flow, it is at its bankfull stage, which is usually the same as its flood stage. The difference between them is the purpose for which they are used. *Bankfull stage* is a term used by scientists and engineers studying rivers; *flood stage* is the term used by meteorologists issuing flood warnings.

Flash floods in dry climates

The land does not need to be soaked for flash floods to occur. If the land is dry, it is rather the intensity of the rainfall that causes the flooding. Water falls to the ground much faster than it can soak into the soil, so it flows directly into previously dry gullies, turning them into fast-flowing, turbulent rivers channeling vast amounts of water into the low-lying ground where people are most likely to have their homes. This is what happened on September 2, 1996, around the town of al-Geili in Sudan. Two hours of heavy rain caused flash floods that destroyed rail lines, bridges, and many houses. The flood left 15 people dead and thousands homeless.

Algiers, the capital of Algeria, receives about 30 inches (762 mm) of rain in an average year. More rain falls in winter than in summer, and around 5 inches (127 mm) usually falls in November. November 2001 was different, however. It began with a drought that had lasted several weeks; water had even been rationed since the middle of October. Then, about 5 inches fell in a 24-hour period beginning on November 9. Muddy water rushed waist high through the city streets. Buildings were demolished in Bab el-Oued, a densely populated, working-class district, leaving many people buried beneath rubble. Others drowned when they were trapped in their cars. Homes that had been constructed unofficially in dry riverbeds collapsed as the suddenly sodden ground swelled beneath them, and the rubble was then washed downstream into the city. More than 750 people lost their lives. The cleanup involved shifting nearly 71 million cubic feet (2 million m^3) of mud.

Whether the ground is wet or dry, a big storm that brings enough rain in a short enough time will cause flooding. Rain of this required intensity is often called a "cloudburst." Before the storm arrives, the air is warm and moist (in Lynmouth, for example, it was summer and had been raining, although it is the air that should be moist, not necessarily the ground). If the sky starts to clear, high-level cloud gradually covers it. This is the "anvil" at the top of the storm cloud and extending a long way in front of it. More usually, the sky is already cloudy or hazy and just becomes a little darker. Any wind that has been blowing may cease, because air is now being drawn into the base of the storm cloud, canceling out the wind. This is the "calm before the storm."

It then grows much darker (in Lynmouth they turned on lights in the middle of the day). This is because the cloud now overhead is densely packed with water droplets and reaches to a height of 35,000 feet (10.7 km) or more, blocking out the sunlight. Next, the wind starts again and the sky lightens (although in Lynmouth it was evening by then). Overhead, the cloud now consists mainly of water drops, much bigger than cloud droplets and less opaque, and falling in the downdraft of air from the cloud which produces the wind. With a cloud of this size there is often lightning and thunder as well (see pages 43–49).

Landslides and mudslides

Enough water rushing down a steep hillside will dislodge rocks and soil, so in a flood, it is not only the water that people fear but also the landslides and mudslides. In two days in July 1996, 20 inches (508 mm) of rain fell along the border between North and South Korea. In this area, the South Koreans had built military barracks into the steep hillsides. A mudslide caused by the rain buried more than 20 soldiers in one of these barracks, and landslides and mudslides engulfed three other units, one an air force base, as well as several guard posts. In North Korea, the floods destroyed much of the rice crop.

A week later at Biescas on the Spanish side of the Pyrenees, the mountain range between France and Spain, more than 70 vacationers died in a flash flood at a crowded campsite and trailer park. Light rain that suddenly turned into a torrential cloudburst sent floodwater, rocks, and mud through the Vírgen de las Nieves site. Cars, tents, campers, and trailers were carried away in the swiftly flowing rivers of mud and rock, and trees were torn from the ground and scattered. Rescuers said that the scene, when they arrived, was like a battlefield.

At the same time as the Biescas flash flood, Jhagraku, a remote village about 55 miles (88 km) northeast of Katmandu, Nepal, was also being devastated in the same way. The rains triggered landslides that carried away dozens of homes and killed at least 40 people.

Such events are common, and there was nothing unusual about the summer of 1996. In addition to the floods in Korea, Spain, and Nepal, between June and August there were flash floods and landslides around

Lake Maggiore, Italy; a mudslide buried a house in the La Baie area of Quebec; and flash floods caused widespread damage on either side of the Saguenay River, 200 miles north of Montreal. At Buffalo Creek, Colorado, the South Platte River overflowed suddenly, destroying a bridge and two roads. Near the Italian ski resort of Cortina d'Ampezzo, landslides and mudslides filled homes with rocks and mud, and in southeastern England a flash flood left parts of Folkestone, in Kent, under 6 feet (1.8 m) of water.

There are floods of this kind every year. In January 2000, at least 28 people died in floods and landslides caused by heavy rain in southeastern Brazil. On May 21, more than 20 died in the same way in Colombia, and nearly 60 died in northeastern Brazil in late July and early August. Europe did not escape that year, either. Flash floods caused a mudslide in Calabria, Italy, on September 10. It destroyed a campsite, killing more than 12 vacationers. In the middle of October, heavy rains caused floods and landslides in the Italian and Swiss Alps. Northern Tanzania, in East Africa, suffered its heaviest rains in eight years in December; the resulting floods killed more than 30 people.

The Putnam flood

When flash floods sweep through towns they always cause a huge amount of damage, but sometimes there is one that is even more devastating than most. The Lynmouth tragedy in England has its many equivalents around the world. In August 1955, Putnam, Connecticut, suffered a similar disaster.

A manufacturing town, with a population then of upward of 8,000, Putnam lies on the Quinebaug River, which divides the town into two parts connected by three bridges. Rainstorms delivered 4 inches (102 mm) of rain, and a week later the dying remains of a hurricane added a further 8 inches (203 mm) in 24 hours. Upstream of Putnam there was a series of old dams. The increased water flow built up behind the first, broke through it, and carried debris from it to the second. One by one the dams collapsed, releasing a wall of water moving at up to 25 miles per hour (40 km/h) and throwing waves several feet high over the riverbanks. As it swept through the town, the river carried away all three bridges, many roads including the main street, and railroad tracks, and damaged about one-quarter of all the buildings. It also caused huge explosions when it washed through a warehouse stocked with barrels of magnesium. This exploded on contact with the water, and the river carried blazing barrels downstream.

It was a week before the flood subsided and the extent of the damage could be assessed. The cost was estimated at $13 million; fortunately, no lives were lost. The emergency services had acted swiftly to evacuate people as soon as there was a risk of the dams failing.

Large rivers in the lowlands can and do overflow, but they do so gently. The rising waters give warning. It is small rivers, carrying water a short distance down steep slopes, that are most likely to be overwhelmed by a sudden increase in the volume of water flowing into them and cause devastating flash floods.

RAINSTORMS

Storms and cloudbursts

Only one type of cloud can deliver enough rain fast enough to cause a flash flood; it is called a "cumulonimbus," and it is a monster. A big cumulonimbus, with a base just a few hundred feet above the ground, can tower to a height of 60,000 feet (18.3 km), or even higher. The top of the cloud is sometimes called a "thunderhead"—and with good reason, for this is the cloud that produces thunderstorms.

As one of these giants moves overhead, the sky darkens. Streetlights, fitted with electronic devices to detect low light levels, may switch on. People will glance nervously upward. The cloud contains water, some liquid and some frozen, and that is all it contains. Water and ice are more or less transparent, so why is the cloud so dark?

To solve that riddle, you must imagine yourself out in space, looking down on the storm from above. The cloud will be easy to recognize because of its size and "cauliflower" top. It will be brilliantly, dazzlingly white. You have probably seen satellite photographs of clouds like this, and you may have flown above cloud in a plane, although you will not have flown above a giant cumulonimbus, because pilots are very careful to avoid them. The cloud is bright because it is made from ice crystals and water droplets that reflect sunlight. Obviously, reflected sunlight cannot reach the ground below the cloud, so the cloud shades the ground. The bright part is only the top of the cloud, however, and although much of the light is reflected, some penetrates deeper. Down inside the cloud the light strikes more ice crystals and water droplets, so it is also reflected. Not all the light is reflected upward. Much of it is reflected to the sides, where it strikes other crystals or droplets and is reflected again. How many times the light is reflected depends on the density of the crystals and droplets in the cloud. The denser the cloud, the more of the incoming light that is scattered in all directions and that is prevented from reaching the ground below.

The darkness at the bottom of the cloud, the side you see from below, is an indication of the amount of water through which light must pass. Meteorologists refer to the amount of light that is intercepted in this way as the optical depth, or optical thickness, of an atmospheric layer or a cloud.

How a storm is born

Warm air is less dense than cold air. This means that any given volume of warm air contains fewer air molecules than does a similar volume of cold air. Since it contains fewer molecules, the warm air has less mass. In other words, warm air is lighter than cold air, volume for volume, so the denser air sinks beneath it, forcing the lighter air to rise.

When air rises it expands and cools. The rate at which it cools is known as the lapse rate (see sidebar). What happens next depends on whether the air is stable or unstable. If it is stable, the rising air will cool faster than the air surrounding it, making it denser too, and it will sink back to its former level. Unstable air, in contrast, cools more slowly than the surrounding air. As it rises, it is always warmer and therefore less dense than the air around it, so it continues to rise. If the air remains unstable all the way from the surface to the tropopause, the boundary between the lower (troposphere) and upper (stratosphere) atmosphere, it is said to be "absolutely unstable." Air can also be conditionally unstable. Conditional instability occurs when stable air is forced to rise, for example by crossing high ground, cools sufficiently for its water vapor to start condensing into cloud, and condensation releases latent heat (see sidebar) that warms the air, causing it to continue rising. More vapor condenses, releasing more latent heat, and so once the air has been made unstable by being forced to rise, it remains unstable.

Lapse rates and stability

Air temperature decreases, or lapses, with increasing height. The rate at which it does so is called the "lapse rate." When dry air cools adiabatically (without exchanging heat with the surrounding air), it does so at about 5.5°F for every 1,000 feet (10°C per km). This is known as the dry adiabatic lapse rate (DALR).

When the temperature of the rising air has fallen sufficiently, its water vapor will start to condense into droplets. This temperature is known as the dewpoint temperature, and the height at which it is reached is the lifting condensation level. Condensation releases latent heat, which warms the air. Consequently, the air cools at a slower rate, known as the saturated adiabatic lapse rate (SALR). The SALR varies, but averages 3°F per 1,000 feet (6°C per km).

The actual rate at which the temperature decreases with height is calculated by comparing the surface temperature, the temperature at the tropopause (about –67°F [–55°C] in middle latitudes), and the height of the tropopause (about 7 miles [11 km] in middle latitudes). The result is the environmental lapse rate (ELR).

If the ELR is less than both the DALR and SALR, rising air will cool faster than the surrounding air, so it will always be cooler and will tend to subside to a lower height. Such air is considered absolutely stable.

If the ELR is greater than the SALR, air that is rising and cooling at the DALR and later at the SALR will always be warmer than the surrounding air. Consequently, it will continue to rise. The air is then absolutely unstable.

If the ELR is greater than the DALR but less than the SALR, rising air will cool faster than the surrounding air while it remains dry, but more slowly once it rises above the lifting condensation level. At first it is stable, but above the lifting condensation level it becomes unstable. This air is conditionally unstable: it is stable unless a condition (rising above its lifting condensation level) is met, whereupon it becomes unstable.

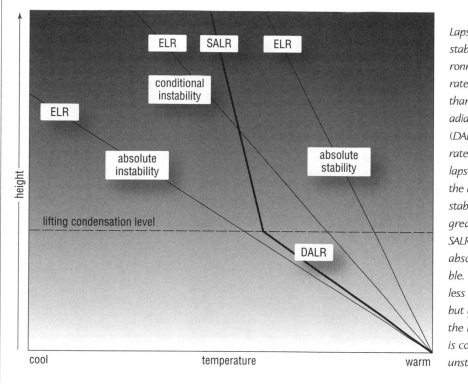

ELR SALR ELR

conditional
instability

ELR

absolute
instability

absolute
stability

lifting condensation level

DALR

height

cool   temperature   warm

Lapse rates and stability. If the environmental lapse rate (ELR) is less than both the dry adiabatic lapse rate (DALR) and saturated adiabatic lapse rate (SALR), the air is absolutely stable. If the ELR is greater than the SALR, the air is absolutely unstable. If the ELR is less than the SALR but greater than the DALR, the air is conditionally unstable.

Cumulonimbus storm clouds form only in very unstable air. The ground or sea surface must be warm, which is why storms occur late in the day more often than in the morning. Storms can also occur after dark, when the top of a growing cloud cools, allowing air below to rise further. In addition, the air must be very moist, and something must start it rising. Many storms in the United States are caused when warm, moist air drifting northward from the Gulf of Mexico moves beneath warm, dry air over the continent and then is lifted as advancing cold air from the north undercuts it. Both the dry and moist air rise, and it is when the instability in the moist air becomes sufficiently vigorous to break through the cap of overlying dry air that huge storm clouds form. Storms also occur along cold fronts, where a wedge of cold air is moving beneath a mass of warm, moist air.

The growth of the storm cloud

As the rising air reaches a height at which its temperature is low enough for its relative humidity to reach 100 percent, water vapor starts to condense into droplets (see sidebar, page 16). This marks the base of the cloud. Inside the cloud, warm air is rising, drawing in more air from below

Latent heat and dew point

Water can exist in three different states, or phases: as gas (water vapor), liquid (water), or solid (ice). In the gaseous phase, molecules are free to move in all directions. In the liquid phase, molecules join together in short "strings." In the solid phase, molecules form a closed structure with a space at the center. As water cools, its molecules move closer together, and the liquid becomes denser. Pure water at sea level pressure reaches its densest at 39°F (4°C). If the temperature falls lower than this, the molecules start forming ice crystals. Because these have a space at the center, ice is less dense than water and, weight for weight, has a greater volume. That is why water expands when it freezes and why ice floats on the surface of water.

Molecules bond to one another by the attraction of opposite charges, and energy must be supplied to break those bonds. This energy is absorbed by the molecules without changing their temperature, and the same amount of energy is released when the bonds form again. This is called "latent heat." For pure water, 600 calories of energy are absorbed to change 1 gram (0.035 ounces) from liquid to gas (evaporation) at 32°F (0°C) (expressed as 600 cal g^{-1}, or 2,501 joules per gram—joules [J] are the units scientists use). This is the latent heat of vaporization, and the same amount of latent

heat is released when water vapor condenses. When water freezes or ice melts, the latent heat of fusion is 80 cal g^{-1} (334 J g^{-1}). Sublimation, the direct change from ice to vapor without passing through the liquid phase, absorbs 680 cal g^{-1} (2,835 J g^{-1}), equal to the sum of the latent heats of vaporization and fusion. Deposition, the direct change from vapor to ice, releases the same amount of latent heat. The amount of latent heat varies very slightly with temperature, so this should be specified when the value is given. The standard values given here are correct at 32°F (0°C). The diagram illustrates what happens.

Energy to supply the latent heat is taken from the surrounding air or water. When ice melts or water evaporates, the air and water in contact with them are cooled, because energy has been taken from them. That is why it often feels cold during a thaw and why our bodies can cool themselves by sweating and allowing the sweat to evaporate.

When latent heat is released by freezing and condensation, the surroundings are warmed. This is very important in the formation of the storm clouds from which hurricanes and tornadoes develop. Warm air rises, its water vapor condenses, and this warms the air still more, making it rise higher.

Warm air is able to hold more water vapor than cool air can, and the amount of water vapor

the cloud base. Provided the incoming air is moist enough to provide a continuous supply of water vapor, the process continues. Condensation releases latent heat, warming the surrounding air and making it rise more. This cools it again, causing more condensation and more warming of the surrounding air, and the air rises still further so that each surge of incoming air raises the top of the cloud higher.

This is the first stage in the development of the storm, sometimes called the "cumulus stage." The cloud is growing, and within it, the air is moving vertically upward. The updrafts are moving at up to 100 miles per hour (160 km/h), which is why pilots avoid storm clouds. So far, there is no precipitation falling from the cloud.

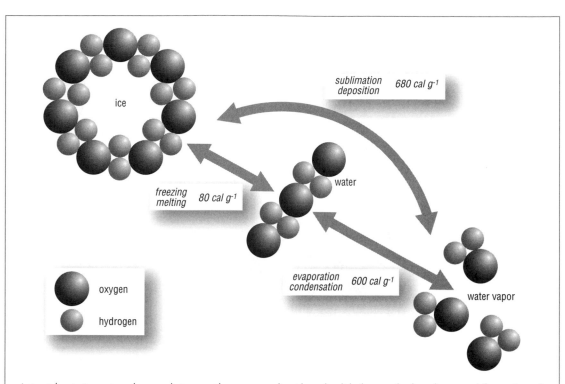

sublimation
deposition   *680 cal g⁻¹*

ice

freezing
melting   *80 cal g⁻¹*

water

oxygen

hydrogen

evaporation
condensation   *600 cal g⁻¹*

water vapor

Latent heat. As water changes between the gaseous, liquid, and solid phases, the breakage and formation of hydrogen bonds linking molecules releases or absorbs energy as latent heat.

the air can hold depends on its temperature. If moist air is cooled, its water vapor will condense into liquid droplets. The temperature at which this occurs is called the "dew point." It is the temperature at which dew forms on surfaces and evaporates from them.

At the dew point temperature, the air is saturated with water vapor. The amount of moisture in the air is usually expressed as its relative humidity (RH). This is the amount of water present in the air expressed as a percentage of the amount needed to saturate the air at that temperature.

Eventually the air rises to a height beyond which it cannot rise, because it is at the same density as the air above it. This level marks the cloud top. In a storm cloud, where the rising air currents are very vigorous, the top of the cloud is so high that water vapor changes directly into ice, forming tiny crystals. In its final dissipating stage, when upward movement has almost ceased, high level winds sweep some of these from the top of the cloud, forming the anvil shape often seen at the top of large cumulonimbus storm clouds.

The crystals fall slowly, but as they do so, they grow at the expense of liquid droplets. In the upper part of the cloud, these are supercooled to just below freezing temperature. Water evaporates from them and is deposited on the ice crystals. When they reach a level where the air is warmer, the crystals melt. Melting absorbs latent heat, cooling the air and making the air sink further, and friction between the droplets and air drags cold air downward. The movement of air inside the cloud also draws in cold air from outside, a process called "entrainment," and this air is also dragged downward.

The cloud then contains both updrafts and downdrafts, as shown in the drawing. Falling water droplets collide and merge with one another, like the drops that trickle down a windowpane. They grow larger, but only the heaviest of them continue falling all the way through the cloud and out

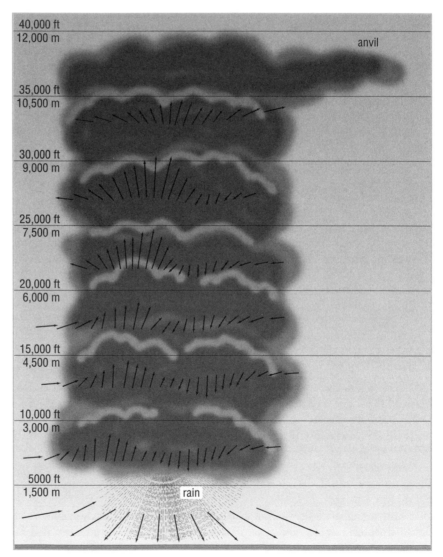

Air currents in a storm cloud.

of the base, as rain. If the temperature is below freezing throughout the cloud, ice crystals remain frozen and as more ice is deposited onto them they grow into snowflakes. When they are too heavy to be supported by the updrafts, they fall from the cloud as snow. The other raindrops and snowflakes are picked up again by updrafts and swept to a higher level, from where they start their descent again. The cloud is now mature, and heavy precipitation is falling from it.

Storm clouds always give a warning when the rain, snow, or hail is about to start falling: the downdrafts arrive ahead of the water. They hit the ground as strong, cold gusts of wind that spread to the sides, so they blow in all directions. Eventually, however, the updrafts and downdrafts conflict. The downdrafts suppress the updrafts. This robs the cloud of the mechanism by which it grew and sustained itself. Usually, the rain will continue for a time as the cloud dissipates and vanishes. A cumulonimbus cloud rarely survives more than an hour or so, but if the conditions that produced it continue, another will form to take its place.

Cloudburst

With some clouds, however, the end is more dramatic, although it all happens too quickly for it to be possible to identify the individual short-lived cloud that will die violently. In this case, the updrafts cease, so there are only downdrafts, and the cloud collapses, releasing all its water droplets. This is what produces the extremely heavy shower dubbed a "cloudburst," and if the cloud was very large, the rain may continue for some time.

There is a lot of water to release. A fully developed, large cumulonimbus cloud may contain 250,000 tons (227,000 metric tons) of water or more. If all of that water falls over an area of 10 square miles (26 km²), it will amount to almost 40 tons per acre (90 metric tons per hectare). That is equivalent to 4 inches (102 mm) of rain, and as one cloud collapses, another is likely to be forming, so the rain continues.

How much rain or snow can a single storm deliver? Most deliver no more than an inch or two of rain, but you must multiply this by 10 to convert rainfall into an equivalent amount of snow. There are exceptions, however. On the night of July 31–August 1, 1976, a storm over Big Thompson Canyon, Colorado, dropped more than 12 inches (305 mm) of rain in six hours. That storm sent a wall of water 30 feet (9 m) high surging through the canyon, killing more than 130 people. On July 18, 1942, a storm at Smethport, Pennsylvania, dropped almost 31 inches (782 mm) of rain in four and a half hours, and almost 43 inches (1,092 mm) fell on the French island of Réunion, in the Indian Ocean, on February 28, 1964, in the space of nine hours.

Cloudbursts can also be spectacular. At Guadeloupe, in the West Indies, 1.5 inches (38 mm) of rain fell in one minute on November 26, 1970.

Thunder and lightning

Around the world, there are about eight flashes of lightning every second. In the United States, the ground is struck by lightning some 30 million times a year. Most thunderstorms happen in summer, but if they were spread evenly through the year, this would amount to one lightning strike every second. Only one lightning flash in every five travels between a cloud and the ground, so the actual number of lightning flashes over the United States is around 150 million a year.

When lightning does strike the ground, it can do a great deal of harm. Lightning kills about 100 Americans every year, as well as causing damage to property costing about $40 million (in insurance claims) and destroying timber worth around $50 million. Lightning causes damage because it releases a huge amount of energy. The electric charge that causes the spark we see as a lightning flash builds up to an average of about 20 coulombs (C). (The coulomb is the scientific unit of electric charge equal to the quantity of charge transferred in one second by a steady current of 1 ampere.) The flash, traveling at up to 10 miles (16 km) per second, carries a current averaging 30,000 amperes and often much more, and the temperature inside the flash reaches about 50,000°F (28,000°C). That is five times hotter than the visible surface of the Sun. Lightning, for example, can cause a tree to explode, because the strike heats the water inside the tree so strongly that it vaporizes instantly and expands with so much force that it shatters the wood and other plant tissue around it. It is not a good idea to stand beside a tree during a thunderstorm.

You would not think it possible to survive being struck by lightning, and, indeed, most victims are killed instantly, but not all of them. Some have survived. Roy Sullivan, a ranger in Yosemite National Park, California, was struck by lightning in 1969, and it only singed his eyebrows. In 1972, he was struck again, and this time it set his hair alight. Lightning seemed attracted to him, because it hit him a total of seven times. He survived them all and died in his bed in 1983. A farmer in New York State who was struck by lightning while driving his tractor survived the strike. A short while later, the ambulance taking him to hospital was also struck by lightning, which made it crash, and the farmer died of injuries inflicted in the accident. On occasion, British policemen (bobbies) have also fallen victim to lightning strikes, as some wear helmets with metal spikes that act as lightning conductors (helmet designs vary from one local police force to another).

Huge cumulonimbus clouds often produce thunderstorms as well as rainstorms, although the two can occur separately. A nimbostratus cloud—a low-level, gray, featureless cloud that produces steady rain or snow—will also generate lightning and thunder occasionally.

What is lightning?

Forked lightning is seen as a jagged flash between the base of a cloud and the ground or an object on the ground. Sheet lightning is a brilliant white flash that seems to have no focus. The latter usually lasts for about 0.2 second and is caused either by a flash between two regions inside a cloud, or between two clouds at a place that is hidden from view.

Thunderstorms are usually accompanied by heavy rain or snow, but not always. Sometimes the air below the cloud is very dry, and precipitation falling from the cloud evaporates before it reaches the ground. Lightning that accompanies such conditions is called "dry lightning" and is often the cause of forest or brush fires, because it happens when plant material on the ground is very dry. Heat lightning is silent as well as being dry. It illuminates whole clouds and is red or orange in color. This is lightning produced by a storm that is too far away for its precipitation to be visible. It is also too far away for its thunder to be audible. All lightning emits white light made up of all the colors of the rainbow, but air scatters blue light, so when light travels a long distance through the air most of the blue is lost, leaving the red and orange. Sunsets are often red or orange for this reason.

Hot lightning, not to be confused with heat lightning, earns its name from the forest fires it ignites, while cold lightning does not. Lightning is a series of electric sparks in rapid succession. In hot lightning, the current is sustained for long enough to heat dry plant material sufficiently for it to catch alight. Cold lightning consists of an interrupted current. It can explode trees, but not set them on fire.

What happens during a lightning flash?

A flash of forked lightning, sparking between a cloud and the ground, lasts for less than a second and looks like a single event. It may seem to flicker very slightly, however, and this is a clue to what is happening. High-speed photography has revealed the whole story: a lightning flash is not one event, but at least three and often more, separated by about 50 milliseconds and each one lasting about 0.2 second. Cameras recorded one flash that consisted of 26 separate strokes. The sequence of events is illustrated in the drawing.

First, electric charges separate inside the storm (see sidebar), and the negative charge in the lower part of the cloud induces a positive charge on the ground below (A in the illustration). This is static electricity, an electric charge that is not flowing, like the charge you can accumulate if you slide the sole of a leather shoe across a nylon carpet on a dry day, or stroke an inflated party balloon against the sleeve of your sweater. The charge cannot flow because air is a good electrical insulator and blocks it. Eventually, though, the accumulated charge becomes so large that it overcomes the resistance of the air. That is when it sparks between regions of opposite charge.

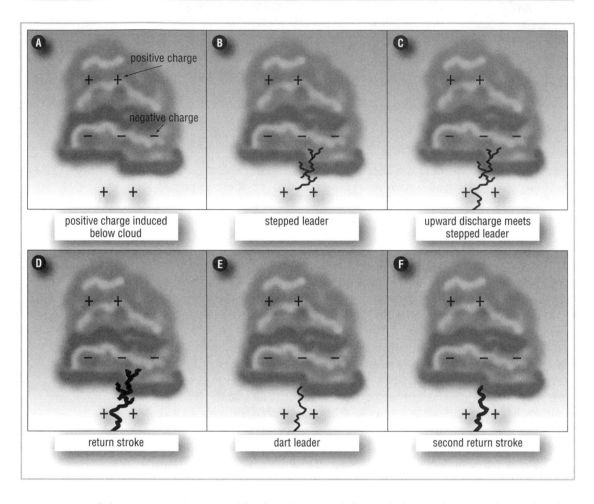

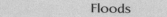

Stages in a lightning flash.

A stepped leader (the initial flow of charge that sets the path other parts of the flash will follow) emerges from the base of the cloud (B in the drawing). Traveling at about 60 miles per second (100 km per second), it follows a branching path downward, jumping in steps that give it its name. As the negative charge moves downward, the positive charge on the ground intensifies, and electrons (particles with negative charge) are freed from air molecules along the path of the stepped leader. An atom or molecule that has gained or lost electrons is said to be "ionized." Ions carry electric charge, and the stepped leader creates a path of ionized air about 8 inches (20 cm) in diameter, the width of a lightning stroke.

As it nears the ground, the stepped leader is met by an upward discharge from the positively charged surface (shown in C). This short-circuits the cloud to the ground, and it follows the shortest route across the resistant air, from the point closest to the cloud that is also in contact with the ground. It will leap from the top of a tall tree, a high building, or any other structure.

Charge separation

A lightning flash is an electric spark, and like any flow of electric current, it travels between two regions of opposite charge. These regions form inside cumulonimbus, and occasionally nimbostratus, clouds in snowstorms, dust storms, and in the clouds of material ejected by volcanic eruptions.

In a cumulonimbus storm cloud, positive charge usually accumulates near the top of the cloud and negative charge near the bottom. There is also a small area of positive charge, of uncertain origin, at the base of the cloud. The drawing illustrates this distribution of charge.

Scientists are uncertain just how this separation of charge occurs, but probably several processes are involved. Some separation may be due to the fact that the ionosphere, in the upper atmosphere (above about 37 miles [60 km]), is positively charged, and in fine weather the surface of the Earth is negatively charged, with a steady, gentle downward flow of current. This means it is possible that a positive charge is induced on the underside of cloud droplets (by the negative charge below) and a negative charge on their upper surfaces. If the droplets then collide in such a way as to split them, the charges may separate. It is also possible that falling cloud particles may capture negative ions.

The most important mechanism is believed to occur when water freezes to form hail pellets. A hailstone forms when a supercooled water droplet freezes. This happens from the outside inward. Hydrogen ions (H^+) then move toward the colder region, so the hailstone contains a preponderance of H^+ in its outer, icy shell and of hydroxyl (OH^-) in its liquid interior. As freezing progresses, the interior of the hailstone expands, bursting the outer shell. This releases tiny splinters of ice carrying positive charge (because of the H^+). Being so small and light, these splinters are carried to the top of the cloud by updrafts. The heavier hailstone centers, with their negative charge (OH^-), sink to a lower level.

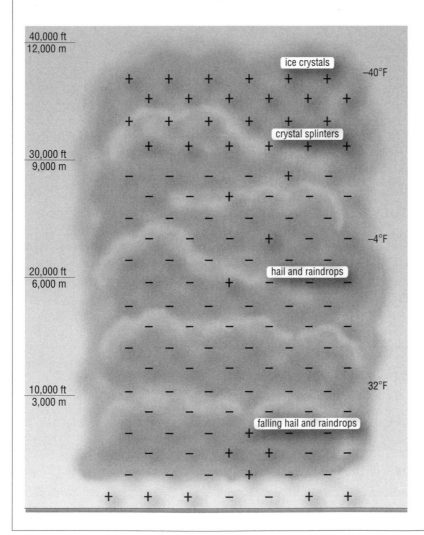

Charge separation inside a thunderstorm.

This is immediately followed by the return stroke (drawing D), which travels at about 60,000 miles per second (100,000 km per second) and is brilliantly luminous. This is the flash that we see. It is called the return stroke because it propagates upward. As the positive ions gather electrons, more electrons move downward from a higher level, so the upward return stroke accelerates the downward flow of electrons, but the luminosity of the stroke travels upward.

The return stroke neutralizes the lower part of the cloud to a height of about 3,300 feet (1 km) and deposits a strong negative charge on the ground. It is followed by small streamers of lightning inside the cloud that reestablish the negative charge near the base and induce a fresh positive charge on the ground. A dart leader then emerges from the cloud, following the ionization path established by the first stroke (drawing E). It is followed by a second return stroke (F).

This description applies to most lightning flashes, and their effect is to reduce the negative charge in the lower part of the cloud. These are called "negative flashes." It can happen, though, that the usual distribution of charge is reversed, so there is an accumulation of positive charge at the base of the cloud. In these cases, lightning lowers the positive charge in the lower part of the cloud in a series of positive flashes. On average, 96 percent of lightning flashes are negative, and 4 percent are positive.

Very occasionally a tall structure or even a space rocket immediately after launch can trigger a stepped leader that travels upward from the ground to the cloud. Aircraft flying through electrified clouds can trigger lightning in this way.

Thunder

A lightning flash happens very fast, and the energy it carries heats the air. The temperature at the center of the return stroke is about 50,000°F (28,000°C). Air expands when it is heated and when it is heated as strongly as this and as fast, the expansion is huge and very rapid. In fact, the air around the lightning stroke explodes.

As the air expands, it compresses the adjacent air. This generates a series of compressive waves that propagate outward in all directions from the center of the expansion. Our ears are sensitive to compressive airwaves. We recognize them as sound. Thunder is the sound of the explosion caused by lightning.

We hear an explosion as a loud bang, which is what thunder sounds like, but only if the storm causing it is directly overhead. If the storm is farther away, thunder makes a rumble rather than a bang.

Why does thunder rumble?

Sound waves travel at about 770 miles per hour (1,238 km/h) in air at 68°F (20°C), and all of them travel at the same speed. As the illustration shows, however, not all the sound waves produced by a lightning flash travel the same distance to the ear of the person who hears them. The flash originates inside the cloud and continues downward along an irregular path all the way to the ground, and it makes the air explode over the entire length. Sound from the base of the cloud, high above the observer's head, has farther to travel than sound starting at a lower level. Consequently, the sound from the lower level, with the shorter distance to cover, arrives first to the ear.

It is true, of course, that the sound at the top of the flash is produced before the sound lower down, but this makes no difference. The flash travels at speeds measured in miles per second—thousands of times faster than the speed of sound—so in effect all the sound from the flash is produced at the same moment, and the distance it travels is all that matters. The sound is produced along the whole of the flash, so it arrives as a continuous series of waves, a rumble.

That is not quite the whole story, however. The flash travels so fast that our eyes see it as almost instantaneous. This would appear to indicate that the thunder should occupy no more time than the flash, and we should hear it as a slightly prolonged bang and not as a deep, menacing rumble. It rumbles, nonetheless, because reflections delay the arrival of some of the sound. Sound reflects from surfaces, just as light does. An echo, for example, is caused by sound reflection. On their way from the

Why thunder rumbles. Sound waves from the lightning stroke travel at the same speed but varying distances to the observer. Consequently, they do not all arrive to the observer's ear at the same time.

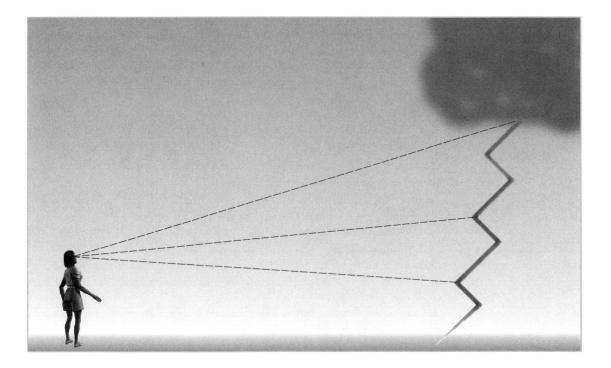

lightning to the observer's ears, some of the sound waves strike buildings, trees, cars, the ground, or water surfaces and are reflected by them. The reflecting surfaces are in different places, at different heights, and the sound strikes them at different angles, so the sound waves are reflected in all directions. Reflections greatly increase the distance the waves travel and thereby extend the prolonged bang into a much longer rumble.

Light travels so fast that the time it takes to reach your eyes from a lightning flash on the horizon is so brief that you see the flash virtually at the instant it happens. Sound travels much more slowly; consequently, you see distant lightning an appreciable time before you hear the thunder it produces. You can use this time delay to calculate how far away the storm is. Start counting seconds the instant you see the flash and stop when you hear the start of the thunder. Every five seconds you counted is equal to approximately 1 mile (1.6 km). If the thunder arrives 10 seconds after the lightning flash, the storm is 2 miles (3.2 km) away. If you perform this calculation several times, you can tell whether the storm is coming closer.

Why is some lightning silent?

As sound waves travel through the air, the air around them and surfaces that reflect them absorb some of their energy. This process is called "damping," and you can watch it happen when you throw a small pebble into the middle of a big pond. Ripples, which are similar to sound waves, travel outward, but the farther they are from the point where the pebble entered the water the smaller they are. Finally, beyond a certain distance they disappear. This is because the kinetic energy released when the pebble hit the water has been absorbed by the water and dispersed. The steady reduction in the size of the waves is called "attenuation."

Sound waves are not all the same size, and they do not all attenuate at the same rate. The distance between the crest or trough of one wave and that of the next is called the "wavelength," and the number of crests or troughs that pass a fixed point in a given time is called the "frequency." Since all sound waves travel at the same speed, the wavelength and frequency are proportional to each other. We hear short-wavelength, and therefore high-frequency, sound waves as high-pitched sounds and long-wavelength, low-frequency waves as low-pitched sounds.

As sound travels through the air, its high frequencies attenuate first. This means that the high-pitched sounds are gradually lost. All natural sounds, including thunder, are made up of a range of frequencies. The farther you are from the source of the sound, the deeper the sound that you hear, because the higher sounds are being lost. When someone is playing music loudly but a long way away, all you hear are the bass sounds, such as the drums. This explains why distant thunder is heard as a deep rumble.

Eventually, though, even the low frequencies become so attenuated as to be inaudible. The air and surfaces have absorbed all of the sound. Distant music can no longer be heard, and neither can distant thunder, even though you may still be able to see the lightning. The distant storm is no more silent than any other storm, but it is too far away for you to be able to hear it.

WHEN THE SEA RISES

Tsunamis

Soon after 10 o'clock on the morning of August 27, 1883, a wall of water 120 feet (37 m) high, racing across the sea, struck the coasts of Java and Sumatra, two of the islands that make up present-day Indonesia. Towns and villages in its path were demolished, and about 36,000 people died. Similar waves, though too small to cause harm, were recorded in Hawaii and South America, thousands of miles away.

It was the kind of wave that people dread more than any other. Waves of this type are much bigger than ordinary sea waves, although rarely as high as the 1883 one, and they arrive without obvious warning, traveling very fast. People used to call them "tidal waves," because they arrive like an incoming tide, but these waves have nothing to do with the tide. Others called them simply "great sea waves," but out at sea they are so small sailors are unaware of them as they pass, so that name is not really appropriate. In Japanese they are known as *tsunamis*, or "harbor waves." This is a much more accurate description and the name now generally used.

There are some every year

Tsunamis are not common, but every year there are a few. A tsunami comprising between three and five separate waves struck southern Peru on June 23, 2001, between the coastal towns of Atico and Matarani. Camaná, a town midway between them, was badly affected. In places, the biggest wave was more than 23 feet (7 m) high, and the water traveled more than half a mile (1 km) inland. It destroyed hundreds of homes, hotels, and restaurants in the holiday resort of La Punta. Fortunately, June is the middle of the Southern Hemisphere's winter, so there were few vacationers in the town. Meanwhile, a wave more than 8 feet (2.5 m) high associated with the Camaná one was recorded approximately 1,400 miles (2,253 km) south at Talcahuano, Chile. Peru is no stranger to tsunamis: in 1996, there was one that killed 12 people, and there have been many others.

Indonesia suffered again on June 3, 1994, when a tsunami struck during the night, killing more than 200 people while they slept. On May 4, 2000, a series of tsunamis devastated several Indonesian coastal villages in the province of Central Sulawesi on Celebes Island and on the islands of Peleng and Banggai. Those waves killed at least 40 people and demolished about 15,000 homes.

Papua New Guinea was struck by a tsunami on July 17, 1998. This one generated waves 23–33 feet (7–10 m) high, and in some places along a 25-mile (40-km) stretch of coast, the waves reached up to 50 feet (15 m) high. They destroyed several villages and were reported to have killed at least 2,500 people.

About 60 people were killed by a tsunami in northern Honshu, Japan, on May 26, 1983, and another struck the coast of Nicaragua on September 1, 1992, killing 105 people and injuring 489. These disasters are not confined to coasts facing the Pacific, however, although that is where most occur. Two tsunamis, up to 10 feet high (3 m), struck a 60-mile (96-km) stretch of the French Mediterranean coast on October 16, 1979. Eleven people were swept away in Nice and one in Antibes and were presumed dead.

Tsunamis are often destructive and sometimes extremely so. At Sanriku, Japan, a tsunami in 1896 killed about 25,000 people and then went on to cause severe damage in California, Chile, and Hawaii. The largest in the 20th century occurred in April 1946 in Hawaii. It destroyed the waterfront in the city of Hilo, killing 96 people.

Not all tsunamis are big and dangerous, however. An eyewitness might have noticed the 32-inch (80-cm) tsunami that reached Port Vila, Vanuatu, on January 4, 2001, but only as a harmless curiosity. Another tsunami recorded at Hachijo Island, Japan, on September 5, 1996, was only 10 inches (25 cm) high, and still smaller ones were registered on other offshore islands. A 10-inch (25-cm) wave will harm no one and might even go unnoticed by the untrained eye; nevertheless, it is a tsunami. Many can be detected only by the most sensitive instruments.

Waves and their characteristics

Tsunamis are not tidal, but they certainly are waves and obey the laws governing the behavior of waves. There are several kinds of waves. Fasten one end of a long rope to a support, hold the other end and move it up and down, and a series of waves will travel along the rope. You will notice that the waves travel, but the rope itself moves only up and down and does not jump from your hand and gather itself in a tangle against the support. Sea waves also travel, but like the rope, the water itself moves up and down, not forward. If it did, all the sea would pile up on land. Throwing a stone into the still water of a pond also demonstrates this principle: the waves will move outward from the disturbance as a series of circles, and leaves floating on the surface will bob up and down as each wave passes, but they will not travel with the wave. The illustration shows the effect, in cross section.

What moves forward, therefore, is not the water, but the energy that set it in motion. The amount of energy imparted to the water can be calculated from the characteristics of the waves produced. The amplitude of a wave is the vertical distance from the lowest point in each trough to the highest point on each crest. The height of the wave is the vertical distance from the midpoint to the crest of each wave. As the name suggests, it is the height the wave reaches above the average level of the surface, and

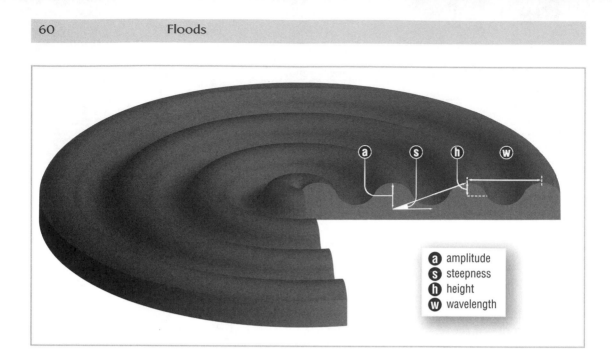

a amplitude
s steepness
h height
w wavelength

Properties of waves.

therefore it is equal to half the amplitude. The distance between one wave crest and the next is the wavelength.

As small children soon learn in the bathtub, big disturbances make big waves. At sea, waves are produced by the wind, and the stronger the wind, the bigger the waves it will make. A wind blowing steadily over a long enough stretch, or fetch, of water will raise waves proportional to the wind force. A moderate breeze, for example, blowing at about 20 miles per hour (32 km/h), will produce waves about 5 feet (1.5 m) high. A fresh gale, blowing at about 40 miles per hour (64 km/h), will raise waves about 25 feet (7.6 m) high, and a wind of 75 miles per hour (121 km/h), just strong enough to be deemed hurricane force, will generate waves 50 feet (12.25 m) high. Real hurricanes can drive waves to even greater heights (see pages 73–77).

Bathtubs may be too small to demonstrate the fact, but the size of the disturbance may also affect the speed with which waves travel. This is measured as the frequency or period. The frequency is the number of wave crests that pass a fixed point in a given time, usually one second, and the period is the time that elapses between one crest passing and the next. Finally, the steepness of the wave is important. This is calculated by dividing the height by the wavelength, but in fact it is the angle to the horizontal made by a line drawn from the trough of one wave to the crest of the next.

How waves move

Careful observation will show that when a stone is thrown into a pond, not all the waves are the same. Some have a longer period than others, and if the pond is big enough, you can see that the slow-moving, long-period waves travel ahead of the faster, short-period waves. The short-period waves move from the site of the disturbance, overtaking the waves ahead of them until they reach the front, but as they do so their period increases and they slow down. The group of waves as a whole travels at half the speed of the individual short-period waves, and at sea, waves always travel as groups. Over the open sea, eventually only the long-period waves remain as ocean swell, and this can travel very long distances. Storms in Antarctic waters have been detected as swell as far away as Alaska.

Back at the pond you may also notice that the floating leaves rise and fall as each wave passes, but they also move forward a little with the crest and back again with the trough. This is because the water itself is moving in small circles, forward with the crest and backward with the trough. You can think of this circular motion, shown in the diagram, as the movement of small "particles" of water. The size of the circles they describe at the surface is related to the height of the waves. Beneath the surface, the size of the circles decreases with depth until they disappear entirely at a depth equal to half the wavelength.

Waves are caused by disturbance. That disturbance transfers energy to the water, and the energy moves away from the source, being passed from one set of water particles to the next. For most waves, the wind is the original source of energy, but not for tsunamis. The energy that causes them originates not at the surface but on or below the seabed.

Water movement beneath waves.

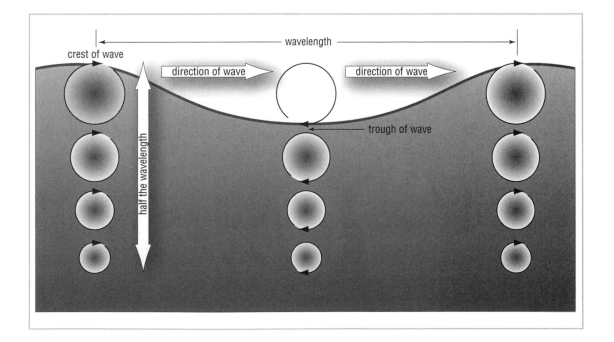

Tsunamis are caused by submarine earthquakes, volcanic eruptions, or the sudden sliding of huge amounts of sediment down a slope. It was an immense earthquake centered near the coastal town of Ocoña that generated the 2001 Peruvian tsunami. The magnitude of earthquakes is measured on the Richter scale, devised by U.S. geologist and physicist Charles Francis Richter (1900–85). It is a logarithmic scale, which means that an increase of 1.0 in magnitude represents a 10-fold increase in the energy released. The magnitude of this Peruvian earthquake, for example, was measured at between 8.3 and 8.4 on the Richter scale. It was possibly the biggest earthquake anywhere in the world in more than 30 years. The earthquake that caused the 1998 tsunami in Papua New Guinea was measured at 7.0.

Coasts bordering the Pacific Ocean experience more tsunamis than any other part of the world. This is because earthquakes and violent volcanic eruptions are so frequent around the Pacific boundaries that the ocean is sometimes described as being surrounded by a "ring of fire." Seashells, pieces of coral, and large rocks that have been found several miles inland from the Australian Pacific coast and up to 100 feet (30 m) above sea level are evidence of past tsunamis, some of which happened 1,000 years ago. Australia has experienced tsunamis more than 100 feet (30 m) high.

Shock waves

Movies about World War II at sea often include encounters between surface warships and submarines in which the surface ships use depth charges. These are bombs, thrown from the ship, which explode deep below the surface. Next time you watch one of these movies, look closely at the water surface when a depth charge explodes. You will see what looks like a tremor traveling outward as a disk. The water itself does not seem to move and there are no big waves, but the tremor is clearly visible as a whitening of the water, moving very fast. In fact, the tremor is a series of surface waves, but they are very small. After this, a great gush of water is thrown into the air. The tremor is a shock wave, produced by the explosion and just like the shock wave that causes tsunamis, although much weaker. The tsunami wave it generates is very different from an ordinary wave.

Shock waves cross the ocean very fast. Typically, a tsunami travels at about 450 miles per hour (724 km/h), although some travel at up to 590 miles per hour (950 km/h), and because it originates at the seabed, it affects all of the water, not just the upper layers. A wind-generated wave can be detected down to about 500 feet (150 m) below the surface (half the wavelength of the surface wave). Below that, the water does not move. In the case of a tsunami, however, the entire ocean vibrates, from the surface all the way to the bed, no matter how deep that may be.

It is a very long wave, with a wavelength between 70 and 300 miles (113–483 km); therefore, it has a long period, up to 20 minutes, elapsing between the passage of one wave crest and the next. The long wavelength means the particles of water disturbed by the waves describe much bigger circles than those of other waves, sometimes with a diameter of 30 feet (10 m). The wave height, on the other hand, is tiny, just like those in the tremor caused by a subsurface depth-charge explosion. Usually, they are no more than 3 feet (almost 1 m) high and often less. They have not the slightest effect on ships, and sailors seldom even notice them.

This is how they travel across the open sea, but their behavior starts to change as they enter shallower water. The captain of a ship moored out at sea in deep water watched the tsunami that struck Hawaii in 1946. The wave had passed his ship without his feeling it.

The wave grows higher as it approaches the shore

As the height of the seabed increases, the circles described by the particles of water near the bottom are flattened. This slows the wave, but more waves continue to arrive at the same speed from deeper water farther out at sea, so the wave period becomes shorter in the shallower water. The same amount of energy is moving, and if the waves at the front are slowing down, the energy carrying them forward is translated into making them higher.

Wave height increases, and because the tsunami is traveling so fast, the wave can grow very high indeed. When the wavelength has been reduced to 5 miles (8 km), the wave at the front will be about 10 feet (3 m) high. Depending on the slope of the seabed, at this stage the tsunami may still be a long way from shore. Closer to shore, where the bed slopes more steeply, the wave may be slowed to no more than 20 miles per hour (32 km/h), but behind it the shock wave is still traveling at 450 miles per hour (724 km/h), and water literally piles up.

As the wave height increases and the wavelength decreases, the waves become steeper. At the same time, the water particles move faster in their circles. It can happen that the particles at the crest of the wave are moving faster than the wave itself, but in the same direction. When this happens, water spills from the front of the wave, producing a breaker.

Tsunamis sometimes arrive like this, as a huge plunging breaker, and that is the way they are usually portrayed in movies. You might wonder why anyone would call what looks like a huge breaker a "tidal wave," and you would be right, but that is not how most tsunamis arrive. Even close inshore, their wavelengths are so long they are more similar to an incoming tide that rises and then goes on rising much faster than a real tide and, of course, to a much higher level. When a tsunami appears as a single, huge breaker, it is merely a foretaste running ahead of the main wave. The latter will arrive a few minutes later and will be much bigger.

After the tsunami has rushed inland, the water subsides and flows back into the sea. The volume of water is huge, and as it flows seaward it meets the next wave. The collision slows the incoming wave and makes it even larger.

Know when a tsunami is coming

Tsunamis are not all the same size. The greater the magnitude of the seabed event that caused them, the bigger they will be, and as the shock wave spreads, it also weakens. Friction in the water dissipates its energy, and the further it travels from the source of the disturbance, the greater the area over which its energy is spread.

Anyone living near the coast can watch for signs that a tsunami is approaching. Ordinarily, waves break on the shore, then rush back into the sea. If, for no apparent reason, the water retreats much farther than usual, exposing rocks that normally remain covered even at spring tides, one should beware. A few minutes later the water will return, rising much higher up the shore than it did before and remaining there for several minutes before flowing back into the sea. If the water rises more than 3 feet (90 cm) beyond its normal level, remains there for a few minutes, and then retreats to more than 3 feet below its normal level, you have been warned and should move immediately to high ground inland and warn everyone else. No time should be wasted in collecting possessions; some miles away out at sea, but approaching fast, there is a tsunami. Eventually you will see it as a wall of water on the horizon, but by then it may be too late to escape. Within just a few minutes its full force will arrive.

Along the coast of Oregon and Washington, Native Americans have a legend about a huge flood that swept inland one cold winter night when the ground shook. A few years ago, Japanese scientists checked the legend against old records in their own country and found reports of a tsunami 7–10 feet (2–3 m) high that flooded rice fields and a storehouse and damaged houses at around midnight on January 27, 1700. There was no record of an earthquake associated with this tsunami, but the scientists checked records from many other parts of the world. Eventually they identified the culprit: it was a massive earthquake centered a little way off the coast of Oregon, Washington, and British Columbia that happened at 9 P.M. local time on January 26, 1700, just as the local legend describes. Not only did the research show that the legend was based on fact, but it implied a warning. That earthquake was a giant, much bigger than any that the region has experienced in modern times, and it could happen again. If it did, rocks might rupture along a 600-mile (965-km) belt, and the tsunamis could be more than 60 feet (18 m) high.

Tsunamis are one more hazard to which people living along coasts, especially Pacific coasts, are exposed (see sidebar). Like flash floods, it is their habit of striking suddenly and with devastating force that makes them terrifying, and although more happen in the Pacific than elsewhere, they can and do occur in all oceans.

Tsunami Warning System

At present, scientists know too little about the ocean floor to provide accurate, reliable warnings, but the situation is improving as more instruments are installed to detect the changes associated with tsunamis. The Tsunami Warning System (TWS), in which 26 nations collaborate, covers the Pacific with a network of stations monitoring the ocean floor and waters.

The National Oceanic and Atmospheric Administration (NOAA) of the United States oper-ates two warning stations, one at Palmer, Alaska, covering the west coast of Canada and the United States, and the other, the Pacific Tsunami Warning Center, at Ewa Beach, Hawaii. Tahiti is the site of the Centre Polynésien de Prévention des Tsunamis. If a tsunami is detected there, for example, the authorities are notified. They issue warnings, as do the NOAA Weather Radio System and the U.S. Coast Guard.

Tides

Twice every day, the sea rises to cover part of the shore, and twice every day, it recedes again. This is flooding, but it is so ordinary that no one thinks of it in this way. Occasionally, though, other factors may add to this regular movement, and then there can be real and severe flooding extend-ing some distance inland (see pages 73–77).

The regular rise and fall of the sea is due to the tides. It is not the same everywhere. In some places, two high tides occur 12 hours apart, whereas in parts of the China Sea, they may occur more than 24 hours apart. There are also places, such as Southampton, England, where the high tide is fol-lowed by a small ebb and then a second high tide.

Usually, the tide ebbs to about the same distance as it rises, but the size and timing of the tides vary day by day, and some coasts experience much bigger tides than the ones that flow and ebb along others. Along Mediter-ranean shores, for example, tidal movements are very small, seldom exceeding 2 feet (60 cm). At London Bridge, in London, and for some dis-tance inland on the tidal stretch of the Thames River, the average tidal movement is about 15 feet (4.5 m) and sometimes reaches 21 feet (6.4 m). At the head of the Bay of Fundy, on the Canadian eastern coast, the tide sometimes rises more than 50 feet (15.25 m). The Bay of Fundy has the biggest tidal movement in the world. All bodies of water have tides, but in any body smaller than a large sea, the effect is too small to be noticed.

Tide-generating forces

Clearly, tides are complicated, but their underlying cause is fairly simple. They are caused by gravity and occur whenever two massive bodies orbit each other. On Earth, the tides move the oceans, but elsewhere in the solar system, their effect is more dramatic. Io, for example, is one of the moons of Jupiter, so it is much farther from the Sun than Earth is. Scientists were startled when they saw the first pictures of Io's surface transmitted by the two *Voyager* spacecraft. They expected Io to be similar to other moons— cold and pock marked with craters. Instead, the pictures revealed a moon covered with volcanoes and volcanic craters called "calderas." What is more, during the four months that elapsed between the arrival of *Voyager 1* and *Voyager 2*, some of the volcanoes ceased erupting and others started. Io is cold: the average surface temperature is about –226°F (–143°C), but in some places it is up to 4,125°F (2,275°C).

Clearly, the interior of Io is hot and what heats it is gravity. Io is pulled this way and that by the gravitational attraction of Jupiter, its parent planet, and also by the gravity of two of Jupiter's other moons, Europa and Ganymede. Like Earth's moon, Io always presents the same face to Jupiter, but the pull of Europa and Ganymede stretches and relaxes it by as much as 330 feet (100 m). This alternate pulling and relaxing is a tidal force and generates heat beneath the surface.

It is the combined effects of the rotation of the Earth and the gravitational attraction of the Moon and Sun that produce Earth's tides. If you swing a bucket of water in a circle, the water will not spill, because once a body is set in motion, it tends to continue moving in a straight line, so the bucket of water tends to fly away. This tendency of any body to resist changes to its state of rest or motion is called "inertia." The rope by which it is swinging exerts a centripetal force acting in the opposite direction, and it is this that prevents the bucket of water from flying away (see sidebar). Provided the centripetal force is equal to or greater than the inertial force, the bucket will continue to swing. Should the inertial force exceed the centripetal force, the rope will break and the bucket will escape, and if the centripetal force should exceed the inertial force, the bucket will fall, spilling the water.

Earth spins on its axis, so the water in the oceans is rather like the bucket of water. The oceans have inertia, tending to throw their water off

Laws of motion

English physicist and mathematician Sir Isaac Newton (1642–1727) discovered three laws that govern the behavior of moving bodies.

1. Unless it is acted upon by external forces, a body at rest will remain at rest, and a moving body will continue moving in a straight line.

2. The momentum of a moving body will change at a rate proportional to and in the same direction as the force causing it to move.

3. If one body exerts a force upon another body, the latter will exert a force called a "reaction" of equal magnitude and in an opposite direction on the former.

into space in a straight line at a tangent to the circumference of Earth. In this case it is the gravitational attraction of Earth that exerts the centripetal force, and it is strong enough to prevent us from losing all our oceans into space. The gravitational centripetal force is strong enough to hold the oceans, but their inertia acting in the opposite direction reduces their weight. Consequently, the oceans bulge outward. Their bulge is biggest around the equator, because that is where they are traveling fastest and, therefore, their inertial force is greatest.

The pull from the Moon and Sun

The Moon and Sun also exert a gravitational pull. Like the inertial force due to Earth's rotation, this pull acts in the opposite direction to the centripetal force; therefore, it also reduces the weight of the oceans and increases the size of the bulge. Gravitational force is proportional to the mass of the two or more bodies and inversely proportional to the square of the distance separating them. Although the Sun is much bigger than the Moon, it is also much more distant, so its gravitational influence is less than that of the Moon. It is mainly the Moon that is responsible for tides— for pulling the oceans outward, into a bulge.

In fact, there are two bulges. As the first diagram shows, at the point on the surface of the Earth directly facing the Moon, the gravitational pull from the Moon draws up one bulge. On the other side of the Earth, at the point directly opposite the Moon, there is a second bulge. Both bulges are of equal size, because the forces producing them are equal in magnitude, but act in opposite directions. The gravitational force acting between two bodies is directly proportional to their masses and inversely proportional to the square of the distance between them, and it draws together the centers of both bodies. Consequently, although we think of the Moon orbiting the Earth, in fact both bodies rotate about an axis

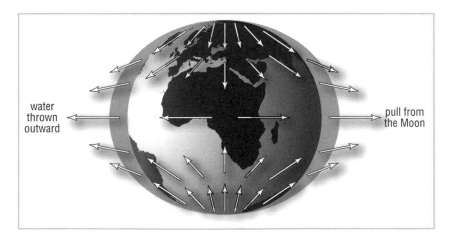

Tidal bulge on Earth caused by the Moon.

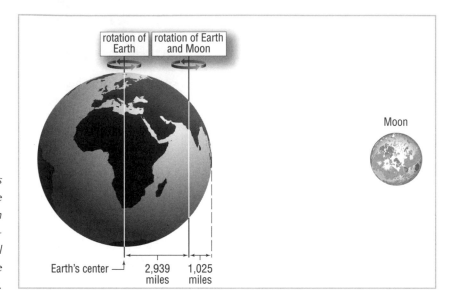

Tides. The Earth spins about its own axis. The Earth-Moon system spins about an axis passing through the mutual center of gravity of the two bodies.

passing through their mutual center of gravity. Earth is 81.3 times more massive than the Moon, so as the second diagram shows, the axis lies inside the Earth but some distance from its center. It is about 2,939 miles (4,729 km) from the center of the Earth and 1,025 miles (1,649 km) beneath the Earth's surface, along a line drawn from the center of the Earth to the center of the Moon.

All the water in all the oceans is drawn by gravity toward the center of the Earth. The Moon offsets this attraction by an amount proportional to the distance from the center of the Moon to the Earth's surface to the Earth's center. The distance between the Earth's surface and its center, one Earth radius, is the same for the point directly beneath the Moon and the point on the other side of the world directly opposite. Directly beneath the Moon its attraction is greatest, and on the opposite of the Earth it is least, by the same amount (proportional to one Earth radius) at both points. This produces the two bulges. At every other point on the surface, water is drawn by smaller forces toward the nearer bulge.

Spring and neap tides

As the Moon circles the Earth—taking 24 hours, 50 minutes, and 28 seconds to complete each orbit—the two bulges follow it. This suggests that one bulge is located directly beneath the Moon, and the other occupies an equivalent position on the opposite side of the Earth; however, as you will know if you have ever helped to push a car that refuses to start, objects do not move the instant a force is applied to them. They are sluggish, due to inertia.

The oceans possess this type of inertia. If the tidal bulge were to remain directly beneath the Moon and the point opposite, it would have to move as a wave through water that is about 12 miles (19 km) deep.

The oceans are much shallower than this, so they slow the wave. The tidal bulge consequently lags four minutes behind the position of the Moon. During those four minutes, the Earth turns 1° on its own axis, so there is an angle of 1° between two lines drawn from the center of the Earth, one to the center of the Moon and the other to the center of the bulge. This delay also acts as a braking mechanism, gradually slowing the Earth's rotation.

The bulges move around the Earth from east to west. They raise the water level as they cross the oceans, but when they arrive at the eastern coasts of the continents their progress is checked. The rocks of the solid Earth respond to tidal forces, but their movement is extremely small. Effectively, the land masses absorb the energy of the tides, and the bulge reappears when the tide crosses the western coast.

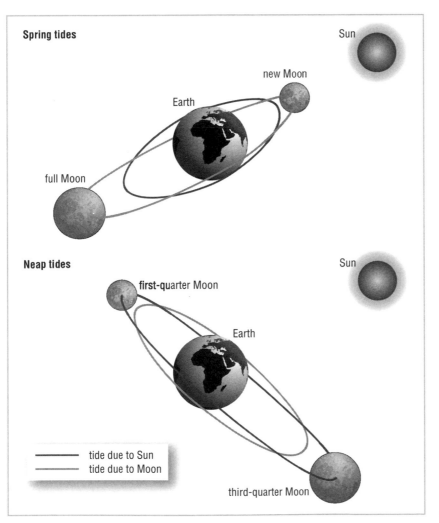

Spring and neap tides.

Absorbing the kinetic energy of the tides also slows the Earth's rotation. The two tidal effects combined slow down the rotation by 0.000015 second per year, so the days are very gradually growing longer. At the beginning of the Cambrian period, around 570 million years ago, the days were about 21.5 hours long, and there were 408 days in a year. This slowing of the Earth's rate of rotation is also causing the Moon to move away from the Earth by about 1.5 inches (4 cm) a year. Fortunately for us, the distance between the Earth and Sun remains constant.

It is the passage of the two bulges that produces two tides a day, 12 hours, 25 minutes, and 14 seconds apart. This is called the "equilibrium tide," and it is what would happen if the entire Earth were covered by oceans and the Moon were always directly overhead at the equator. Obviously, neither is true, so the real situation is more complicated. The tilt of the Earth's axis means the Moon is sometimes to the north of the equator and sometimes to the south by up to 28.5°. This displaces the tidal bulge, and the magnitude of the tides, therefore, changes from day to day.

Although the Moon is the more important influence, the Sun also exerts a gravitational pull on the oceans, producing tidal bulges like those produced by the Moon but smaller. Sun and Moon do not always pull in the same direction, however. Sometimes the Sun pulls against the Moon and makes the tides smaller; sometimes both pull together to make them larger. Tides reach their maximum height at spring tides and their lowest height at neap tides.

At the time of spring tides, the Moon and Sun are aligned. When the Moon is new, it lies almost directly between the Earth and Sun, so the two tidal pulls act in the same direction, and the bulges combine. When the Moon is full, the Moon, Earth, and Sun are also aligned, but this time the Moon is on the side of the Earth opposite the Sun. The bulge on the side of the Earth opposite the point directly beneath the Sun is in the same place as the bulge directly beneath the Moon, so again the tides are high. Neap tides occur when the pulls of the Sun and Moon act at right angles to one another. This happens at the first and third quarter of the Moon. The diagram illustrates the alignments for spring and neap tides.

The effects of coasts and islands

All this would be fine if there were no continents, but there are and they have coastlines, aligned in every direction and with headlands, bays, and offshore islands. The tidal bulges move around the Earth like waves—in this case true tidal waves—but coastlines deflect and reflect them, and like other waves, their characteristics change when they move from deep to shallow water (see pages 58–65).

In small seas almost enclosed by land, tidal waves may enter from more than one direction, meet, and then move back and forth in a complicated manner. This happens in the North Sea, for example, where tides from the Atlantic enter in the north around the north coast of Scotland and in the south through the English Channel and Straits of Dover. The tides then behave like ocean currents and are influenced by the Coriolis effect (see sidebar). This deflects them so that they end by circulating around a point, called an "amphidromic point," at which there is no tidal movement whatsoever. There are three amphidromic points in the North Sea, situated between eastern Britain and continental Europe. Their locations are shown on the map. The solid lines in the drawing are cotidal lines, indicating the time of high water measured in lunar hours (approximately 1 hour, 2 minutes) after the Moon has passed the Greenwich meridian. The broken lines are corange lines, indicating the average distance between high and low tides.

Coastlines are seldom aligned at right angles to the tidal waves, so the tides reach one part of the coast first, then travel along it as a current flowing parallel to the coast. This is a longshore current, and a curve in the coastline can deflect it back out to sea as a rip current. Such currents

The Coriolis effect

Any object moving toward or away from the equator and not firmly attached to the surface does not travel in a straight line but is deflected to the right in the Northern Hemisphere and to the left in the Southern Hemisphere. Furthermore, moving air and water tend to follow a clockwise path in the Northern Hemisphere and a counterclockwise path in the Southern Hemisphere.

The French physicist Gaspard-Gustave de Coriolis (1792–1843) discovered the reason for this in 1835, and it is therefore referred to as the Coriolis effect. It happens because the Earth is a rotating sphere and as an object moves above the surface, the Earth below is also moving. The effect used to be called the "Coriolis force" and is still abbreviated as CorF, but it is not a force. It results simply from the fact that we observe motion in relation to fixed points on the surface.

The Earth makes one complete turn on its axis every 24 hours. This means every point on the surface is constantly moving and returns to its original position (relative to the Sun) every 24 hours. But because the Earth is a sphere, different points on the surface travel different distances to do so. If you find it difficult to imagine that New York City and Bogotá (in Colombia)—or any other two places in different latitudes—are moving through space at different speeds, consider that if this were not so the world would tear itself apart.

Choose two points on the surface, one at the equator and the other at 40° N, which is the approximate latitude of New York and Madrid. The equator, latitude 0°, is about 24,881 miles (40,033 km) long. That is how far any given point on the equator must travel in 24 hours, which means it moves at about 1,037 miles per hour (1,668 km/h). At 40° N, the circumference parallel to the equator is about 19,057 miles (30,663 km). The point there has less distance to travel, so it moves at about 794 miles per hour (1,277 km/h).

An object on the surface travels with the surface and therefore at the same speed. When it leaves the surface, it continues to travel in an easterly direction at the same speed as it had while it remained on the surface. If it moves into a different latitude, however, the surface below it will be moving faster or slower. Consequently, the path of the moving object across the surface will appear to be deflected.

The size of the Coriolis effect is directly proportional to the speed at which the object moves and the sine of its latitude. The effect on an object moving at 100 miles per hour (160 km/h) is 10 times greater than that on one moving at 10 miles per hour (16 km/h). Because sin 0° = 0 (the equator) and sin 90° = 1 (the poles), the Coriolis effect is greatest at the poles and zero at the equator.

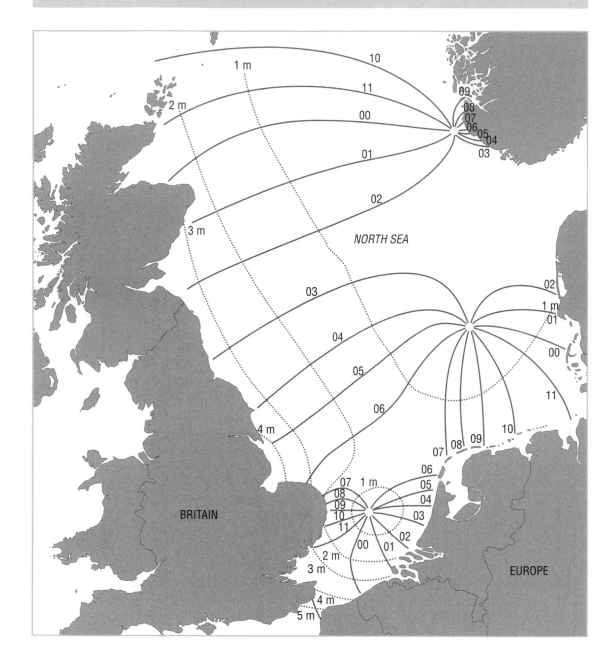

Amphidromic points in the North Sea.

are common and make it very dangerous to swim or surf on certain parts of many beaches. They also explain why the times of high and low tides are different along different parts of the same coastline.

When the tidal wave approaches the shore, it enters shallow water, and as with any other kind of wave, its wave height increases. The waves flow with some force up the beach and as they return can carry with them material from sandy or gravel beaches that has been disturbed by their turbulence.

Longshore currents can then remove this material and deposit it elsewhere. The process is called "littoral drift." It results in coastal erosion in some places and extensions of the coast in others. Of course, it is also waves, generated by wind and tides, that form beaches in the first place, by constantly battering coastal rocks until boulders break away from them and are then slowly reduced to small pebbles and eventually sand.

Waves may also move material higher up the beach. This sand or gravel may then accumulate along a line marking the highest point strong waves commonly reach, making a ridge called a "berm." Berms can be quite high, and they shelter the land behind them, making it an apparently attractive place to build. It is not always a wise place to build, however. The sea that built the berm can just as easily demolish it, and it can do so in the course of a single storm.

Tidal surges

Think of a hurricane, and the first image that springs to mind is probably of the fierce wind. Hurricanes generate winds of terrifying force that can cause great damage. It is not usually the wind that does the most harm, however, but rather the water. Storms deliver heavy rain, which can cause flash floods (see pages 37–42), but they also produce storm surges, sending the sea crashing through coastal communities. When Hurricane Fran struck Cape Fear, North Carolina, and then moved northward along the coast on September 6, 1996, the wind and rain were accompanied by a storm surge of 12 feet (3.7 m) and in some places of 16 feet (4.9 m).

Fran was a big but typical hurricane, and its storm surge was no bigger than those produced by earlier hurricanes. Hurricane Opal, which crossed the coast of the southeastern United States in October 1995, for example, caused a 12-foot (3.7-m) storm surge. In 1992, Tropical Storm Polly, not quite strong enough to be rated a hurricane, produced a storm surge of 20 feet (6.1 m) at Tianjin, in southeastern China. A hurricane that struck Galveston, Texas, on September 8, 1900, cost more lives than any other natural disaster in the history of the United States. More than 6,000 people died, and perhaps as many as 10,000—no one is certain—and most were killed by the 20-foot (6.1-m) storm surge. That hurricane occurred before hurricanes were given names.

A hurricane—or, to give it the name scientists use, a tropical cyclone—is an intense depression, or region of low atmospheric pressure. Such storms are classified on the five-point Saffir-Simpson Hurricane Scale. Category 5 hurricanes, which are the most severe, generate storm surges of more than 18 feet (5.4 m), but the size of the surge depends on the configuration of the seabed. Despite its big surge, the Galveston hurricane would probably have been rated category 4 because of the strength of its winds.

Depressions, which meteorologists call "cyclones," are familiar in middle latitudes. They usually travel from west to east, bringing low clouds and rain or snow, sometimes with strong winds. They are associated with bad weather, but not dangerous weather, and some are so weak they do not even produce much cloud and precipitation. Nevertheless, the atmospheric pressure at their center is lower than that away from the center. They are what are known as lows.

Air pressure and sea level

Tropical cyclones are also depressions but on a much bigger scale. This means that as a tropical cyclone develops, the pressure at its center falls much further than it would in a milder mid-latitude depression. The average atmospheric pressure at sea level is 29.9 inches of mercury (in. Hg), or 1,013 millibars (mb), or 14.5 pounds per square inch (lb in^{-2}). In the eye of a category 1 hurricane, which is the gentlest type of tropical cyclone, the pressure is 28.9 in. Hg (980 mb; 14.0 lb in^{-2}) or lower. Fran, the 1996 hurricane that caused serious damage in the Carolinas, Virginia, and West Virginia, was a category 3 hurricane. It produced steady winds of 115 miles per hour (185 km/h), and the pressure at its center was between 27.9 and 28.4 in. Hg (945–964 mb; 13.5–13.8 lb in^{-2}). The pressure in the center of Mitch, one of the fiercest storms of modern times that devastated the Caribbean, especially Honduras, in 1998, at one point fell to 26.72 in. Hg (905 mb; 12.9 lb in^{-2}). Mitch was a category 5 hurricane, which requires that the central pressure is always lower than 27.1 in. Hg (920 mb; 13.2 lb in^{-2}).

This is an average drop in pressure of no more than 5–7 percent. Even Mitch had a central pressure only about 11 percent below normal. It is quite small, but its consequences are not. Atmospheric pressure is due to the weight of all the air, right to the top of the atmosphere, pressing down on a surface (see sidebar). When the water is still, the surface of a small pond is absolutely level, and you can even see reflections in it. This is because the air is pressing down on it to the same extent everywhere.

Suppose, though, that there was a little less air over one small part of the pond. You could measure this as a lower atmospheric pressure. If there is less air, and the pressure is lower, the air is pressing less heavily

Air pressure—highs and lows

When air is warmed, it expands and becomes less dense. When air is chilled, it contracts and becomes more dense.

Air expands by pushing away the air around it. It rises, because it is less dense than the air imme-diately above it. Air flows in to replace it, lifting it upward, and in turn is warmed by contact with the surface so that it also expands and rises. If you imagine a column of air extending all the way from the surface to the top of the atmosphere, warming

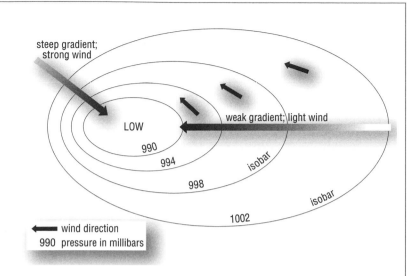

Pressure gradient and wind speed. A wind that blows at right angles to the isobars, like water flowing down a hillside, is a gradient wind. Above the ground, winds flow parallel to the isobars and are known as geostrophic winds.

steep gradient; strong wind

weak gradient; light wind

LOW

990

994

998

1002

isobar

isobar

← wind direction
990 pressure in millibars

from below causes air to be pushed out of the column, so it contains less air (fewer molecules of air) than it did when it was cooler. Because there is less air in the column, the pressure its weight exerts at the surface is reduced. The result is an area of low surface pressure, often called simply a "low."

In chilled air the opposite happens. The air molecules move closer together, so the air contracts, becomes denser, and sinks. The amount of air in the column increases, its weight increases, and the surface atmospheric pressure also increases. This produces an area of high pressure, or called simply a "high."

At sea level, the atmosphere exerts sufficient pressure to raise a column of mercury about 30 inches (760 mm) in a tube from which the air has been removed. Meteorologists measure this pressure at sea level as one bar and break it down into millibars (1,000 millibars [mb] = 1 bar = 10^6 dynes cm^{-2} = 14.5 lb in^{-2} = 29.9 in. Hg = 760 mm Hg) to measure atmospheric pressure. Millibars are still the units quoted in newspaper and TV weather forecasts, but the international scientific unit has changed to pascals (Pa); 1 mb equals 100 Pa.

Air pressure decreases with height because there is less weight of air above to exert pressure. Pressure measured at different places on the surface

is corrected to sea level pressure, to remove differences due only to altitude. Lines are then drawn, linking places where the pressure is the same. These lines, called "isobars," allow meteorologists to study the distribution of pressure.

Like water flowing downhill, air flows from high to low pressure. Its speed, which we feel as wind strength, depends on the difference in pressure between the two regions. This is known as the pressure gradient. On a weather map, it is calculated from the distance between isobars, just as the distance between contours on an ordinary the steepness of hills to be measured. As the diagram shows, the steeper the gradient, the closer together the isobars are and the stronger the wind.

Moving air is subject to the Coriolis effect (see sidebar, page 71), which swings it to the right in the Northern Hemisphere and to the left in the Southern Hemisphere, with the result that clear of the surface, winds flow parallel to the isobars rather than across them. It is also affected by friction with the surface. This is greater over land than it is over sea. The result is that surface winds do not flow parallel to the isobars. They cross them at about 30° over the oceans and at about 45° over land.

on that part of the surface, so the water will rise a little. In fact, a drop in pressure of (0.03 in. Hg 1 mb; 0.01 lb in^{-2}) will allow the water to rise about 0.4 inch (1 cm). At the center of a tropical cyclone, the fall in pressure is much greater than this. At its peak, Hurricane Mitch had an eye pressure that was about 3.2 in. Hg (108 mb; 1.6 lb in^{-2}) below the average sea level pressure. This would allow the water beneath the eye to rise by about 43 inches (1.1 m).

We think of water as "finding its own level," so ignoring waves, the surface of open water must be absolutely level. This is not so. The sea surface is higher in some places than it is in other places owing to differences in atmospheric pressure. Weather satellites use radar to measure how the height of the sea surface varies from place to place, because these variations allow the surface atmospheric pressure to be calculated.

Add the tidal effect

When a tropical cyclone crosses a coast, the sea level will rise due only to the fall in pressure in the center of the storm. A rise of 2 feet (60 cm) or so may not be very important in itself, but suppose it happens at high tide or, even worse, at the height of a spring tide. Then this small rise might be enough to flow over the top of a sea wall.

This is not the only effect of a difference in atmospheric pressure. It will also cause air to flow, as wind, spiraling into the low-pressure center with a force proportional to the difference in pressure inside and outside the low. It is known as the pressure gradient because it resembles the slope on a hillside, with air flowing down the gradient like water flowing downhill. It is the large pressure gradient that generates the hurricane winds. At sea, winds also produce waves. A sustained wind of more than 110 miles per hour (177 km/h) will generate waves more than 30 feet (9 m) high. These move away from their source, with a fairly long period (see pages 58–65), and as they slow down they are overtaken by waves that are moving faster. If several waves combine so that crests coincide with crests and troughs with troughs, the waves will grow even bigger.

A storm surge results from the combined effects of the sea level rise due to low pressure and the wind-generated waves. If the arrival of the surge at the coast coincides with a high tide, it becomes a tidal surge. When a surge is forecast, its height is given as the vertical distance by which the sea will rise above the predicted high tide on an open coast. In a sheltered bay or estuary, the rise may be half as great. If the high tide is a spring tide, the surge will be still higher. The worst surges are associated with storms occurring around the time of full moon or no moon.

Flood barriers

Storm surges are not confined to those parts of the world affected by tropical cyclones. At Woolwich, downstream from the center of London, there is an array of floodgates, called the Thames Barrier, constructed in 1982 at a cost of about $758 million to protect London from flooding due to storm surges. There are likely to be more constructed in years to come because the land is sinking in this part of eastern England, and the high-tide level has risen by more than 5 feet (1.5 m) since 1780. Back in 1663, the English diarist Samuel Pepys recorded that much of central London was under water.

The most serious storm surge of modern times occurred in 1953, when the sea level at Southend, on the coast, rose by 9 feet (2.7 m) two and a half hours before high tide; by high tide, it was still 5.5 feet (1.7 m) above its normal level. This surge traveled around the North Sea, causing damage and loss of life in England and the Netherlands.

Both tides and surges move around the North Sea in a counterclockwise direction. Tidal water enters from the Atlantic in the north and south, so two tides flow in opposite directions and meet. This can set up a complicated oscillation of water, as it sloshes back and forth, but its movement is affected by the rotation of the Earth, the Coriolis effect (see sidebar, page 71). This results in a counterclockwise flow around three centers, the amphidromic points where there is no tidal movement at all (see pages 70–71). If a deep depression crosses the northern part of the sea, producing a gale blowing from the north, it can generate long-period waves traveling around the sea, while the low pressure also raises the sea level. When these combine with the tidal flow, the resulting surge can be large.

Tides cause the sea level to rise but in a regular, predictable way. Storms also cause the sea level to rise, because of the reduction in atmospheric pressure at their centers. In addition, storms produce wind-generated waves. When the rise in sea level due to a storm coincides with high tide, the result is a surge of water that can flow over coasts with great force.

COPING WITH FLOODS

Monsoons

It is April. Spring has arrived in the middle latitudes of Europe and North America. Leaves are bursting forth on the trees, gardens are a riot of bright flowers, and everywhere there is the promise of summer soon to come.

In India and Pakistan, it is not spring. It is the hot season—something very different. The ground is parched after the long, dry months of winter, and now the Sun is almost directly overhead and the temperature is rising. It soon passes 90°F (32°C), except near the coast where the proximity of the ocean moderates the intense heat. For several months, the prevailing winds have been from the northeast, bringing dry air from the Himalayas. Now, they have slackened, and most of the time, the air is fairly still. Sometimes the relative humidity falls as low as 1 percent (see sidebar, page 16).

Temperatures continue rising through May, and the heat is fiercest in the north. In Jacobabad, Pakistan, the average daytime temperature in May is 111°F (44°C), and it has been known to reach 123°F (51°C). It is impossible to work in this climate during the hottest part of the day. The night brings a little relief. The average nighttime temperature is 78°F (26°C). In Bombay, India, the average daytime temperature is 91°F (33°C), falling to 80°F (27°C) at night. It is somewhat cooler in the south. In Sri Lanka, the temperature seldom rises above 100°F (38°C) by day, although the nights are no cooler than those in the north, and the air is much more humid. There is frequent, heavy rain in the south of the subcontinent, but further north conditions remain dry.

As May gives way to June, the dry heat becomes unbearable, but soon the sky changes. Until then it had been grayish white from the permanent dust haze, but by the end of the first week of June, clouds start to appear. They grow during the day and move from east to west, then dissipate by nightfall without bringing any rain. Day after day, the clouds appear, and each day, they grow bigger and darker. The humidity rises, and dry heat is replaced by an oppressive, sticky heat that is even worse.

Finally, the weather breaks. The winds increase, this time from the southwest, and the skies open. Bombay receives an average 0.7 inch (18 mm) of rain in May and none at all in April. By the end of June, however, more than 19 inches (483 mm) have fallen, and the rain continues through the summer, decreasing in September to an average 10.4 inches (264 mm) and falling to 2.5 inches (64 mm) in October. Jacobabad, much farther inland than Bombay and therefore inevitably drier, has an average 0.1 inch (3 mm) of rain in May and 0.3 inch (8 mm) in June, but in July and August this increases to 0.9 inch (23 mm). Cherrapunji, India, 4,309 feet (1,313 m) above sea level in the mountains of Assam, is one of the wettest places in the world. It receives an average of 425 inches (10,798 mm) of rain a year.

Of that total, 366 inches (9,302 mm), amounting to 86 percent, fall between May and September.

These are extreme seasonal differences. They are most marked in southern Asia, but they also occur in other parts of the Tropics. West Africa experiences them, and so do parts of the United States. Since the 18th century, the rainy season has been known as the monsoon, but strictly speaking there are two monsoons: the dry winter and wet summer monsoons. The word is probably derived from the Arabic word *mawsim*, which means "season."

Trade winds and the winter monsoon

During the winter, the interiors of continents become very cold. The land does not retain heat the way water does. Warmth radiates away, and as the ground cools, the air in contact with it is also chilled. The cold air contracts, its density increases, and it forms an extensive area of high pressure. In Eurasia, this anticyclone is centered over Mongolia, to the north of the Himalaya mountains.

Throughout the winter, the intertropical convergence zone (ITCZ) is situated far to the south of the subcontinent (see sidebar). This means that

---

Intertropical convergence and the equatorial trough

The trade winds blow toward the equator in both the Northern and Southern Hemispheres. Consequently, there is a region close to the equator where the winds meet. When two bodies of air flow toward each other, they are said to "converge." The meeting of the trade winds is therefore the intertropical convergence, and the region where it happens is the intertropical convergence zone (ITCZ). Because the ITCZ forms a boundary between air from the two hemispheres, it is sometimes called the intertropical front (ITF), although it is not strictly a front as found in middle latitudes between polar and tropical air.

The ITCZ is more strongly developed over the oceans than over the continents, and even over the

(*continues*)

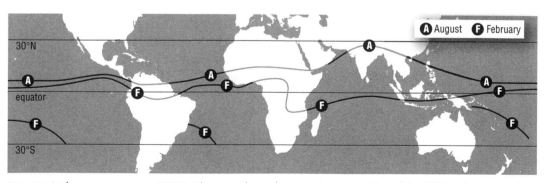

Intertropical convergence zone (ITCZ). The map shows the approximate position of the ITCZ and equatorial trough in February and August.

(continued)

oceans, it is evident only as an average. The convergence of the trade winds varies in strength, as disturbances form in it and travel westward. The ITCZ rarely occurs in the areas affected by the doldrums, sea areas where the winds are light and variable and often there is no wind at all, although the calm weather is sometimes interrupted by violent storms.

The position of the ITCZ changes through the year. The map shows its approximate location in February and August, as revealed by bands of clouds that are clearly visible on satellite images. The ITCZ is more often to the north of the equator than to the south, and it seldom coincides with the equator itself. Instead, its position coincides with the thermal equator, the region where surface temperature is highest. Any change in the sea-surface tem-

perature is likely to cause the ITCZ to move. The highest sea-surface temperature also produces the most highly developed convection, with the formation of convective clouds and heavy rain.

Both convergence and convection cause air to rise. This reduces air pressure near the surface and produces a region of high pressure in the upper air, where air diverges. The diagram shows what happens. The low surface pressure is known as the equatorial trough. The trough does not coincide precisely with the ITCZ, but is a short distance from it, on the side furthest from the equator.

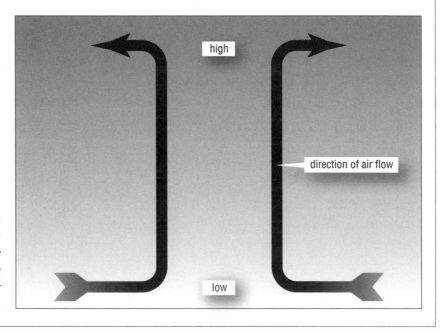

Convergence. Air converges and rises, producing low surface pressure and high pressure in the upper troposphere.

over tropical southern Asia, the prevailing winds are the northeasterly trade winds. These are intensified by the flow of air out of the winter anticyclone. The winds are dry because they originate over the center of the continent, and the little moisture they contain is lost as they cross the Himalayas. On the southern side of the mountains, the air descends. The descent causes the air to warm adiabatically as it is compressed, thus reducing its relative humidity still further. Air that began dry becomes even drier as it sweeps across the central plains to the Indian Ocean. Some rain falls in the south of the subcontinent because it is exposed to trade winds blowing from Myanmar and Thailand that have crossed the Bay of Bengal, where they gathered moisture.

To the north of the Himalayas, the Tibetan Plateau is nowhere less than 12,000 feet (3,660 m) above sea level. Its high elevation compared with the much lower land in India increases the contrast in temperature. The average January daytime temperature in Lhasa, Tibet, at an elevation of 12,090 feet (3,685 m) is 44°F (7°C). Further north, Ürümqi, 2,972 feet (906 m) above sea level in the Tian Shan Mountains of China, has an average January temperature of 13°F (–11°C). Compare this with the Indian cities of Delhi, 714 feet (218 m) above sea level, where the average temperature is 70°F (21°C) and Hyderabad further south, elevation 1,778 feet (541 m), where it is 84°F (29°C). January, nonetheless, is the coldest month in all four cities.

The low temperatures over central Asia and the Tibetan Plateau intensify the anticyclone, but the high pressure is quite shallow. A trough of low pressure extends over eastern Asia, and in the upper troposphere, the winds are from the west, with the jet stream blowing from west to east near the tropopause. The jet stream is divided into two, passing to the north and south of the Himalayas. The location of the more northerly jet stream is extremely variable from one year to another. It is also the weaker of the two. The two jet streams join on the lee side of the mountain range, over northern China and southern Japan.

It is the subsidence of air beneath the westerly jet streams that feeds the low-level anticyclone and generates the dry winds that blow from the northwest over Afghanistan and Pakistan, from the northeast over most of India, and from the east over southern India. The map shows the winds in winter and summer.

Summer rains

By March, the ITCZ has begun its seasonal northward migration. Near the tropopause, the belts of westerly winds are also moving northward, but the southerly jet stream remains to the south of Tibet, gradually weakening. As the Sun moves into the Northern Hemisphere, the sunshine intensifies, and surface temperatures start to rise.

For a time, India lies beneath subsiding air that is sinking on the northern side of the equatorial trough. At the same time, however, the rising surface temperature generates convection and local areas of low pressure. The weather becomes unsettled, and there are squalls and storms in some places. These occur mainly in the northeastern part of the Indian subcontinent, where cold air from the north moves above warm, moist, low-level air over the sea. The moist air becomes highly unstable, and squall lines develop. A squall line comprises storms that join together, forming a line that advances at right angles to the line itself. They are especially common in March and April. In the Ganges Delta, they are known as nor'westers.

The southern jet stream continues to weaken, then to break down altogether, until in May and June, it moves fairly abruptly to the northern side of the Tibetan Plateau. As the jet stream weakens, the equatorial trough

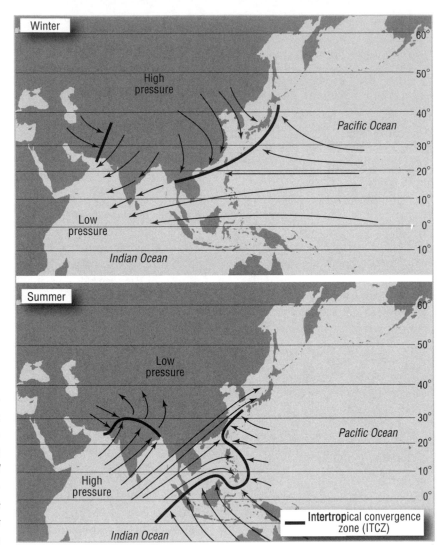

Asian winter and summer monsoons. In winter, high pressure over central Asia generates dry winds blowing from land to sea. In summer, pressure is higher over the sea, and moist winds blow over the continent.

continues its northward migration. Convection intensifies, finally overwhelming the subsiding air. This marks a complete change in the distribution of pressure and winds. Subsiding air and high-surface pressure over the continent has given way to rising air and low pressure. The low-surface pressure draws air inward.

The ITCZ finally lies along the southern side of the Himalayas. The surface winds now blow from the southwest, but the upper winds blow from the east, and an easterly jet stream becomes established between 10°N and 15°N at a height of about 50,000 feet (15 km). The westerly jet stream moves south of the equator.

Rain arrives suddenly in what is aptly called the "burst of monsoon." Southwesterly winds blowing from the Arabian Sea at 25–30 miles per hour (40–48 km/h) bring thick, dark clouds and violent storms. The rains begin in the southeast and advance steadily in a northwesterly direction. In most years, they reach southern China and Taiwan around May 10. By May 20, rain is falling along a line from about the Andaman Islands to Hong Kong, and by May 25, it has reached Sri Lanka. To the east of the Himalayas, the monsoon advances through China, Korea, and Japan, arriving in the vicinity of Beijing by the end of July. South of the mountains, the rains cross India and reach Pakistan by about July 15.

Monsoon floods

The rain is heavy and prolonged. Farmers depend on it. In years when the monsoon rains arrive late or fail to arrive at all, the resulting drought destroys crops and may even make sowing them impossible. This impoverishes the growers and sometimes causes famine. Too much rain is as bad as too little, however. All too often the monsoon rains bring severe flooding.

The year 2000 seemed perfectly ordinary. The monsoon arrived at its usual time and brought the usual amount of rain. In the middle of May, however, the rains combined with a tidal surge (see pages 73–77) to cause floods in West Timor, Indonesia, that left about 20,000 people homeless and killed at least 140. One month later, at least 20 people died in monsoon floods in the northeastern Indian states of Assam and Arunachal Pradesh. On July 12, the rains caused a landslide in a settlement near Bombay, killing about 80 people. The following day, there was a mudslide in Shaanxi Province, China, that buried houses and killed more than 120 people. A few days after that, some 140 people died in floods in the states of Maharashtra, Gujarat, and Andhra Pradesh, India. At least 70 people lost their lives in further floods in Andhra Pradesh in August, but the worst floods of the year occurred in September and October in West Bengal, India, and in Bangladesh. Those floods cost more than 900 lives in India and about 150 in Bangladesh, where some 5 million people were left homeless.

Vietnam, Laos, and Cambodia also suffered, from late July until early October, when the delta of the Mekong River experienced the worst floods in 40 years. At least 315 persons died in them. Nearly 200 people were killed in late October and early November when monsoon rains caused flooding in Indonesia, Thailand, and Malaysia. 2000 was a fairly typical year.

Monsoons in other parts of the world

Alternating dry and wet monsoon seasons are caused by changes in the distribution of pressure associated with the seasonal movements of the equatorial trough. These affect many parts of the world, so the monsoons are not confined to Asia. They are strongest in Asia because the extent and height of the Tibetan Plateau and the Himalayan mountain range intensify them, but other parts of the world experience less extreme monsoon conditions.

The trade winds blow from the northeast on the northern side of the equatorial trough. In winter, they reach West Africa after crossing the Sahara. Not surprisingly, they are dry. At Conakry, on the coast of Guinea, an average of 1.9 inches (48.26 mm) of rain falls during the five months between December and April.

As the trough passes, the wind direction changes. Moist air from the Atlantic flows across the region, and from the beginning of May to the end of November, Conakry receives 167 inches (4,244 mm). The temperature remains constant throughout the year, however, averaging 82–90°F (28–32°C) by day and 72–75°F (22–24°C) by night.

This climate is similar to that of India and occurs over most of West Africa. The main difference between the African and Asian monsoons concerns the onset of the rains. Africa has no east-west mountain range comparable to the Himalayas to block the migration of the equatorial trough. Consequently, it is able to move steadily northward in spring, and the rains begin more gently. There is no sudden burst of monsoon. It is the summer monsoon that brings rain to the parched lands along the southern margin of the Sahara Desert.

Parts of the United States also have a monsoon climate, but with the seasons reversed. In summer the subtropical anticyclone moves northward over the Pacific ahead of the equatorial trough. This brings dry weather to most of the area west of the Rocky Mountains. Los Angeles, for example, receives an average of only 2.3 inches (58.4 mm) of rain between the beginning of April and the end of October. In winter, however, the anticyclone follows the equatorial trough southward, so Los Angeles receives an average 12.7 inches (322.6 mm) between November and March.

On the eastern side of the country, the seasonal changes are smaller, although they do exist. In summer, the strengthening of the anticyclone centered over the Azores combines with the convergence of air over the center of the continent to bring a southeasterly flow of moist air across the Gulf of Mexico and into the states bordering the gulf. In winter, when the subtropical high is weaker, winds blow more often from the north or northeast, and the climate is somewhat drier.

Failure of the African monsoon brings drought to the semiarid lands bordering the Sahara, whereas heavy rains can cause flooding, but floods are much less common there than in southern Asia. In the United States, failure of the winter rains may cause water shortages in California. Floods there are more often caused by El Niño (see sidebar, pages 7–8) than by unusually heavy seasonal rainfall.

Aquifers, springs, and wells

Slowly, the water below ground flows downhill, inching its way through the porous soil or rock. The subterranean water itself is called "groundwater."

The material through which it flows is an aquifer, a word that means "water-bearing," from the Latin *aqua* (water) and *ferre* (to bear).

Not all rocks will allow water to flow through them, even though they may be fully saturated. A rock that prevents or seriously restricts the flow of water through it is either an aquitard (or aquiclude) or an aquifuge. Water moves slowly and with difficulty through an aquitard, so-named because it retards the water. An aquifuge, as its name suggests, neither absorbs water nor allows it to pass through but rather expels it or drives it away.

If an aquifer meets either of these types of rock, the passage of groundwater will be slowed or halted completely at the boundary. This will cause water to accumulate on one side of the boundary, and as it does so, the water table will rise until it is higher than the top of the aquitard or aquifuge. Then the flow of groundwater will resume above the obstruction. The aquifer therefore lies above a partially impermeable layer of material and is said to be "perched."

Whether a layer of rock comprises an aquifer depends on the size of the pore spaces between particles, called the "porosity" of the rock, and as far as geologists are concerned, soil is a type of rock. The relative ease with which a rock allows water to pass through it is called its "permeability." Porosity and permeability are not the same thing. A porous rock is not necessarily permeable, although a permeable rock must be porous.

Soil particles and the pore spaces between them

Where the pores are large, water flows easily, but where they are small, water moves by capillarity (see pages 17–23). In the capillary fringe, above the water table, capillarity draws water upward, but it also ensures that the pores remain filled with water, and this is what impedes the horizontal flow. Water molecules are attracted to the sides of the pores with a force greater than that of gravity. Clay, composed of minute particles, can become saturated with water yet severely impede the movement of groundwater.

If the pore spaces are too large to allow water to be seriously affected by capillarity, the rate at which water flows through them is proportional to the fourth power of the radius of the spaces. Take two glass tubes, for example, one with a radius double (2×) that of the other; water flows through the larger tube 16 times (2^4) faster than through the narrow one.

Soil particles come in many shapes and sizes, but they are classified into seven principal types—spheroidal, crumb, platelike, blocklike, subangular blocky, prismlike, and columnar—as shown in the illustration. Spheroidal particles are small and pack together to produce a fairly nonporous soil. Crumbs are similar but produce a more porous material. Platelike particles often overlap one another to produce a very impermeable structure; clay is made from microscopically small platelike particles. Blocklike, subangular blocky, prismlike, and columnar particles are bigger and form more porous and permeable soils. Soil does not consist of loose particles, of course. Chemical substances in the soil cement particles together to form small lumps, called "aggregates," or "peds." These may stick together forming larger lumps that are called "clods."

You can measure the amount of pore space in a sample of soil by weighing the soil with an accurate scale or balance. First, weigh a small pan onto which you will place the sample and record its weight. Next, place the soil sample on the pan, and add water until the soil is thoroughly soaked but no water is lying on the surface. Weigh the wet soil, deduct the weight of the pan, and write down the weight of your sample. Now place the pan of soil in the oven on a low heat and leave it there for a couple of hours or more. Later, remove the pan of soil; allow it to cool; weigh it again, remembering to deduct the weight of the pan; and compare the second weight with the first. Divide the second weight ($W2$) by the first weight ($W1$) and multiply the result by 100: $(W2 \div W1) \times 100$. The result tells you the amount of pore space as a percentage of the total weight of soil. You can convert this into the percentage of the total volume if you know how densely soil particles pack together. In most soils, there are approximately 1.52 ounces of particles in every cubic inch of soil (2.65 grams per cubic centimeter), so the calculation becomes $(W2 \div W1) \div 1.52 \times 100$, if the units are ounces and cubic inches, or $(W2 \div W1) \div 2.65 \times 100$, if they are grams and cubic centimeters.

If you wish to know the actual volume of pore space in the sample, you will need to know the two weights in grams (grams = ounces × 28.4). $W2 - W1$ gives you the weight of water that was present in the saturated soil. One gram of water occupies a volume of one cubic centimeter, so the weight of water in grams is equal to the same number of cubic centimeters, and that is the volume of pore space in the sample (to convert back, $1 \text{ cm}^3 = 0.061 \text{ in}^3$).

Soil particles. The size and shape of soil particles strongly affect the ease with which water moves through the ground. Particles are classified into seven basic types.

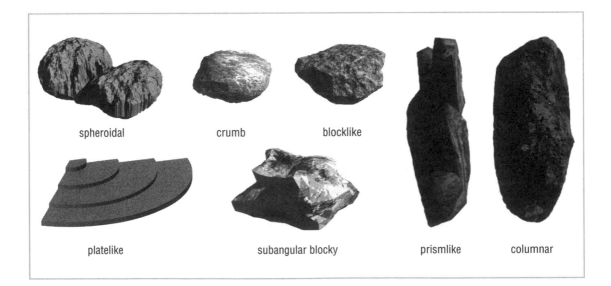

spheroidal

crumb

blocklike

platelike

subangular blocky

prismlike

columnar

CLASSIFICATION OF SOIL PERMEABILITY

Class	Permeability (inches per hour; centimeters per hour)
Slow	
very slow	less than 0.05; less than 0.13
slow	0.05–0.20; 0.13–0.51
Moderate	
moderately slow	0.20–0.80; 0.51–2.03
moderate	0.80–2.50; 2.03–6.35
moderately rapid	2.50–5.00; 6.35–12.7
Rapid	
rapid	5.00–10.00; 12.7–25.4
very rapid	more than 10.00; more than 25.4

Permeability

The rate at which water will move through a particular type of material is a measure of the permeability, also called the "hydraulic conductivity," of that material; the permeability of different soil materials is classified as slow, moderate, or rapid. The table shows what these classifications mean in terms of the speed with which groundwater moves.

Rivers, springs, seeps, and aquifers

Prolonged, heavy rain usually brings no immediate change to a river. If the land on either side is cultivated you may see pipes discharging water from fields where farmers have installed underground drainage systems for this purpose, but you will see little or no water flowing across the surface and spilling over the banks. The river continues to flow as before, and the water level does not begin to rise until some time has elapsed. It is not until hours or even days later, when the rain may have ceased, that the river starts rising and there is a risk of flooding.

The reason, of course, is that the river is fed not by surface flow and drainage from fields but by underground aquifers. Water draining into the aquifer over the whole drainage basin, or the part of it experiencing the heavy rain, increases the thickness of the saturated layer, raising the water table, but it takes time for the additional water to reach the river. How long it takes depends on the distance it must travel, the permeability of the aquifer, and the gradient.

As the first drawing (A) in the illustration shows, rivers flow where the part of the ground surface comprising the river bed lies below the water

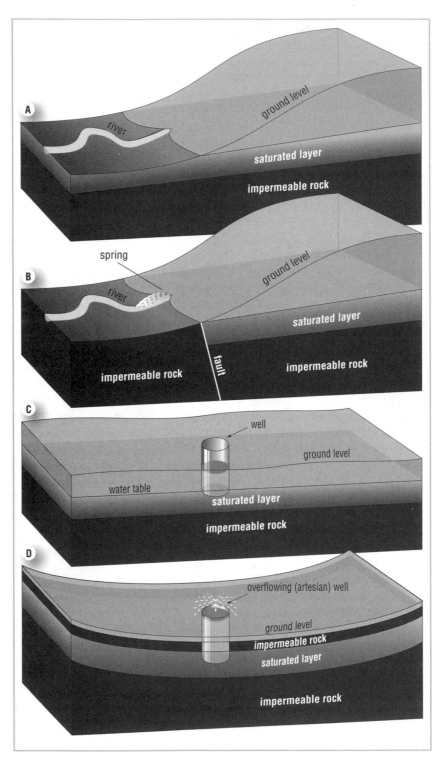

*Water below
ground. A) River.
B) Spring. C) Well.
D) Overflowing well.*

table. When heavy rain increases the content of the aquifer, water enters the river from the rising water table beneath the bed, not from above the bed. If the material composing the aquifer is the same over a large area and the water therefore flows through all of it at the same rate, the water level will rise simultaneously along an entire stretch of the river.

Suppose, though, that the aquifer meets an obstruction. Perhaps the composition of the soil changes, with sand giving way to clay, for example, forming an aquitard. Or suppose that the rock of the underlying impermeable layer is faulted, so part of it has been raised or lowered and the aquifer meets an impermeable wall, an aquifuge. Water will accumulate, the water table will rise, and the flow will resume over the top of the obstruction. It may be, however, that the higher water table lies at or very close to the ground surface, as in drawing B. In this case, groundwater will flow out over the surface. Depending on the type of surface, water may fill a small pool or soak into a patch of adjacent ground, making it permanently muddy. In either case it will then overflow. If the ground surface remains below the level of the water table, the emerging water will feed a small stream. If the ground rises again further down the slope, water will soak back into the ground and rejoin the aquifer. The place where groundwater reaches the surface is called a "spring" if the water forms a stream filling a pool or flowing away downhill or a "seep" if it soaks a small area of soil without emerging visibly from below ground.

Springs and seeps can occur anywhere. They result from the formations of rock and soil below ground, and although all rivers start as springs or seeps in the uplands, these can also be found in valleys and on the plains. Some are more dependable than others, but there are many which have never been known to run dry. That means the aquifers feeding them are never seriously depleted.

Heavy rain or melting snow on higher ground can turn a gentle spring into a raging torrent. The spring marks the place where the water table reaches ground level. Should it rise even higher, because the addition of more water has increased the thickness of the saturated layer, water will pour freely over the surface. It no longer has to make its way slowly through porous rock or soil, so its rate of flow is determined only by gravity and the saturated layer will drain rapidly. What had been a small stream is then transformed into a fast-flowing river, often dividing and rejoining as it courses down a hillside, and its water is delivered quickly to the larger river of which it is a tributary. This will raise the level of the main river much faster than water that travels all the way below ground.

Wells

If no river is nearby, you need not hunt for a spring in order to find water. Almost certainly there is water lying under foot that can be reached by digging a hole. As drawing C shows, it is a simple matter, at least in principle, to dig a hole from ground level down to below the water table, where the bottom of the hole will fill with water that can be extracted with a bucket or pump. This is a well. In practice, it may not be easy, because the water table may be at a considerable depth, and digging a deep hole is always hard work. In Australia, where water is a scarce and highly valued commodity, some wells are approximately 6,000 feet (1,830 m) deep. In the world as a whole, most wells are less than 100 feet (30 m) deep, but even those are the result of a great deal of hard digging.

An aquifer lying beneath permeable soil is said to be "unconfined." A confined aquifer flows between two layers of impermeable material. It is possible for an unconfined aquifer and a confined aquifer to occur in the same place. This happens when a layer of solid rock forms the base, a layer of densely compacted clay lies above the saturated layer, sealing it from above, and the upper impermeable layer lies beneath a deep layer of permeable soil. A second saturated layer may then develop, producing two aquifers separated from each other by an impermeable layer. The lower aquifer is thus confined, and the upper one, unconfined.

Layers of rock are often undulating, so they form depressions and domes. When groundwater flows into a depression in the underlying impermeable layer, it will accumulate there until the water table rises high enough for the flow to spill over the opposite edge. If the aquifer is confined, however, the water table cannot rise beyond the base of the overlying impermeable layer. The aquifer will become saturated, and the weight of water flowing into it will exert enough pressure to force it up and over the opposite lip. In the situation illustrated by drawing D, the aquifer is full, and the pressure on the water in the depression increases toward the center because of the weight of water pushing against it. If it were unconfined, the water level in the depression would rise until the water table was at the same height in the depression and to either side of it.

If you drill a hole from the surface and through the upper impermeable layer, this is what will happen. Once the pressure is released in a particular place, water will rise at that point. A well sunk into the lowest point in the depression will yield water without any need for buckets or pumps. The well will overflow, and if it pierces the depression at a level markedly lower than that of the impermeable rock to either side, as in the drawing, water will gush from it with some force. You can demonstrate this for yourself using rubber or plastic tubing to represent the confining layers.

At Lillers, a small town not far from Lille in northern France, a well of this kind was dug in the year 1126. Lillers is situated in what was then the province of Artois (now the department of Pas-de-Calais). The Roman name for Artois was Artesium, which gave the French their adjective *artésien*, which in English becomes *artesian*. Overflowing wells, which need no pumping because they tap into groundwater that is held under pressure, are often called "artesian wells."

If you live near a river in the plains or in a valley several miles wide, heavy rain need not worry you. It is not the rain falling on the plain or in the valley that will cause the river to flood, but rain falling over a large part of the area the river drains, or snow melting in the far-off mountains. The floodwaters may travel many miles below ground before they emerge, possibly with little warning, to inundate fields and homes.

Vegetation and natural drainage

July and August are the rainy months in Nepal. That is when the Asian summer monsoon brings torrential downpours (see pages 78–84). The monsoon is not altogether reliable: in some years, the rainfall is much higher than it is in others. In 1996, it was high.

Late on Monday, August 5, the rains triggered landslides that swept away dozens of homes in the village of Jhagraku, about 55 miles (88 km) northeast of the capital, Kathmandu. At least 40 people were killed, bringing to 218 the number of Nepalese people who had died in landslides and floods so far in 1996.

Nepal is a small country, a little larger in size than Arkansas, sandwiched between India and Tibet, in the Himalayas. The map shows its location. It has eight of the 10 highest mountain peaks in the world, including Everest, Kanchenjunga, and Annapurna, but also relatively

Nepal, which lies between India and Tibet.

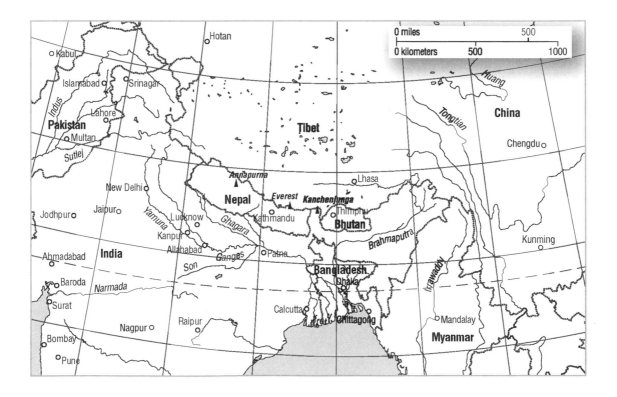

low-lying, level ground at the foot of the mountains in the southern part of the country. Much of this area is cultivated, growing mainly rice. On higher ground, corn, wheat, millet, sugarcane, and other crops are planted in terraced fields; farmers also raise cattle for milk and water buffalo for meat.

At one time, the mountainsides were densely forested with pine and juniper, giving way to juniper shrubs and grassland at higher altitudes. Little by little, however, poor farmers were forced to extend the area of cultivated land further up the slopes, clearing the forest to make way for their fields and homes.

Then, in 1953, Sir Edmund Hillary, a mountaineer from New Zealand, and Sherpa Tenzing Norgay climbed to the summit of Mount Everest, and Nepal attracted the attention of the world just as it was seeking to develop its economy. Homes, hospitals, and schools were built, and roads and bridges for access to them, and later an airfield. The improved access brought tourists and climbers. They had to be accommodated and, in the mountain climate, they needed fuel for warmth and cooking. The fuel and building materials came from the forests. By the 1970s, foreign visitors to the Everest region were arriving at the rate of 5,000 a year, and three times that number of Nepalese moved into the area to provide the services the outsiders needed. Most of the forest was cleared.

Today, with international aid, the Nepalese are planting forests to replace some of those that were lost in the 1970s. Despite this, between 1990 and 2000, forests were still being cleared at the rate of about 193,000 acres (78,000 ha) a year, mainly for fuel. In 2002, deforestation continued at a rate ranging from 1.3 percent of the total forest area in the low-lying areas to 2.3 percent in the hills and 4.8 percent in shrub land. Forests cover approximately 40 percent of the total land area, but at least one-quarter of the forest is in poor condition. The price of so much forest clearance is still being paid. The villagers of Jhagraku are among those who are paying.

Each year, the monsoon rains flow down the mountainsides almost unimpeded because of deforestation. They carry with them soil washed from the surface (see pages 131–137) that ends in the Ganges, which discharges it into the Bay of Bengal. So much soil has been carried over the last quarter of a century that it has made new islands in the river. Before it reaches the Ganges, however, the mixture of mud and rock destroys everything in its path.

Forests and floods

Nepal is far from unique. The mountains of Greece were once densely forested, too, but forest clearance was already well advanced by about 500 B.C.E., and people living in the lowlands had to endure the floods, landslides, and mudslides that resulted. In China the effects of deforestation continue to this day. Between the Great Wall and the high, grassland plateau of Mongolia, there is a plain formed by a deep, yellow soil called "loess," deposited by winds from central Asia. At one time, this plain was forested, but between the seventh and ninth centuries C.E., the forest was cleared. Rains then began to wash the soil into the Yellow (Huang) River, named after the loess. Nowadays, in the lower stretches of the river, every cubic foot of water carries an average of 2.3 pounds of silt (37 kg m^{-3}). As the soil has settled on the riverbed, the river has become shallower and overflowed its banks more often. It still causes catastrophic flooding (see pages 1–8).

The Apennine Mountains, in Italy, were also once forested. Roman troops, however, became wary of the cover the forests afforded enemy forces. As Florence expanded in the 12th century, the trees were felled to provide building material and were never replaced. The hillsides were left bare, and since 1117, when the first flood was recorded, the Arno River, carrying water draining from the Apennines, has repeatedly caused catastrophic floods (see pages ix–xi).

Transpiration

Plants greatly reduce the risk of flooding and mudslides by capturing water and returning it to the air before it can drain away. The process is called "transpiration" (see pages 1–8), and it moves a surprisingly large amount of water. During the six months that elapse from the time its seed germinates until it releases its own seeds and dies, a sunflower plant may transpire more than 50 gallons (189 l) of water. A birch tree may transpire 95 gallons (360 l) of water a day, and an oak tree, 180 gallons (680 l). Indeed, trees are able to move so much water that species that grow naturally on river banks and in other wet places and can tolerate very moist soils are often planted to help dry out wet ground. Through the combined effects of transpiration and evaporation, a forest immediately returns to the air about 75 percent of the rain that falls on it. The precise amount varies according to the temperature and humidity of the air above the treetops.

When it rains, those leaves and stems that are exposed to the rain are wetted. Some of the moisture evaporates from them, and some drips from leaf tips or runs down stems to fall on leaves and stems at a lower level, from which more evaporates. At the same time, and all the time, water is entering plant roots and moving through the plant. The water carries nutrients to each cell and by filling the cells gives them rigidity. Woody plants, such as trees and shrubs, have rigid stems and branches, but other plants, such as herbs and grasses, are able to stand erect only because of the water flowing through them. The water must continue to flow, which means it must leave the plant and be replaced by more water drawn from the soil. It passes through pores called "stomata" in leaves and "lenticels" in roots, stems, and branches, and evaporates from the surface. That is transpiration.

It is possible to measure the amount of water a plant transpires over a given period, but this is feasible only under laboratory conditions. Outdoors it is very difficult to distinguish between water vapor that enters the air by transpiration and water vapor that evaporates from exposed surfaces. In practice, therefore, the two are usually measured together, and the combined process is known as evapotranspiration.

Microclimates

If you walk through a forest on a hot day, you will notice that the air is cooler and stiller than the air outside. It is also moister. The trees provide shade, of course, and shelter from the wind, which accounts for part of the difference, but transpiration also contributes. As transpired water evaporates, the latent heat of vaporization (see sidebar, page 46) is taken from the plant surfaces and surrounding air. This has a cooling effect. In addition, all this water moving into the air above a forest increases its humidity (see sidebar, page 16), so clouds tend to form. This is another climatic effect forests have. Altogether, a forest produces a climate that is different from the climate of the surrounding, unforested area.

It is not only forests that produce a local climate, or more precisely a microclimate, different from the climate of their surroundings. All types of vegetation do so, including grasses, but if you walk across grassland, you will not be aware of this because the microclimate does not extend very far beyond the top of the grass, so most of your body is outside it. At ground level, however, the temperature, humidity, and wind are altered in just the same way as they are in a forest. The effect, however, is smaller because, being much smaller plants, grasses transpire much less water than trees transpire. By day, most plants transpire from 0.4 to 7.3 fluid ounces of water per hour from each square yard of leaf surface (15–250 grams per square meter), and they transpire 0.03–0.59 fluid ounces per square yard per hour (1–20 g h^{-1} m^{-2}) by night. If there are 12 hours of daylight and 12 hours of darkness, this amounts to approximately 0.096–1.56 cubic inches of water per square yard (1.8–30.0 cm^3 m^{-2}) through the day and 0.006–0.12 cubic inches (0.12–2.4 cm^3 m^{-2}) through the night.

Roots

If transpiration is the first line of defense plants provide against floods, their roots are the second. Roots penetrate the soil and actively search for water. In most plants, the roots first grow in length, then later produce side roots, dividing into ever smaller branches only when they find water. Like all living things, roots die and decompose, but for a time, the passages they have forced through the soil remain. These increase the amount of pore space in the soil (see pages 84–91), allowing surplus water to drain downward more easily and join the groundwater.

Roots are hidden below ground, so most of the time we are unaware of them. Try digging anywhere near trees, however, and you will soon see just how extensive they can be. Even then, unless you are able to dig a deep trench, which is difficult, you will find only those roots that are close to the surface and you may not notice the smaller roots, because your spade will cut through them.

Most coniferous trees have fairly shallow roots. This makes them much more likely to be blown down by strong winds than broad-leaved trees, such as oaks and beeches. When a conifer is blown down, its roots are exposed, but you see only a part of the whole root system, because the smaller roots break as the tree falls. Although the roots are not deep, they extend sideways further than the tree's branches. Broad-leaved trees, on the other hand, have roots that penetrate more deeply, some species producing conical taproots that grow vertically downward to a considerable depth.

For most plants, the total mass of the root system is at least equal to the mass standing above ground. If you could stretch out all the roots and root hairs of a tree end to end, they would reach hundreds of miles and fill thousands of cubic feet of space. Even small plants often have huge root systems. The roots of a single wheat plant might extend more than 40 miles (64 km) if they were all joined together in a single line, and those of a rye plant would reach about 50 miles (80 km). A corn plant growing by itself, with no other plants to crowd it, will use its roots to "claim" more than 100 cubic yards (76.5 m³) of soil. The roots of a full-grown wheat plant penetrate 6 feet (1.8 m) or so beneath the surface and some prairie grasses root even deeper—to 8 feet (2.4 m) or more.

Roots allow air to penetrate the soil, and as the roots die, they leave vegetable matter to feed small animals and tunnels to help them move around. The animals, especially worms, then make more tunnels of their own, lining them with mucus that prevents them from collapsing. This, too, helps the soil to drain, but if there are no plants, there is no food for the animals, so they leave.

Effect of removing the plants

Removal of all the vegetation changes the situation quickly. Transpiration and evaporation from plant surfaces cease immediately, and all of the rain falls to the ground and remains there, with only evaporation from the soil surface and natural drainage to remove it.

Just above ground level, the microclimate becomes warmer, because there are no longer plants to shade the surface and evapotranspiration to cool the air by removing latent heat. As the ground warms, the decomposition of dead plant material accelerates, because the chemical reactions by which soil organisms break down large, complex molecules into smaller, simpler ones work two to three times faster for every increase of 18°F (10°C) in temperature. Decomposition ordinarily releases nutrients that are absorbed by the roots of living plants, but in the absence of plants, the nutrients accumulate. For a time, the soil becomes very fertile, but if there are no plants to take advantage of the nutrients, the situation does not last long. The nutrients are soluble, and the rain washes them out of the soil and away. After a few years, the soil has lost its fertility, and it is very difficult to grow plants in it.

Below ground, roots decay. The spaces they made fill with soil particles washed into them from above, and there are no new roots to maintain the amount of pore space. Worms and other animals die or leave, and their tunnels also fill. Gradually the soil loses its structure and becomes less permeable.

If the original vegetation was forest, felling and removing the trees scars the surface. Vehicles move among the trees, and timber is removed by dragging whole trunks across the ground. Small plants are destroyed, and the layer of soil beneath the surface layer is packed down, or compacted, by the weight of the traffic moving over it. The routes along which logs have been hauled and those most used by vehicles are worn into gullies.

Heavy rain pounds the soil, churning it into mud. Water drains downward, but slowly and with difficulty because of the reduction in soil permeability. Before long, most of the surplus water flows directly over the surface and along the gullies, turning them into small rivers.

These problems can occur anywhere, but they are especially severe on high ground. This is because rainfall there is usually heavier than at lower levels (see sidebar, page 25). Air is forced to rise as it crosses high ground, and when it rises, it cools, on average by 5.5°F for every 1,000 feet (10°C per km). Cool air can hold less water vapor than warm air can, so as it cools, the rising air may become saturated. Cloud will then form, and rainfall will be greater than at the lower level. As you know if you have ever walked in the mountains, fog and rain are common at high altitudes, even when the weather is dry down in the valleys. Caracas, Venezuela, lies 3,418 feet (1,042 m) above sea level, and its annual rainfall is 33 inches (838 mm). Maracaibo, not far away and in the same latitude, is at 20 feet (6 m) above sea level and has about 23 inches (584 mm) of rain a year. The difference, of 10 inches (250 mm), results from the different altitudes of the two cities.

Soil erosion

Rain in the hills falls onto sloping ground, often onto steep slopes. If the ground is bare and the soil has lost its permeability, water will flow directly over the surface, plunging into the valleys and quickly filling rivers. At the same time, because there are no longer plant roots to trap and hold soil particles, the flowing water gathers soil and washes it into the rivers. There, it settles on riverbeds, raising their level and in that way further increasing the likelihood of flooding down in the valleys.

This is why the Italian city of Florence, villages in Nepal, and the towns and villages along the floodplain of China's Yellow River suffer so frequently from floods, landslides, and mudslides. The forests that once cloaked the mountainsides and protected them, and many other towns and villages on every continent, have been removed, and the best way to reduce flooding would be to restore them. In some countries, reforestation is under way, but it is difficult, expensive, and uncertain unless the problem is recognized and addressed before the soil deteriorates to the point at which reforestation requires large fertilizer applications to compensate for the lost nutrients. Even so, in the long run, it is probably the most effective remedy.

FLOODS AND AGRICULTURE

The Nile floods and the Aswân Dams

Every year when the star Sirius, which the ancient Egyptians knew as Sothis, appeared on the horizon, the river overflowed its banks. Sothis was the star of Isis, wife of Osiris and the goddess who was believed to have discovered wheat and barley. It was Isis who created and became all vegetation. She was the cultivated field itself, and when the reapers cut the first sheaves of the harvest, they beat their chests and called upon her, mourning the spirit their sickles had slain.

The river, of course, was the Nile, and unlike the Tigris and Euphrates, the two other great rivers of the ancient world, its floods were fairly dependable. The peoples of Mesopotamia living between the Tigris and Euphrates, suffered sudden, violent flash floods (see pages 37–42) that caused appalling destruction and strongly influenced their outlook on the world. Mesopotamian priests spent much of their time studying the sky and state of the rivers, and they developed many techniques aimed at divining what the waters were about to do. Politically, this need to be constantly alert to natural phenomena led to the emergence of strong governments and laws as well as the beginning of science. For the Egyptians, on the other hand, life was much more predictable. Their mainly peaceful and prosperous civilization flourished beside the banks of the Nile, in what was in effect a long, narrow oasis bordered by desert to the east and west, and the way of life of ordinary people changed little for almost 3,000 years.

Apart from its many tributaries, two principal rivers combine to form the Nile. The White Nile, which is the longer, rises in Burundi, and the Blue Nile, which carries the greater volume of water and is the main source of the annual flood, rises in the highlands of Ethiopia (see map). The two Niles meet at Khartoum, capital of Sudan, and about 200 miles (322 km) further downstream, they are joined by the Atbara River. This, and its own tributaries, are no more than strings of pools in the dry season, but in the rainy season, the Atbara is large and muddy and an important source of the silt on which Egyptian farmers used to rely.

The annual flood

Egypt has a dry climate. Cairo has an average annual rainfall of barely more than 1 inch (2.5 cm), and Aswân, 555 miles (893 km) to the south,

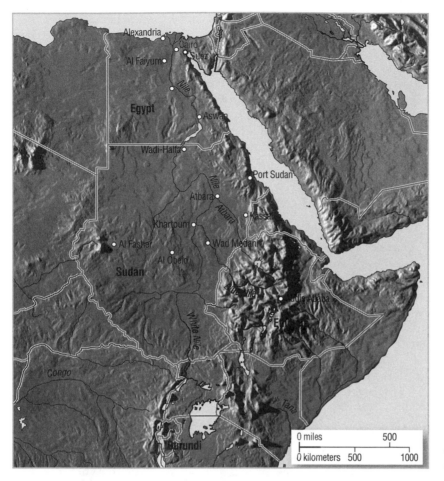

The "Nile countries" of Egypt, Ethiopia, Sudan, and Burundi.

rarely receives any rain at all. Further upstream, however, the rainfall increases, and the average over the highland sources of both Niles is about 50 inches (270 mm). The Nile owes its great size to the huge area it drains—more than 1 million square miles (2.59 million km²)—rather than to a rainy climate in any large part of its basin. The rainfall over the part of its basin in Sudan and Ethiopia, in fact, is strongly seasonal, with a maximum in July and August. This sends a surge of water into the river, reaching its maximum flow in Egypt in late August and early September, which is when the river floods.

North of Aswân, the annual floods have formed a floodplain, covered by a layer of rich, alluvial (river-borne) soil, more than 60 feet (18 m) thick near the Mediterranean coast. Each year, the flood brought a further 110 to 160 million tons (100–145 million metric tons) of silt. Some of the silt settled on the land to replenish it, and the rest was carried into the sea. Nevertheless, the Nile is not exceptionally muddy. During the flood, the water carries an average of about 1,600 parts silt to 1 million parts water, which is less than that in the Colorado and Missouri Rivers. This flood-plain, nowhere more than 12 miles (19 km) wide, opens north of Cairo into a delta, extending 100 miles (160 km) to the Mediterranean and reaching a maximum width of 155 miles (249 km). The floodplain and delta provide the farmland. Traditionally, embankments running from the river to the edge of the desert divided the land to the south of the delta into basins, ranging in size from 2,000 acres (809 ha) to more than 80,000 acres (32,376 ha). Short canals led from the river to the basins. Dikes sealed the canals and were not opened until the river was in flood.

Nilometers

Ancient farmers had advance warning of the flood, because regular readings were taken of the water level at various points upstream by means of Nilometers. The most accurate of these was located at Roda Island, in Cairo. The drawing shows how it worked. River water was fed along a tunnel into a cistern. Because water finds its own level, the level in the cistern was always the same as the level in the river and was not disturbed by waves, so it could be read easily. In this example, the water level is read from a graduated obelisk in the center of the cistern. Other Nilometers used graduations on the side of the cistern itself. Nilometer records have survived; the most complete series, from Roda, covers the years 622 to 1522, excluding some gaps.

When word came that the river was rising, as indicated by Nilometers, muddy water was allowed to flow along the canals and covered the basins to a depth of several feet. The water remained there for several weeks, during which the mud settled and the water soaked into the ground. Then, as the river fell, surplus water drained back into it, leaving behind its soft, sticky mud into which the farmers planted their seeds. When the mud dried it became very hard. Once the river level had fallen, water had to be lifted from wells to provide any additional irrigation the crops needed.

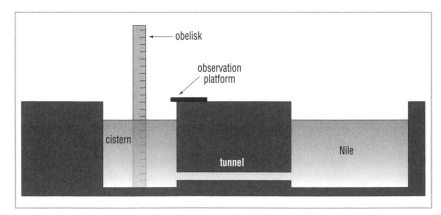

One type of Nilometer.

Sustainable—but with risks

This ancient system must have come close to what people mean nowadays when they talk of "sustainable farming." It produced only one crop a year, but it did so year after year for thousands of years, and there was no sign of the soil deteriorating.

Unfortunately, it had one drawback. Although the Nile flood was reliable, the extent of it was not. Sometimes the water it brought would not be enough to fill all the basins. When that happened, the harvest was poor, and there was often famine. Occasionally, the flood failed for several years in succession, and the famine was catastrophic. Records from the Nilometer at Roda show periods of several years when levels were high and others when they were low, but with no obvious pattern to the changes. When the flood was higher than normal, it might breach the embankments, sending water coursing into homes and threatening to destroy the entire system.

That is why around the middle of the 19th century, low dams were built to hold back the Nile waters from the canals leading from the river. The idea behind the project was to release small amounts of water every few weeks, as it was needed. This system allowed farmers to grow two or three crops a year, and little by little, the Nile and its tributaries were brought under control. It was possible to cultivate a bigger area of land more dependably, and the result was that agricultural production increased.

Even with this improvement, however, it was still impossible to grow crops throughout the year, and in the latter part of the 19th century, six dams were constructed with the aim of increasing control of the river and extending the growing season. The last of these dams was built at Aswân, 3.5 miles (5.6 km) downstream of the town (see map). It was completed in 1902 and heightened twice, in 1907 and between 1929 and 1934. In its day, it was one of the largest dams in the world, with a granite wall 1.5 miles (2.4 km) long that can fill a lake extending 150 miles (240 km) upstream with more than 6.4 billion cubic yards (5,351 m³) of water. There are 180 sluices in the wall. These allow most of the floodwater to pass almost unimpeded, taking its silt with it. Then, after the flood has peaked, the sluices are closed and water is stored for use during the dry season.

Dams can do more than just store water, however. A regular flow of water through or beside the wall can spin turbines and generate electricity. In 1960, a generating plant was fitted to the Aswân Dam and began producing power.

The Aswân High Dam

That was the same year work began on an even more ambitious project, the Aswân High Dam, 4 miles (6.4 km) upstream of the other dam. Built to a West German design subsequently modified by Soviet engineers, its purpose was to free Egypt once and for all from its dependence on the

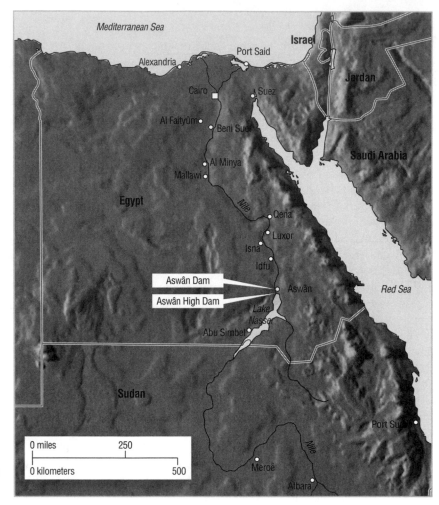

Nile River and the Aswân dams.

annual Nile flood, to increase greatly the area of available farmland, and to generate a substantial amount of electrical power. It took eight years to build the dam wall and two more years to complete the installation of the 12 generating turbines. These were made in the Soviet Union, which also sent 400 technicians to work on the project and contributed one-third of the $1 billion cost. At one point, the dam's construction employed about 33,000 workers.

On January 15, 1971, the dam was officially declared open. Its wall is 364 feet (111 m) high, more than 3,000 feet (915 m) thick at its base, and 2.3 miles (3.7 km) long. It is difficult to imagine the size of the dam, but its volume is about 17 times that of the Great Pyramid at Giza. Its hydroelectric generators can produce 2.1 gigawatts (GW) of power (1 GW = 1 billion watts), which is enough to supply Egypt with 25 percent of its electricity.

Behind the dam lies its reservoir, Lake Nasser, named after Gamal Abdel Nasser, president of Egypt when the dam was built. It averages 6 miles (9.6 km) in width and is 310 miles (500 km) long, nearly one-third of it located across the border in Sudan.

Costs and benefits

From its inception, the dam project was controversial. All dams involve the flooding of low-lying land to form the reservoir. This is inevitable and always unpopular, but the valley that was flooded to fill Lake Nasser contained many ancient sites of great historic importance. An international project was launched in 1960, headed by the United Nations Educational, Scientific, and Cultural Organization (UNESCO), to save the 19 most important monuments. Several temples, including that at Abu Simbel, together with its huge statues, were removed entirely and reconstructed on high ground close to the new lake, and all the endangered monuments were preserved and can be visited at their new sites. The valley was also inhabited, of course, and all 100,000 people living there had to be evacuated and resettled.

Severe environmental problems were also predicted. Some materialized and are described below; others did not. The aim in building the dam was to supply enough irrigation water to increase the area of farmland by about 900,000 acres (36,420 ha). Work toward this goal went under way, but a drought began in 1979 and lasted for several years, lowering the water level in the lake by 20 percent. The water supply to farms had to be curtailed, and the power output was almost halved. Despite this setback, the output of corn and wheat increased steadily during the drought years, although rice production did not do so well.

The table shows the annual yield of these crops from 1971, the year the dam was completed, to 1999, excluding 1987, 1990, 1996, and 1998. Yields are measured in two ways: the amount produced (in thousands of metric tons; 1 metric ton = 1.1 tons) and as indices, which are useful for comparing the output in different years. Yields for one base year—in this case, 1971—are given a value of 100, and yields for other years are calculated as percentages of the yield in the base year. In 1983, for example, the corn yield was 150 percent of the 1971 yield; the wheat yield, 115 percent; and the rice yield, 96 percent.

As the table shows, corn and wheat yields increased steadily, but then leapt ahead around 1990. By then they had more than doubled since 1971. Rice yields lagged, often not reaching their 1971 level (index less than 100), but then they too began to increase around 1990, and in 1999, they were more than double the 1971 figures.

Whether yields continue to rise at these rates depends on major improvements in irrigation schemes. Egyptian farmers were used to cultivating basins watered by the annual flood. Perennial irrigation calls for different techniques.

EGYPTIAN ANNUAL PRODUCTION OF THREE CEREAL CROPS
(in thousands of metric tons; figures in parentheses are indices, 1971 = 100)

Year	Corn	Wheat	Rice
1971	2,342 (100)	1,729 (100)	2,534 (100)
1972	2,421 (103)	1,618 (94)	2,507 (99)
1973	2,508 (107)	1,838 (106)	2,274 (90)
1974	2,600 (111)	1,850 (107)	2,500 (99)
1975	2,600 (111)	2,033 (118)	2,450 (97)
1976	2,710 (115)	1,960 (113)	2,530 (100)
1977	2,900 (124)	1,872 (108)	2,270 (90)
1978	3,197 (136)	1,933 (112)	2,351 (93)
1979	2,937 (125)	1,856 (107)	2,507 (99)
1980	3,230 (138)	1,796 (104)	2,348 (93)
1981	3,308 (141)	1,806 (104)	2,236 (88)
1982	2,709 (116)	2,016 (117)	2,287 (90)
1983	3,510 (150)	1,996 (115)	2,440 (96)
1984	3,600 (154)	1,815 (105)	2,600 (103)
1985	3,982 (170)	1,874 (108)	2,800 (110)
1986	3,801 (162)	1,929 (112)	2,450 (97)
1987	Figures not available		
1988	4,088 (174)	2,839 (164)	1,900 (75)
1989	3,748 (160)	3,148 (182)	2,680 (106)
1990	Figures not available		
1991	5,270 (225)	4,483 (259)	3,152 (124)
1992	5,226 (223)	4,618 (267)	3,908 (154)
1993	5,300 (226)	4,786 (277)	3,800 (150)
1994	4,883 (208)	4,437 (257)	4,582 (181)
1995	5,178 (221)	5,722 (331)	4,789 (189)
1996	Figures not available		
1997	5,180 (221)	5,600 (324)	4,900 (193)
1998	Figures not available		
1999	5,500 (235)	6,347 (367)	5,900 (233)
2000	6,395 (273)	6,534 (378)	5,996 (237)

Figures from Britannica Book of the Year (*published annually by* Encyclopaedia Britannica)

When water is supplied to the surface, it drains quickly through the sandy soil. It is lost to the crops but accumulates as groundwater, causing the water table to rise slowly. In some parts of Egypt, it is rising at 6 to 10 feet (1.8–3.0 m) a year and has already reached the root zone of plants. Effectively, the soil is becoming waterlogged. When that happens, plant roots are deprived of air, which they need for respiration. Evaporation from the surface then draws water upward, but as it evaporates salts dissolved in it are deposited in the upper layer of soil. Most crop plants can tolerate only small concentrations of salts, and if those are exceeded, the crops die. The remedy to both waterlogging and salt accumulation, or "salination," as it is called, is to install efficient drainage. This removes surplus water. Unfortunately, it is expensive.

Environmental costs and unanticipated benefits

In the hot, dry climates of Egypt and Sudan it was feared that much of the water in Lake Nasser would be lost by evaporation. Indeed, each year, the lake loses an estimated 9.3 cubic miles (15 km^3) of water in this way. It is replenished, of course, but this is wasteful nevertheless.

Aquatic plants have grown rapidly in the lake. They clog irrigation channels and create areas of stagnant water in which insects breed, including disease-carrying species. The water in the lake is warm and rich in plant nutrients carried into it by the river. A diverse and abundant population of microscopic plants and animals has established itself in the lake. Fish were introduced, and other fish species arrived by themselves to feed there. Lake Nasser now supports a thriving fishing industry.

As well as water, the dam traps and holds the silt carried by the Nile. This settles to the bed of the lake. Eventually it will raise the bed so much that the dam will be useless, but it will be several centuries before that happens. This is partly because much of the silt is collecting at the southern end of the lake. One day this will reach the surface and dry, providing a small area of land for the use of the Sudanese. Downstream, of course, the fields no longer receive their annual load of nutritious sediment. Farmers have to compensate for the loss of nutrients by using factory-made fertilizer.

Now that water flows at much the same rate throughout the year, the Nile itself has changed. Its water has become more salty, because of salts entering from adjacent fields, and it is contaminated by fertilizer and pesticides. This has reduced the number and variety of fish, partly offsetting the national economic benefits of the Lake Nasser fishery and causing hardship to the people who formerly fished the river downstream and a very long way from the lake. The dam has also reduced the quality of water people use for washing and drinking. The lack of silt has led to erosion along the banks of the river and in the delta, where the coast is receding and salt water is infiltrating into the groundwater (see pages 120–125). Silt no longer reaches the Mediterranean, where it used to nourish organisms supporting an important sardine fishery. Sardine fishing in the eastern Mediterranean has almost disappeared.

Finally, the presence of water throughout the year has led to an increase in diseases transmitted by aquatic organisms. Schistosomiasis (or bilharzia) is probably the most widespread of these. It is not fatal, but its victims become weak and apathetic, and it can lead to more serious secondary infections. It can be treated with drugs, but victims are easily reinfected. It is caused by a microscopically small animal called a fluke, or trematode, belonging to one of three species of the genus *Schistosoma*. Its eggs hatch in water, and the larvae enter the body of an aquatic snail. There, they develop into small fork-tailed animals, called "cercariae," that leave the snail and swim around in the water until they find a mammal, which may be a human. They discard their tails and burrow through the skin, feeding on glycogen in the blood and are carried to the lungs and from there to the heart and liver, growing all the time. When mature they mate and lay eggs that exit the host body in urine or feces, and the cycle begins again. Before the dam was built, many of the snails died during the dry season, and this restricted the numbers of *Schistosoma* flukes. Now more of the snails can survive, and the flukes are spreading. Schistosomiasis has become a serious problem in the Nile delta and it is spreading south along the Nile valley.

Overall, the benefits of the Aswân High Dam greatly outweigh the harm it has done. Nevertheless, the experience shows that interfering with the natural behavior of a river has consequences reaching far beyond those associated with the management of its water flow.

Wet rice farming

Floods usually cause huge amounts of damage to property, destroy crops, and kill people, but some floods are encouraged. Where flooding can be relied on and controlled, it can be useful, and Asian farmers have been using it for thousands of years.

Whenever you eat rice in any form, including rice-based breakfast cereals and snacks, almost certainly floods helped in its production. Oil obtained from rice bran is used in making some margarine, so even that food may have been produced with at least some assistance from floods. In southern and eastern Asia, where rice is the central part of the diet—as bread and other wheat products together with potatoes are in the West—the floods bring life, not death.

Rice is the most important food commodity in the world, in terms of the amount that is grown, with wheat coming in a close second. In 2001, the total world production of wet rice amounted to more than 652 million tons (592.8 million metric tons). Wheat production in that year amounted to about 638 million tons (580 million metric tons). Almost 90 percent of all the world's rice is grown in Asia, and most rice is eaten in the region where it was grown. Of all the wheat grown in the world, about 20 percent is exported, but less than 3 percent of rice is exported. The table shows the amount of wet, or paddy, rice grown in 2001 by each of the main producing countries—those countries that produced more than 1 million tons—arranged in descending order.

Where did it begin?

No one knows where rice was first cultivated, but the modern plant is most probably descended from a plant that once grew wild over much of southern Asia. A different species, native to West Africa, was domesticated there. By 2800 B.C.E., rice was a regular part of the diet in China, and the Chinese may have learned of it from India. Certainly, Indians were eating it at about that time, although it may have been grown even earlier in Thailand. Rice chaff has been found at Non Nok Tha, an archaeological site in northeastern Thailand, and dated to 4500–4000 B.C.E. and traces of chaff have been found in China and dated to around 5000 B.C.E. Neither of these may have come from cultivated rice, however.

Knowledge of rice cultivation spread to the Middle East, and the invading Saracens brought it to Europe in the Middle Ages. Rice is still grown in southern Europe and used in traditional dishes such as paella and risotto. It was first grown in North America in 1685, in South Carolina. Rice growing spread from there to North Carolina and Georgia by the early 19th century, and its cultivation moved westward after the Civil War, to Louisiana, Texas, Arkansas, and eventually to California, where it is now one of the 10 most economically important farm crops. At present, Arkansas is the leading U.S. producer, followed by California, Louisiana, Mississippi, Missouri, and Texas.

Nowadays, rice is grown in many parts of the world, in latitudes as high as 53° (the latitude of Edmonton, Alberta), and in mountains up to 8,000 feet (2,440 m) above sea level, but about 80 percent of all rice is grown in the lowlands in low latitudes. It thrives best and produces the biggest yields in fields that are flooded for part of the year.

Rice is a grass

Rice is a grass related to the other cultivated cereals, but it differs from them in one respect. Like most plants, cereal grasses cannot tolerate waterlogged soil. Their roots need air for respiration, and they drown if the roots are totally immersed in water. The roots of rice plants also need air, but rice stems are hollow, and provided the upper part of the plant stands clear of the water surface, air reaches the roots through the stem. Rice can also be grown on dry land, in the hills beyond the reach of floodwaters. This is known as upland rice. Less than one-fifth of the

WET RICE PRODUCTION, 2001

Country	Amount (millions of tons; millions of metric tons)
World total	652.11; 592.83
Asia total	593.83; 539.842
China	199.67; 181.515
India	145.08; 131.90
Indonesia	55.11; 50.10
Bangladesh	43.02; 39.11
Vietnam	35.12; 31.92
Thailand	27.72; 25.20
Myanmar	22.66; 20.60
Africa	18.67; 16.97
Philippines	14.25; 12.95
Japan	12.45; 11.32
Brazil	11.23; 10.21
United States	10.63; 9.66
South Korea	8.05; 7.32
Pakistan	7.42; 6.75
Egypt	6.27; 5.70
Nepal	4.64; 4.22
Cambodia	4.51; 4.10
Nigeria	3.63; 3.30
Sri Lanka	3.15; 2.87
Madagascar	2.53; 2.30
Malaysia	2.44; 2.21
Laos	2.42; 2.20
Iran	2.41; 2.20
Colombia	2.32; 2.11
North Korea	2.27; 2.06
Peru	2.22; 2.02
Ecuador	1.51; 1.38
Italy	1.34; 1.22
Uruguay	1.13; 1.03
Ivory Coast	1.10; 1.00

Source: Food and Agricultural Organization (FAO) of the United Nations

bread wheat durum wheat rice

Wheat and rice. Bread wheat, used to make bread, is similar in appearance to the wheat used to make cakes and pastries. Durum wheat is used to make semolina for pasta. Rice ears look quite different from either cereal.

world crop is grown this way, however, because upland rice produces much lower yields than "wet" rice, although the rice itself is no different.

Rice also looks rather different from wheat, barley, and rye. These latter cereals bear seeds—the grains that we eat—in ears bunched tightly around the stem of the plant, forming a spike. Rice seeds (and also those of oats) are held much more loosely in a panicle. The drawing shows bread wheat, durum wheat (used to make pasta), and rice.

There are two cultivated species of rice: *Oryza sativa* and *O. glaberrima*. *O. glaberrima*, known as red rice from the color of its bran, is the West African species, but it is little grown elsewhere. American wild rice, also known as Indian rice and Tuscarora rice (*Zizania aquatica*) is also a grass, native to eastern North America. It resembles the rice plant but is not closely related to *Oryza*; botanically, it is not rice at all.

The rice we eat, and the one eaten in Asia, is *O. sativa*, of which there are two types, or subspecies: *O. sativa indica* and *japonica*, which can be broken down into tens of thousands of varieties among each. *Indica* rice has long grains that are separate after cooking. *Japonica* grains are round and stick together when they are cooked. Cooked and dried *japonica* grains are used to make rice flakes, crispies, and puffed rice.

Growing rice

When rice is grown on dry land, the technique is the same as that for growing wheat. The land is plowed and harrowed, and the seeds are sown in rows. For wet rice, the technique is different. In the United States, many rice growers drop seed and fertilizer together from airplanes into flooded fields, then spray pesticide later, also from the air. Together with machines for harvesting, this technique has reduced the number of person-hours per acre from 900 to about seven (from 2,224 to 17 person-hours per hectare).

Traditionally, and until recently in the United States, growing rice is hard, back-breaking work. The seeds, comprising rice grains with their husks, are soaked in water for 24 hours, then stored for a day or two until they start to germinate. At that stage they are sown in dry soil, where they grow for a month. Meanwhile, the wet fields are prepared. They are low lying and surrounded by dikes or banks, called "bunds," and after the surface has been tilled it must be made level. Water is then allowed to flood the fields. Most are flooded to a depth of about 4 inches (10 cm), but for some varieties, the rice is planted into dry ground that is then flooded with deeper water. Once the field has been flooded it is called a "paddy," the same name the rice is given just after it has been harvested. Machines are sometimes used to transplant the seedlings from the nursery into the paddies, but this is often done manually, by women and children who must spend long hours bent almost double with their feet and hands in water. The seedlings are planted about 6 inches (15 cm) apart, in rows about 12 inches (30 cm) apart.

As the crop starts to ripen, the water is drained from the field and the ground dries. With modern varieties, the crop is ready to harvest about 17 weeks after it was sown in the paddies; traditional varieties ripen more slowly. The introduction of new varieties as part of the "Green Revolution" has meant two crops a year can often be grown where only one grew before. In some places, annual yields have increased eightfold.

After harvesting

After harvesting, the rice sheaves (stalks and ears together) are stacked and left to dry for a few days, then the grain is separated by threshing and winnowing to remove the chaff. The grain is next milled to remove the husk. At this stage, it is brown rice, which many people prefer. Brown rice still retains the layer below the husk, called the "bran" (the aleurone layer, rich in enzymes and thiamin) and the "germ" (from which a new plant would grow). A second milling removes these, and the grains are passed through brushes to remove any remaining particles of bran or husk. Once complete, it is white rice. In some countries, the white rice is polished by coating it with talc and glucose.

About one-fifth of the world rice harvest is parboiled before its first milling, a technique that is most popular in India and southern Asia. Parboiling involves soaking the rice, with its husks, for one or two days; heating it for a short time in a sealed vessel with very little water; then allowing it to dry once more before milling. This alters the outer layer of the starchy endosperm, toughening the grains so that fewer break during milling. Parboiled rice takes a little longer to cook, but its grains do not stick together.

It is also more nutritious than non-parboiled rice because the part of the endosperm affected by parboiling absorbs thiamin (vitamin B_1) from the bran, thus reducing the amount that is otherwise lost during cooking.

Water is essential

Obviously, water is the key to wet rice cultivation, and the best rice-growing land is on the floodplains and deltas of large rivers. Rice is grown in the deltas of the Red River and Mekong in Vietnam, the Chao Phraya in Thailand, and the Brahmaputra and Ganges in India and Bangladesh.

Southern Asia is affected by the monsoons (see pages 000–000). During the winter monsoon the climate is dry, but the summer monsoon brings heavy rain to swell the rivers, which tend to overflow their banks. It is this natural flood of which the rice farmers take advantage, allowing the water to inundate the paddies and drain from them once the rains have eased and the river levels have fallen. Elsewhere, the paddies must be flooded artificially, by means of irrigation canals, and outside the monsoon regions many ingenious irrigation systems have been devised over the thousands of years since people first began growing rice.

Despite the fact that rice grows under conditions that would destroy any other cereal crop, rice farmers are as dependent on the weather as any others are. The floods are needed, but only at certain times and to certain depths. Monsoon rains are not always reliable. In some years they arrive late, or fail to arrive at all, and in others they are so heavy as to wash over the paddies and carry away the tender young plants. Outside the monsoon region, drought destroys rice more quickly than it can destroy wheat, and heavy rain or hail shortly before harvest can wreak just as much damage to rice as it can to wheat.

THE COST OF FLOODS

Coastal erosion

After a certain stormy night a few years ago, a married couple who had recently moved into a house beside the north shore of the Firth of Forth, in eastern Scotland, found that half of their backyard had disappeared into the sea. Where the yard had been the evening before there was a large hole filled with seawater. A sea wall between their yard and the beach, built many years ago and thought to be safe, had been breached by the waves.

Hundreds of miles away, on a different coast and at a different time, the grounds of a hotel vanished when the cliff beneath them collapsed. The storm had made the building so insecure that the emergency services allowed the owners of the hotel 10 minutes to remove their belongings and vacate the premises.

Entire villages that were once beside the sea are now beneath it, some distance from the shore. Such disappearances give rise to stories—some of them possibly true—about the sound of ghostly church bells that ring beneath the waves during storms as they are swayed by currents. The eroded material does not simply vanish, however. Often the sea deposits it further along the coast, so that while the coastline is receding along one stretch, elsewhere it is advancing and the land area is growing. There are villages that once had harbors and fishing fleets but are now a mile or more inland.

Why coastlines change

Coasts change constantly. Some scientists define *coast* as a wide belt of land and sea along which the shoreline, the actual boundary between dry land and the sea, shifts back and forth. These shifts occur naturally, but several different forces are involved, and not all shorelines are affected to the same degree.

Part of this change is due to the fact that in some places, the land itself is rising, and in others, it's sinking, a result of the melting of the glaciers and ice sheets from the last ice age. It is this sea level rise due to the glacioisostatic sinking of the land (see sidebar) that increases the risk of coastal flooding along much of the eastern seaboard of the United States and on coasts bordering the southern North Sea. Eastern and southeastern England are vulnerable, too, and this was part of the reason for building the Thames Barrier to protect London from tidal surges (see pages 73–77). Obviously, the risk is greatest where coastal land is low lying. London averages 16 feet (5 m) above sea level, but certain districts are lower, and severe flooding could swamp the subways and sewers, with disastrous

Glacioisostasy

During an ice age, the polar ice sheets expand until they cover a substantial part of the northern continents. At present, we live during an interglacial (the Holocene interglacial), but the ice has not retreated altogether. The Greenland ice sheet is 5,000 feet (1,525 m) thick on average, and the thickness of the ice sheet covering most of Antarctica averages about 6,900 feet (2,100 m).

Ice is heavy, and an ice sheet thousands of feet thick is very heavy indeed. It presses down on the solid rocks of the Earth's crust beneath it. These rest on the hot, slightly plastic rock of the mantle below the crust, and the extra weight of the ice makes them sink into it. At the edges of glaciers and ice sheets, however, the ice pushes the surface rocks upward, so the center of the ice sits in a depression and its edges on a bulge.

When the ice age ends and the ice melts, the weight is removed and very slowly the rocks return to their former level. The diagram shows the result. Rocks that were depressed beneath the center of an ice sheet rise, and those that were elevated near the edges sink. This readjustment, called "glacioisostasy" (*isostasy* is from the Greek words *isos*, meaning "equal," and *stasis*, meaning "station"), began as the ice retreated around 10,000 years ago and is not yet completed. In Scandinavia, the weight of ice depressed the land by about 3,000 feet (915 m), and so far it has risen again by about 1,700 feet (518 m). In parts of Scotland, there are beaches, with seashells embedded in them, that lie 130 feet (40 m) above the present sea level. Northeastern Canada, Greenland, northern Scandinavia, and northern Scotland are still rising, and the sea level is falling. Elsewhere, around the coasts of North America and Europe, the land is sinking meanwhile, and sea levels are rising.

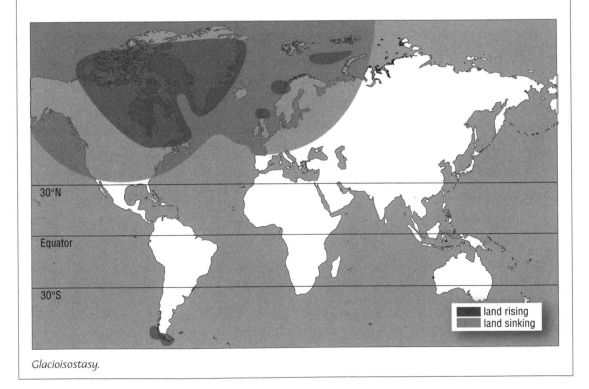

30°N

Equator

30°S

■ land rising
▨ land sinking

Glacioisostasy.

consequences. Some U.S. cities are also at risk. Baltimore is only 14 feet (4.3 m) above sea level; Charleston, South Carolina, 9 feet (2.7 m); Miami 25 feet (7.6 m); and Norfolk, Virginia, 11 feet (3.4 m).

Over the past century, the average temperature has risen slightly throughout the world. This has warmed the oceans, and when water is warmed, it expands. The expansion of ocean water has raised the sea level in many places by about 6 inches (15 cm) compared with its level around 1900. (This is not true everywhere, however; see sidebar.) If global warming continues, the sea level is expected to go on rising, although scientists are unable to estimate by how much. Although glaciers have been retreating in mountainous regions for many years, the polar ice caps are not likely to shrink, and the West Antarctic ice sheet is growing thicker, not thinner. Consequently, melting ice is unlikely to release enough water to increase the volume of the oceans significantly. Nevertheless, even a small rise could make floods more frequent along very low-lying coasts, especially coasts that are sinking through glacioisostatic readjustment.

These changes happen so slowly that no one notices them. Along some coasts, where storms and surging waves seem to be growing bigger or more frequent, sea walls are made higher and stronger, but elsewhere, vulnerable coasts are still considered very attractive places to live.

Isle of the Dead

In the middle of the 19th century, the island of Tasmania, then known as Van Diemen's Land, was a British penal settlement in the South Pacific. Thomas Lempriere, one of the officials in charge of the settlement, maintained careful records of tides and weather. In July 1841, the Antarctic explorer Sir James Clark Ross (after whom the Ross Sea is named) visited Tasmania and met Lempriere. The two men discussed Lempriere's meteorological and tidal records and the problem Lempriere had with tide gauges, devices placed on the shore to measure the extent of the tidal movement. Convicts routinely vandalized the gauges, so he had to keep moving them to new locations. In the course of their conversation, Lempriere and Ross hit upon a plan to make a permanent marker, called a "bench mark," carved into the rock. The bench mark would show the height of the mean tide, the level halfway between the lowest and highest points reached by the tide, and would be impossible to vandalize.

They decided the mark should be made on a small island, about 2 acres (1 ha) in area, located in Port Arthur harbor at a point sheltered from storm-driven waves. Superstitious convicts avoided the island, because it was used as a burial ground and considered spooky. The island was known as the Isle of the Dead.

Lempriere set up a tide gauge on the Isle of the Dead in July 1841; he later carved a bench mark beside it. In the 1990s, John L. Daly, a Tasmanian with a keen interest in climatology, read about the bench mark and decided to explore the shore of the Isle of the Dead in search of it. He found the mark exactly where the records showed it should be and discovered that it still registered the mean tide level. This meant the sea level on this part of the Tasmanian coast had not risen since 1841.

Battering by the waves

Other changes are wrought by the sea itself. Sea cliffs were once rounded hills. Continual battering by waves has worn away the rocks of which they are made, cutting them back and leaving the sheer faces visible today. This process never ceases; along the beach at the foot of a cliff after a storm, you will often see boulders recently torn from the cliff. Eventually, the sea and wind will break them apart again and again until they are reduced to gravel or sand.

A sea wall can protect a cliff against erosion by waves, and many such walls have been built, especially where the cliff is only a few feet high and there are roads and buildings close to its edge. Often they succeed, but sea walls can fail. It was the failure of an apparently secure sea wall that carried away part of that backyard overlooking the Firth of Forth. If the beach between the wall and the sea is low enough for waves to break against the wall itself, the reflection of the waves from the wall will scour away the beach. This lowers the beach further and exposes more of the wall. Lowering the height of the beach reduces the amount of energy that waves dissipate in crossing it, so they have more energy when they strike the wall. In time this can weaken it.

The best protection for a cliff is a high beach. This was demonstrated dramatically in south Devon, England. In 1887, about 810,000 tons (735,500 metric tons) of shingle were mined from a beach there to be used as building material for the construction of new dockyards at Plymouth. This reduced the height of the beach by about 13 feet (4 m) and allowed waves to break with full force against the cliff behind the beach. Between 1907 and 1957, the cliff retreated by 20 feet (6 m). Waves then attacked the village of Hallsand, by that time on the clifftop, eventually leaving it in ruins.

Coasts where there are beaches made from sand or gravel are the most popular places to vacation and to live. They are also the most changeable. How quickly they change depends on the configuration of the coastline and the character of the sea to which it is exposed. There are high-energy and low-energy coastlines. You can tell one from the other by looking at a map. A high-energy coastline will be very irregular in shape, with cliffs, headlands, bays, and small coves, or with sand dunes and big, sandy beaches. A low-energy coastline will be generally low-lying and relatively straight, with wide, shallow bays and spits projecting from it here and there.

Building as well as destroying

It is easy to imagine how waves erode coastlines, but they also build them. Material removed by the sea from one place is usually deposited somewhere else.

As a wave approaches a beach, it enters increasingly shallow water and eventually it breaks (see pages 58–65), then spilling up the beach and expending the last of its energy, with water falling over itself repeatedly.

This turbulence stirs up the sand or gravel, and as the water flows back down the beach and toward the sea, some of this material travels with it, only to be carried back by the next breaking wave. Waves that are generated by winds far out at sea reach the shore quite widely separated, as a regular swell. Ocean swell tends to carry material onto the beach and leave it there, so it builds beaches.

Storms close to the shore produce short, steep waves that carry material away from the beach. Many beaches are eroded by storms, then rebuilt by the ocean swell between storms so that although they are constantly changing, over time building and erosion find a balance. Often, the balance takes place over the year. Winter storms erode the beach, so in spring it is quite small, but calmer weather in the summer and fall rebuilds it.

Furthermore, fine sand grains are easier to shift than large grains or pebbles. One consequence of this is that the larger particles tend to be pushed up the beach rather than carried into the sea. Generally, this means that the bigger the particles from which the beach is made, the steeper it will be.

Longshore currents, littoral drift, and groins

Waves seldom arrive at right angles to a coast. Most of the time they strike obliquely. This produces a longshore current, flowing parallel to the shore. As each wave breaks at an angle, beach material is carried up the beach at one angle, then down the beach at another angle, and some of it is caught in the longshore current. Both on the beach and in the water adjacent to it, sand and even gravel are carried along the coast. The process is called "littoral drift." The diagram shows how littoral drift, produced by wind- and tide-generated waves, shifts beach material along the coast. The wavy line represents the direction in which material is transported by wave action; the pale gray band is the longshore current into which some of the material is swept. The process works steadily, but a brief increase in wave energy can accelerate it dramatically, and a substantial part of a beach can vanish overnight. Further along, where the angle between the shoreline and the waves is different, the current loses energy and drops the material it is carrying. There it accumulates, eventually building into a bar or barrier.

Littoral drift can have alarming implications for people living beside beaches, so it is not surprising that they try to prevent it. It is not only shoreline property that is at risk. The beach itself may be a valuable asset, attracting vacationers. As seaside vacationing became popular in the 19th and 20th centuries, attempts were made to prevent the disappearance of beaches that attracted visitors with money to spend. Groins were a favorite device. Some are still in place, and the remains of others can be seen on many beaches.

A groin is similar to a sea wall but erected at a right angle to the shore, so it lies across the beach, extending as far as the low-tide mark or beyond. Often groins were made from timber, and many of them have now decayed

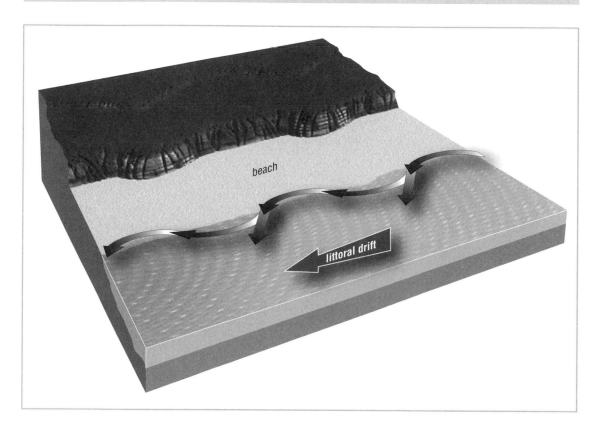

beach

littoral drift

and vanished. Their purpose is to trap the sand or gravel that is being carried by the waves before it can move far enough offshore to become littoral drift.

Groins are little used nowadays, because after they had been in place for some years, it was found they had curious effects. As the upper drawing in the illustration shows, in the absence of groins littoral drift transports material along the beach at the base of the cliffs. A groin, however, captures much of this material, as shown in the lower drawing. This is what it is meant to do, of course, but the groin also breaks the waves. This sends water eddying turbulently around the other side of the groin, adding to the force of the waves there; consequently, the groin reduces beach erosion on one side but increases it on the other. A series of groins along a beach eventually alter the shape of the beach to one with triangular heaps of sand or gravel against one side of each groin and a scooped-out, much smaller beach between groins. More seriously, reducing parts of the beach in this way accelerates the erosion of the cliff behind the beach.

Piers and jetties, projecting into the water at right angles to the shoreline, have a similar effect. They, too, can accumulate beach material on one side and accelerate erosion on the other. Beaches move about naturally, and in most cases, it is probably wise to let them do so.

Littoral drift. Beach material is transported parallel to the beach by wave action.

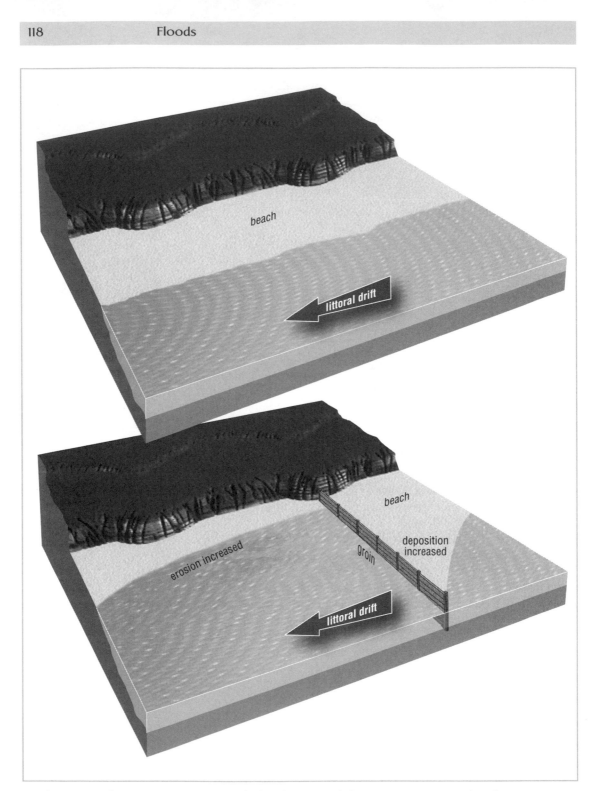

Beach erosion and protection. Groins protect the beach on one side but increase erosion on the other.

Barrier islands

Along much of the eastern seaboard of the United States, the high-energy coast is protected by barrier islands. These are made from sand that is scoured from the coast by waves and then deposited as long strips lying parallel to the shore. Waves sweep right over the lower barrier islands, whereas the higher ones often have wide beaches. The islands absorb the energy of the waves, and in doing so, they constantly change shape and location. Damaging the barrier islands can quickly expose the coast to the full force of the waves, so care is taken to protect them.

Even protection can cause problems, however. In the 1930s, some of the barrier islands off the North Carolina coast were protected by sand fencing, built to trap sand and prevent it from being swept away during storms. The sand dunes grew taller and plants were established to stabilize them. Waves could no longer lose their energy gradually by flowing over and between unstable dunes; instead, they expended it all at once on the permanent dunes. The beaches over which the waves flowed became narrower and steeper, erosion increased, and behind the islands, water driven into Pamlico Sound by northeasterly winds could no longer drain across the islands to the sea. Now it accumulates and floods the coastal area.

Rivers and erosion

Large rivers also extend coastlines and protect them from erosion and flooding. Rivers carry soil particles that are washed into them from land all along their courses. As they flow into the sea, chemical reactions between the chlorine in seawater and the particles cause them to cling together in lumps (the process is called "flocculation"). These lumps settle to the bottom. Gradually, the sediment grows thicker until it is capable of absorbing a substantial part of the energy of waves crossing it. In some places, the sediment lies so close to the surface that the land can be reclaimed from the sea.

Inland, however, soil erosion from farmland is a serious problem (see pages 131–137), and great efforts have been made to reduce it. These have been successful, but reducing erosion means the rivers no longer carry so much soil. Between the 1930s and 1960s, the amount of soil transported by the four principal rivers of Texas (the Brazos, San Bernard, Colorado, and Rio Grande) fell by 80 percent, and it remains low. There has also been a large reduction in material carried by the Mississippi. This has greatly reduced soil erosion from farmland, but it has also reduced the volume of sediment that is deposited in the Gulf of Mexico and thereby increased coastal erosion. Over the last century, Texas has lost four times more land along its coast than it has gained by reclamation, and this is due partly to the success of its soil conservation policies inland. River discharges have been reduced in this way right along the Atlantic coast of the United States.

Most of us enjoy walking and playing on the beach. The sea attracts many people, and not surprisingly, some of those who are able to make the move choose to live there. If they relocate to a stretch of low-energy coast, where the sea is gentle, all may be well, but high-energy coasts can be dangerous places, where the shoreline moves back and forth, cliffs collapse, new land emerges from the sea, and flooding can occur at any time.

Saltwater infiltration

Some years ago, the Dutch authorities deliberately allowed some of the polders (tracts of low land) bordering the North Sea to be flooded. They feared that a rise in the sea level would cause salt water to infiltrate below ground, contaminating the groundwater. Had this happened and been allowed to continue, the contamination might have affected a large area, and in time, it would have made the soil infertile.

Most crop plants are very intolerant of salt. Plants absorb water through the tips of their root hairs. At the same time, they absorb mineral nutrients dissolved in the water present in the soil. This soil solution is more dilute than the solution inside the plant, so water passes readily through the cell walls of the root hairs by osmosis (see sidebar). For most plants, this works only if the soil solution is based on freshwater. (Some are adapted to salt water.) The presence of salt makes the solution more concentrated, and water does not need to be very salty before it is more concentrated than the solution inside cells. In that case, osmotic pressure causes water to move in the opposite direction, out of the cell. This is why if you drink only seawater, you will become increasingly thirsty as the cells of your body lose water and dehydrate. It is also why most plants die in salt water, and salt renders soils infertile.

Osmosis

Certain membranes are partially permeable: some molecules can pass through them, but not others. Many biological, naturally occurring membranes are of this type, but they can also be manufactured industrially.

If a partially permeable membrane separates two solutions of different strengths, there will be a pressure across the membrane that forces solvent molecules (molecules of the substance, such as water, in which the solute is dissolved) from the weaker to the stronger solution until both are at the same strength. This is called "osmotic pressure," and osmosis is the process by which molecules cross the membrane under osmotic pressure. The most common solutions occurring naturally are of substances dissolved in water, so the movement across membranes is most commonly of water.

Cells are enclosed within partially permeable membranes and contain substances dissolved in water. If the solution outside the cell is stronger than that inside, water will pass out of the cell. If the solution inside the cell is the stronger, water will pass into the cell.

The Dutch remedy was to seal off the coastal polders lying on the landward side and flood them with freshwater to keep out the salt water. What were once fields are now freshwater lakes. As an amenity they are valuable, but making them has required the loss of farmland. It was a deliberate manipulation of flooding. Causing a flood at the surface prevented a much more serious flood below ground.

Polders

Polders are fields made by reclaiming land from the sea. The Netherlands is renowned for them, and the word itself is of Dutch origin. People who had settled on the river deltas and along the adjacent, low-lying, marshy coast of what is now the Netherlands were at constant risk from floods. As early as the first century C.E., they were building mounds to protect their land from the rivers and the sea. The first dikes may have been built in the eighth or ninth century. By the end of the 13th century, dikes enclosed substantial areas of farmland. More have been added and more land reclaimed in the centuries since then.

Between 1920 and 1932, part of the Zuider Zee inlet of the North Sea was closed by building a dam 18.5 miles (29.77 km) long, called the Afsluitdijk, giving the country more than a half million acres (about 202,000 ha) of additional farmland. The southern part of the Zuider Zee is now known as the IJsselmeer, and the part to the north of the Afsluitdijk that adjoins the North Sea is called the Wadden Zee. The resulting Dutch polders now occupy 2,500 square miles (6,475 km²)—almost one-fifth of the total land area of the Netherlands—and much of this land lies below sea level. Prins Alexander Polder, the lowest point in the country, is 22 feet (6.7 m) below sea level. The map shows the location of the Netherlands in northwestern Europe.

The Dutch are especially noted for their land reclamation, but people have been reclaiming land from the sea throughout history and no doubt were doing so long before anyone compiled written records. Presently, there are polders in many countries, wherever coastal lands are flat and low lying and farmland is in short supply, such as England, France, Germany, Denmark, Japan, India, Guinea, and Venezuela. In the 18th century, polders could be found in Georgia and the Carolinas, used mainly for growing rice (see pages 106–111). These eventually fell into disuse, and the land reverted to coastal marsh.

To make a polder, the first step is to surround the area with dikes. These are levees (see pages 155–161), high and strong enough to keep out the sea. Then the water must be removed. If the polder is above the high-tide level, surface water can be allowed to drain away at low tide, and the polder resealed. If it lies below the low-tide level, the water must be removed by pumping, the purpose of the windmills for which the Netherlands is famous. These lifted water from the polders and poured it into elevated drainage channels that carried it to the sea. Such windmills as remain today mainly serve as tourist attractions, apart from those

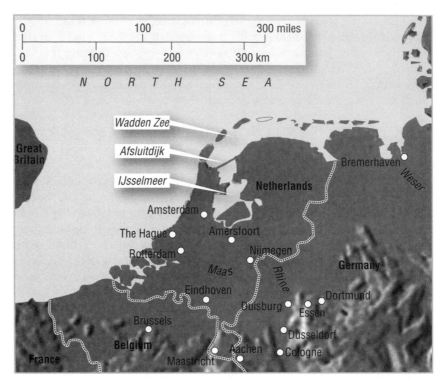

The Netherlands.

generating electrical power or used to grind cereals. At one time there were about 10,000 wind- and watermills in the Netherlands; now about 1,035 windmills and 106 watermills are turning, and engines drive the pumps that do the drainage work.

Once the surface water has been drained away, the salt must be removed from the soil. This is done by pumping freshwater or water containing very little salt onto the surface. As it sinks through the soil, the salts dissolve into it and are carried into the drainage system and away to the sea. In time, a layer of freshwater accumulates below ground and joins the groundwater draining from further inland. Freshwater is less dense than salt water and lies above it. The freshwater and salt water mix slowly, but there is a boundary between them. Above the boundary there is a layer of freshwater that is deep enough to supply the needs of the farmer. As soon as the soil has been treated to make it fertile, the polder is ready for use.

Below the surface

Below ground and within the reach of plant roots, there is fresh groundwater. On the seaward side, however, salt water pushes some distance inland. It is denser than freshwater, so it moves beneath it, usually as a wedge. As the upper drawing in the illustration shows, this may make the land immediately adjacent to the sea infertile, because there the groundwater is wholly salt, while a little way inland plants have adequate access to freshwater. If irrigation is needed, a well sunk into the groundwater will yield freshwater.

It may be, though, that so much freshwater is abstracted that the water table falls, as in the lower drawing. This allows the salt water to intrude further, because there is less freshwater holding it back. Salt water then soaks into the underlying sand, gravel, or rock that formerly held freshwater. Now the well is tapping salt water and the coastal strip that is rendered infertile by salt water below ground is wider.

The drawing suggests that the boundary between freshwater and salt water is sharp. In fact, the two mix, and the line in the drawing represents a midpoint. Moving from left to right in the drawing, the freshwater becomes a little salty, then increasingly so until it is pure seawater. Water is considered unfit to drink if its salt content exceeds 2 percent, so it takes only mild contamination to cause considerable trouble.

Salt intrusion

Saltwater contamination of freshwater is a problem in the Netherlands. Crop irrigation and surface evaporation during periods of dry weather have lowered water tables, and little by little the sea intrudes into the

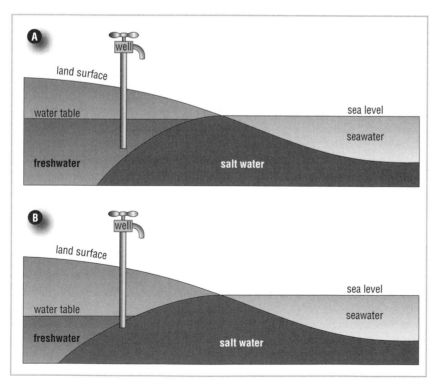

Saltwater intrusion.

groundwater. By flooding polders with freshwater, the intrusion of seawater is checked, protecting the fields on the inland side of the newly made lakes.

The problem of saltwater intrusion is not confined exclusively to the Netherlands. Increased water abstraction occurs whenever people move into an area to live, and as long ago as the 1950s, saltwater intrusion was known to be occurring in the United States. It affected coastal areas in every state bordering the Atlantic and Pacific Oceans and the Gulf of Mexico, as well as in Hawaii.

Coastal wetlands, such as marshes and mangrove forests, trap sediment and often store freshwater, but coastal development usually requires such areas to be cleared of vegetation and drained, to provide building land. This happened many years ago at Sanibel Island, a large, exposed barrier island (see pages 112–120) off the Florida coast. Removing the vegetation led to saltwater intrusion from above, as well as from below. Storm surges poured over the shore to cause flooding inland by salt water. Seawater also penetrated the sand dunes that surrounded and protected the interior. At the same time, salt water intruded into the groundwater.

On the mainland, canals can be built to drain surplus water from farmland and carry it toward the coast, but this can make the situation worse. Instead of carrying freshwater seaward, in dry weather seawater is able to push inland by the same route, so the canals flow backward and salt contaminates the fields.

When people move into coastal areas, they need more than homes and roads; they also wish to use the sea for recreation. This sometimes calls for the digging of channels or deepening of rivers to provide sheltered anchorages linked to the open water. It is seawater that flows into the channels, of course, and the resulting change in the circulation of water and in its chemical composition can allow salt water to infiltrate the groundwater. When deeper channels were cut in the Sacramento River delta, that is precisely what happened.

Nor is it only the coastal strips where groundwater suffers this kind of contamination. During dry weather, when river levels are low, seawater can also move inland beneath riverbeds. Salt water often moves beneath the Hudson as far upstream as Poughkeepsie, New York, and it also follows the Delaware, Potomac, Sacramento, and other rivers.

Saltwater intrusion is a form of flooding, but it is one that takes place below ground. It happens out of sight, and by the time its effects become evident, the harm has already been done, and remedying the situation will be difficult and expensive. As always, prevention is much better than cure. In some places it is possible to insert a layer of impermeable material between the fresh- and salt waters to keep them apart. Elsewhere, sites must be examined before any development starts to trace the way subsurface water moves, and the development then should be planned accordingly. Wetlands (see pages 150–155) should be disturbed as little as possible for this reason alone, as well as for their value as habitat for wildlife. Finally, limits should be set to the amount of fresh groundwater that can be abstracted for irrigation or other uses. If the water table is found to be falling, abstraction should be stopped and freshwater imported from outside the area and poured in to recharge the groundwater.

Flood damage

Beneath the city streets, groundwater moves slowly downhill, and at its upper margin there is a water table. Water moves below ground just as it does everywhere else, with one important difference. When it rains over the city, water soaks vertically downward into the groundwater only from parks, backyards, and other open spaces where there is soil and where plants grow. Rain that falls onto buildings, streets, and parking lots cannot soak downward, so it flows into storm drains that carry the water away, eventually to a river, a lake, or the sea.

Drains are pipes, and there is a limit to the amount of water they can carry. Beyond a certain rate of flow, they can accept no more. Once the drains are loaded to capacity, instead of disappearing through the grills beside roads, water will flow along the road itself. If the storm drains discharge into a nearby river and heavy rain or the rapid melting of snow upstream has increased the volume of water in the river, raising its level, the situation may be still worse. River water may flow back through the drains, forcing the rainwater ahead of it and sending water up through the grills and onto the streets.

Scientists use measurements of rainfall, the type of surface, the height of the water table, and other relevant information to calculate and apply flood peak formulae. These are numbers that are used to predict the maximum rate at which water is likely to drain from an area. This number is much higher in cities than it is in rural areas. In Chicago, for example, the peak flow is up to four times greater in the commercial and industrial areas than it is in residential areas, where water can drain through natural soil. This difference is typical. The measurements and calculations show that flooding is a greater risk in a city than in the countryside surrounding it and that the water rises faster in the city, often much faster.

What water can do to a city

Cities stretch far below ground level. Buildings have basements and cellars, and beneath these are service tunnels of all kinds, carrying telephone and electric cables, gas and water pipes, and sewers. A city's service tunnels flood first.

Floodwater is not clean. Apart from the harm caused by soaking, a flood leaves behind a thick deposit of mud, picked up from the land over which it has swept, together with debris of all kinds. In the 1966 flood in Florence (see pages ix–xi), the Arno River shifted 1 million tons of soil, rubble, furniture, and other debris. It took four weeks to clear it all, using heavy earth-moving equipment.

Floods also hamper rescue efforts. Overflowing rivers sweep away bridges. Water rushing through and beneath a town can lift sections of road and railtrack and smash them, leaving them broken and piled high with rubble. At three o'clock in the afternoon on February 19, 2002, for example, a fierce storm of rain and hail broke over the city of La Paz, Bolivia. It lasted for no more than 50 minutes, but it was so intense that cars were completely buried beneath hailstones. The city is built on the steep side of an extinct volcano, and water rushed down the hillside, turning the streets into fast-flowing rivers that swept away cars and hurled people against lampposts, trees, and cars, causing serious injuries to more than 100 people. The Choqueapu River burst its banks, filling an underpass beneath the main street, El Prado, with mud, hail, and water to a depth of nearly 10 feet (3 m) and killing five people. An underground parking lot was filled to the roof with hail and debris. The water also ripped up streets and ruined the foundations of buildings. The final death toll was 70, with about the same number missing and unaccounted for.

Underground flooding also creates a risk of fires and explosions. The floodwater fractures gas pipes and electric cables, exposing bare live wires that are liable to generate sparks. At the same time as it shuts down these essential services, it also breaks telephone lines. Above ground, poles carrying overhead power and telephone lines are swept away even more easily than trees. Communities can be left isolated, their road and rail links broken, and all the telephone lines down. A region around Omegna, near Lake Maggiore in northern Italy, was briefly isolated in this way by a flood and landslide in July 1996. Fortunately, in these types of situations, emergency workers can communicate by radio and members of the public often can use their cell phones.

The force of water and buoyancy

When water moves, it exerts considerable force (see sidebar, page 28). It is the force of moving water that has carved the Grand Canyon. Niagara Falls appeared about 12,000 years ago, when the ice retreated at the end of the most recent ice age. During its 12,000 years, the water has worn away so much rock at the edge that the falls have retreated by about 7 miles (11 km). Water that can carve out a canyon and cut into a mountainside can easily shift almost any loose object and demolish wooden buildings. Water has another effect, too. It reduces the weight of objects, making them easier to move—some objects even float.

This principle of objects becoming lighter in water is said to have been discovered by the Greek mathematician and engineer Archimedes (c. 287–212 B.C.E.). The story goes that Hieron, the king of Syracuse, to whom Archimedes was related, asked Archimedes to discover whether a new crown the goldsmith had just delivered was pure gold or a mixture of gold and silver, but to do so without damaging the crown. Archimedes had no idea how to undertake the task until one day when he stepped into his bath, which was a little too full, some water overflowed. He realized that the volume of the water that overflowed was precisely equal to the volume of the part of his body that had entered the tub. The minor mishap had revealed to him how to analyze the crown without damaging it. He was so excited that he jumped from the bath and ran naked through the streets of Syracuse to the palace, shouting "Eureka! Eureka! ("I've found it!").

Silver is less dense than gold, so weight for weight, it is bulkier. Archimedes saw that if he immersed the crown in water, measured the amount of water it displaced, and compared this with the volume of water displaced by the same weight of pure gold, he could tell whether the crown contained silver. He weighed the crown, borrowed a similar weight of pure gold from an honest goldsmith, and immersed each to measure their volumes. The crown was bulkier, proving that it contained silver. He informed the king, and the goldsmith was executed.

No one knows whether the famous tale is true, but the principle of buoyancy certainly is. You can easily demonstrate for yourself that when an object is immersed in water, it displaces a volume of water equal to its own volume and experiences a force acting upward that is equal to the weight of the displaced water. Buoyancy is this upward force that water (or any other fluid) exerts on a body immersed in it. One cubic foot of water weighs 62.4 pounds (1 cm^3 weighs 1 g). The density of a substance is the mass of a given volume of the substance, so 62.4 lb ft^{-3} (1 g cm^{-3}) is the density of water. If the density of the immersed object is the same as the density of water, the weight of water it displaces will equal its own weight. The object will then experience neutral buoyancy and remain at the same level in the water. If its density is less than that of water, it will experience positive buoyancy and bob to the surface and float, like a cork. If its density is greater than that of water, it will experience negative buoyancy and sink, like a stone. Even if it experiences negative buoyancy, however, the upward buoyancy force will reduce its weight. Astronauts learn to work outside their space vehicles and do "space walking" by practicing tasks underwater, where they experience neutral buoyancy and are therefore weightless. Buoyancy also allows elephants and hippopotamuses to move gracefully in water and makes it possible for animals the size of whales to exist at all—by reducing their immense weight.

Why some things float

Wood experiences positive buoyancy, in other words, it floats, because it is less dense than water. One cubic foot of oak, for example, weighs about 44 pounds (1 cm^3 weighs 0.7 g). Moving water will raise wooden objects as well as push them forward. Metals are denser than water, and experience negative buoyancy and sink. Whole objects made from metal may also contain air, however, and what matters is the density of the object as a whole, not necessarily the material from which it is made. Steel sinks in water, but ships made from steel contain air, which is why they float.

Automobiles also contain air. Modern cars are well made, with tightly fitting doors and windows that make them almost watertight. Imagine you are sitting in a car when floodwater washes past it. Water splashes into the engine, which stalls, leaving your vehicle immobilized. Suppose the car is 12 feet long and 5 feet wide (3.7×1.5 m) and that with the passengers on board it weighs 1.5 tons (1.36 metric tons). The water rises around you and soon reaches the level of the floor. As it rises higher, the water exerts a buoyancy force on the car. When it has risen 1 foot (30 cm) above the floor level, this force, equal to the weight of the displaced water, will amount to about 1.8 tons (1.6 metric tons). The car at this point weighs less (it is less dense) than the water beneath it. The car will float and once its wheels lose contact with the road surface, there will be no way someone inside can control it. The flood is in charge and will carry you where it will.

Making an allowance for the distance between the floor of the car and the road, when the flood is 2 feet (61 cm) deep all but the heaviest cars will float provided their doors are shut. Open a door and water will fill the car, adding to its weight and sinking it so it stays on the road.

About half of all people killed in flash floods in the United States die because they are trapped in automobiles that have been carried away on the waters. Eventually the vehicle is likely to enter deeper water and, despite its tightly fitting doors, it will slowly fill with water and sink. When the water outside has risen until it is close to the top of the doors, the pressure of the water may make it impossible to open the doors without lowering a window first. That allows the car to fill with water, thus equalizing the pressure on either side.

Trailers, campers, and mobile homes are also liable to float and then he thrown against one another haphazardly but often violently. When the flood also brings down rocks, trees, and other large pieces of debris, the damage is compounded as these objects are hurled with considerable force against vehicles. This happened on July 7, 1996, at a campsite in the Spanish Pyrenees.

Fleeing for safety

People who live in more solid houses and are indoors when the floods arrive can seek shelter on upper floors and eventually the roof. They will survive, but the contents of their homes will be ruined by contact with the water. This is tragic for families, but the damage can be worse. Floodwaters can wash away the ground from around buildings, weakening the structure, and this, combined with the pressure of the moving water against the sides, can cause irreparable structural damage. Floods can even carry away whole houses, when these are not firmly fixed to solid foundations. On the afternoon of Sunday, June 14, 1903, a substantial wooden house in Heppner,

Oregon, was carried six blocks by a flash flood. Its bottom story was reduced to splinters and, of course, the entire house was wrecked. Almost one-quarter of the population of Heppner, about 250 persons, died in that flood.

When the waters start to rise, many people flee their homes. There may have been some warning of the impending flood, giving the authorities time to evacuate the areas deemed to be at risk. The scale of evacuation, part voluntary and part compulsory, is often huge. A total of about 28,000 people were evacuated from their homes in southern Manitoba, Canada, in May 1997, during what was called the flood of the century, but the drama often plays out on a much larger scale in Asia. In August 1996, floods in Bangladesh caused 100,000 people to flee their homes, and the same month, 80,000 evacuated their homes in Hanoi, Vietnam, when the Red River burst through a dike 30 miles (48 km) upstream and flooded the city to a depth of several feet. The following month, tropical storms brought widespread flooding to central Vietnam, and 114,000 people had to leave their homes.

Heavy monsoon rains also devastate vast areas. They inundated 60 villages in the Indian state of Assam in the summer of 1996, forcing an estimated 1.5 million people to flee. The authorities had to establish 120 relief camps to accommodate them. In 1995, summer rains caused floods in three provinces of China that killed at least 1,200 people and left 5.6 million people marooned by the waters. That flood destroyed about 900,000 homes, and accommodation had to be found for 1.3 million people.

When there is no time to escape

Advance warnings usually allow enough time for evacuation, but regrettably this does not always happen. Furthermore, evacuation is possible only if enough transport is available. There may not be time for people to walk to safety. Floods, especially flash floods that arrive very suddenly, almost always cause some deaths. Between November 9 and 17, 2001, for example, 750 people died in floods in northern Algeria, most of the casualties in the Bab el-Oued district of the capital, Algiers. Those floods also left 24,000 people homeless and destroyed at least 1,500 houses in Algiers alone. Nevertheless, the number of fatalities from floods is much lower now than it used to be.

On April 17, 1421, the sea broke through dikes at Dort in the Netherlands, inundated polders (see pages 120–125), and drowned 100,000 people. Asia has suffered disasters on this scale more recently; for example, in 1876 in what is now Bangladesh, a cyclone from the Bay of Bengal brought torrential rain to rivers that were already at their high monsoon levels, and the Ganges and Brahmaputra overflowed. It caused one of the worst natural disasters in modern history, drowning 100,000 people in just half an hour. Similar flooding in the summer of 1996 affected nearly one-third of Bangladesh, but caused only 120 deaths. This is still a large number, but the toll was much lower than that of the 1876 flood.

In rural areas, there are fewer homes for floods to destroy, but when fields lie underwater, the crops in them are ruined. If the water is flowing fast it will carry away soil (see pages 131–137) and along with it, fertilizer, seeds, or growing plants. Still water is no better. It will fill all the spaces between soil particles so there is no air for the roots and the plants will drown. When the waters recede, what remains of the crop will lie dead beneath a thick layer of mud.

Where food supplies are already barely adequate, floods can lead to famine. Floods in the summer of 1996 destroyed about one-fifth of the North Korean rice crop and 2.5 million acres (1 million ha) of crops in China.

The destruction of crops can lead to food shortages, but more immediately it ruins the livelihoods of many people. Nearly 6 million people lost their homes and crops in the 1996 floods in Bangladesh. After such a catastrophe, not only does the government face the problem of replacing the lost food, but it must also help all those who have been left destitute.

Disease

Since floods are caused by too much water, it may seem strange that one of the most serious hazards associated with them arises from a water shortage. Piped water supplies fail when the pipes fracture and there is no power to drive the pumps, and sewers are overwhelmed. Ordinarily, sewage is removed by allowing it to flow under gravity or by pumping. An overflowing river sends water in the opposite direction under great pressure. This pushes back the contents of sewers, which can then overflow into the streets. As the flood subsides it leaves behind large pools of water in low-lying areas on the surface and in the cellars and basements of buildings. This water contains material transported by the flood and is likely to be seriously contaminated with sewage.

These are the conditions in which disease-causing bacteria flourish, and it is all too easy for them to infect people. Diarrhea, nausea, and vomiting are the most widespread symptoms. These are unpleasant and can be dangerous, especially for young children, as they may indicate very serious illnesses. Cholera, dysentery, and typhoid fever are among the diseases that may follow a flood, and unless treated, these diseases can kill. Treatment requires medicines and health workers to distribute them quickly, and the diseases can be checked only by removing the contaminated water and restoring a reliable supply of clean water. The need is urgent, because these diseases can spread rapidly to become epidemics.

The cost

We often measure the cost of any disaster in monetary terms. This is convenient and allows us to compare the severity of one disaster with that of another. Counted in this way, floods are always expensive, with damage running to hundreds of millions of dollars and sometimes more. In 1996 alone, damage due to flooding was estimated to have cost $140 million in Russia, $200 million in Canada, $600 million in South Korea, $2 billion in northern Europe, $2.5 billion in the United States, and $12 billion in China. The cost varies quite widely from year to year, however. During the 1990s the average annual cost of flood damage in the United States was $4 billion. In the world as a whole, flood damage costs approximately $40 billion a year.

A price tag, however, tells only part of the story, and perhaps the less important part. The tag refers to damage to homes, crops growing in fields, factories, and to the streets, bridges, and public buildings that are central to communities. It has risen over the years, in the United States from $1 billion in the 1940s to $4 billion in the 1990s (the figures are adjusted to take account of inflation), mainly because of rising property values and the increasing proportion of all property that is insured.

But the rising waters also damage human lives, and it is ordinary people who pay the real cost in terms of bereavement; the loss of homes and possessions, even of jobs when businesses are destroyed; and livelihoods ruined when crops are inundated and fishing boats smashed and sunk. In some countries insurance may help with the cost of repairing homes and rebuilding lives, but not everyone can afford insurance, and it cannot heal the emotional wounds left by the loss of cherished possessions or the ruination of achievements resulting from a lifetime of hard work. Far less can money compensate the survivors for the lives that are lost.

Floods and soil erosion

Big rivers carry vast amounts of sediment. Every year, 11 million tons (10 million metric tons) of soil particles travel down the Tennessee River and into the sea, and the Missouri transports 176 million tons (160 million metric tons) a year. This movement of soil from the land to the sea continues year in and year out, although the amount a particular river carries depends on the kind of land across which it flows. In all, the United States loses about 4 billion tons (3.6 billion metric tons) of soil a year, around half of which is deposited as sediment in lakes or in the sea just off the coast.

After very heavy rain, river levels rise, and the appearance of river water changes. Rivers that were once fairly clear become opaque as they turn into raging torrents, because the quantity of soil in them increases dramatically. If, then, they overflow their banks so that the floodwaters flow directly over the land, even more soil is carried downhill. This soil is not necessarily lost, because a proportion of it is deposited on land near the bottom of the slope.

Weathering

Soil consists of mineral particles, formed from rock that is split when water freezes inside small cracks, expanding with tremendous force as it does so. Later, when the ice melts, fragments flake away from the rock surface. These are then rolled by the wind and water, and battered and ground down by friction with other particles. The process is called physical weathering and differences in the composition and structure of the original rocks produce soil particles that vary widely in size. (Chemical reactions with rock minerals cause chemical weathering which also contributes to soil formation.)

One ounce of dry sand contains about 2,500 grains (88 per gram) if the sand is very coarse and up to 1.3 million (45,500 per g) as the sand becomes finer. Silt particles are much smaller. One ounce of them contains about 165 million (6 million per g). Clay has the smallest particles of all. About 2.5 trillion of them weigh just one ounce (87.5 billion per g). If plants grow in the soil, it will also contain organic matter made up of their remains and those of animals, together with the products of their decomposition.

Pick up a handful of soil, and unless it is very dry, its particles will stick together in small lumps. While it is in the ground, these lumps are more or less joined to form a soil mass. When water moves soil, however, it must begin by detaching particles or small lumps from this main mass. This is the first stage in erosion.

Once the particles or lumps are detached, the water can shift them. It will do so whenever heavy rain falls onto bare ground and water flows over the surface down a slope. Gradually, the soil becomes deeper at the bottom of the slope and shallower at the top until eventually all of the upper layer of soil, the topsoil, may have been removed from patches at the top of the field, exposing the subsoil. The appearance of exposed subsoil may be the first visible sign that alerts the farmer to what is happening.

Soil removes soil

Erosion feeds on itself. Clear water dislodges very few soil particles, even when it flows quite fast. As soon as it starts carrying particles, however, its power to dislodge more soil increases greatly. The particles themselves do the work, by slamming into particles that are attached to the main soil mass and knocking them free. As the water proceeds down a slope, not only does the load of soil it carries increase, but so does the rate at which it gathers more.

Obviously, the speed of flow is important, because the kinetic energy (energy of motion) of the particles is proportional to the square of their speed (see sidebar, page 28), but the length of the slope is even more important, for two reasons. In the first place, the water has further to travel down a long slope than down a short one, so there is more time during which it can gather soil. In the second place, a larger area of ground is exposed on a long slope than on a short one, and assuming that moving water covers the whole area of the slope, there is more water available to gather and transport soil.

The larger the drainage basin (see pages 24–31) supplying a river system, the less soil that enters it from each acre of land. This does not mean that less soil is transported, but only that more of it is deposited in relatively low-lying areas before it reaches the river. The Mississippi discharges 1 million tons (908,000 metric tons) of sediment into the sea every day, but its drainage basin is so large that this amounts to only 290 tons a year for each square mile (102 metric tons km^{-2}). Much smaller basins in the San Gabriel Mountains of California lose up to 5,000 tons of soil per square mile (1,750 metric tons km^{-2}) annually, and when fires have destroyed the chaparral vegetation, the loss can increase to as much as 100,000 tons per square mile (35,050 metric tons km^{-2}).

Erosion is worst in deserts

Soil is more likely to be stripped from the land surface in regions where the climate is dry than in places where rainfall is spread evenly through the year, even though rain falling in every month adds up to a greater annual total. Where the climate is dry, weeks or months may pass without rain. During this time the soil dries out thoroughly. Except on clay soils, which shrink and harden as they bake in the hot sunshine, drying separates soil particles. The cloud of dust that follows an automobile traveling along a desert road is proof that the soil has turned to dust or loose sand. Few plants can grow when the soil is in this condition, so the vegetation is sparse. Scattered shrubs and clumps of tough grasses are separated by wide expanses of bare ground.

When at last the rain arrives, it often does so as a fierce storm that dumps a huge amount of rain in a very short time. Even a very porous, sandy soil cannot absorb the water fast enough to prevent it from flowing across the surface, and a fine-grained soil quickly turns to waterlogged mud. The flowing water surges over the ground, carrying soil with it and leaving behind deep gulches, arroyos, and dry washes that it carves as temporary channels. These features, common in the Great Plains and western United States, are evidence of the erosive power of torrential rain. Over most of the United States east of the Rockies, storms that are severe enough to be regarded as rare events account for up to 90 percent of the soil particles carried by rivers.

Even so, certain places are more vulnerable than others. In the 1930s, for example, an area to the north of Salt Lake City, Utah, suffered a series of floods that caused a great deal of damage, because the floodwaters brought with them large amounts of sand, gravel, and boulders. This material was later found to have come from particular localities, making up only 10 percent of the watershed over which the waters had flowed, where overgrazing and fires had removed most of the vegetation. Grazing was stopped, the areas were given better protection from fires, and trenches were dug across the slope at intervals of 25 yards (23 m) and sown with tough grasses. Rainstorms have been just as frequent in the years since then, but there have been no more floods carrying large amounts of debris.

Water that flows across the surface in a flood is lost. Floods are caused by too much water, of course, but in deserts and regions of low rainfall, all water is valuable. If it could have been trapped and stored, there would have been water to irrigate crops after the storms had passed (see pages 161–168).

When erosion matters

New soil is forming all the time, so the loss of soil by erosion is significant only if the rate of loss is greater than the rate of soil formation (see sidebar). In recent years, the United States has been losing soil by erosion

---

Soil erosion

The loss of soil from the land surface is an entirely natural process. It commences as soon as soil is exposed to wind and rain and the eroded soil is transported elsewhere. If the soil is carried by water, eventually it usually reaches the sea or a river estuary. At the same time, soil is forming naturally. The rate varies, mainly because of differences in climates, but soil forms at an average of approximately 0.3 inch (8 mm) a year. This amounts to approximately 0.9 ton per acre (2 metric tons ha^{-1}) per year. (This is the approximate weight of 0.3 inch [8 mm] of dry soil over an acre [hectare] of ground.) If the rate of erosion exceeds the rate of soil formation, there will be a net loss of soil by erosion. If the rate of soil formation exceeds the rate of erosion, soil will accumulate.

Agriculture accelerates natural erosion because cultivation loosens the soil, making it more vulnerable to the action of wind and water. It also leaves the bare soil exposed to the weather between the time one crop is harvested and the following crop becomes established. Whether a particular rate of erosion is acceptable depends on the circumstances, but erosion from a thin soil overlying bedrock is much less acceptable than erosion from a deep soil.

Both wind and water erode soils, but water is the more serious cause of erosion. Water accounts for somewhat more than half of all erosion, wind for

about one-third, and the remainder (less than one-sixth) is through chemical and physical deterioration of the soil. The rate of erosion (A) from a field that is to be farmed in a particular way can be estimated in advance from the universal soil-loss equation: $A = R \times K \times L \times S \times C \times P$.

The erosivity of rainfall (R)—its capacity for eroding soil—is determined by measuring the amount and type of rainfall, converting this mathematically to an index number, and reading the value for erosivity from a table. The erodibility of the soil (K)—its susceptibility to erosion—is a number related to the type of soil. The ratio of the length of the field under consideration to the length of a standard field of 25 yards (22.6 m) gives the length factor (L) of the field. The slope factor (S) is the ratio of the amount of soil lost by erosion to the amount lost from a field with a 9 percent gradient and is related to the gradient of the field. The crop management factor (C) is the ratio of the amount of soil lost to the amount lost from a cultivated field that is left fallow, but with the soil bare. It is related to the type of farming, such as arable cropping, temporary grass, rough grazing, etc. The conservation practice factor (P) is the ratio of the soil lost to the amount lost from a field where no steps are taken to reduce erosion. Values for all of these factors are found in tables.

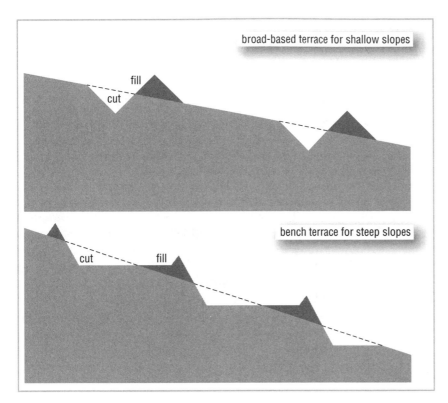

broad-based terrace for shallow slopes

fill

cut

bench terrace for steep slopes

cut   fill

Two types of terracing used to reduce water runoff and soil erosion.

at about 17 times the rate at which new soil is forming, and about 90 percent of the country's cropland is losing soil faster than soil is forming. This is serious, but in parts of Africa, Asia, and South America, soils are eroding at about twice the U.S. rate. Unless the management of farmland improves greatly, the Food and Agriculture Organization (FAO) of the United Nations estimates that by 2010, approximately 346 million acres (140 million ha) of land will be suffering from serious erosion, most of it in Asia and Africa.

Terracing controls the gradient of a slope and is very effective in reducing erosion. Terraces break a slope into a series of level areas, like steps. Water flowing down the slope slows at each terrace, allowing more time for it to deposit its load of soil and to soak into the ground. A ridge along the downhill edge of each terrace, resembling a low wall, traps still more water. As the diagram shows, on a shallow slope, the ideal arrangement involves digging a shallow ditch along the lower edge of each terrace and using the excavated material to make a low ridge. The terraces themselves are broad based and slope gently. On steeper slopes the "bench" terraces are horizontal. There, the material that is excavated along the uphill edge of the terrace to make the terrace level is used to build the low ridge along the downhill edge of the adjacent terrace on the uphill side.

Where does the soil go?

Although dry regions are more vulnerable, few places are immune from floods and the loss of the soil that they remove. It is the upper layers of soil that contain the nutrients plants need, and their loss renders the soil much less productive. Much of the soil removed from sloping ground is deposited at a lower level. This might make it seem that one field's loss is another's gain, but it is not so simple. After the topsoil has been stripped away, less fertile subsoil is likely to follow it and then be deposited on top of the topsoil. The soil that accumulates is often fairly useless for farming, because the less fertile subsoil is at the top, and the entire mass of water-borne soil, deposited as thick mud, buries the cultivated soil and the plants already growing in it. When floods course through a town, large amounts of the soil they carry are left behind as a thick layer of dirty, useless mud filling cellars and coating streets and the floors of buildings.

Not all the soil transported in this way is dumped onto the land. Much of it enters rivers and is carried downstream. As the river crosses almost level ground, its waters flow more slowly. They then have less kinetic energy with which to transport solid particles and these begin to settle on the riverbed. This raises the bed, but not by the same amount everywhere. Piles of sediment collect in particular places until they rise high enough to form bars that interrupt the flow of water. During peak flows, these bars shift this way and that, but by reducing the size of the river channel, they also increase the likelihood that the river will overflow its banks. By carrying away soil, a flood upstream makes it more probable that some time later the river will flood further downstream.

If the river is dammed, the sediment will settle in the reservoir behind the dam. Reservoirs are used to store water and to generate power, and the accumulation of sediment reduces their capacity to do either. About 35 years after it was built, Washington Mills Reservoir, at Fries, Virginia, was able to hold only 17 percent of the volume of water it held originally due to sedimentation. This was an extreme case, but most reservoirs are made by damming rivers, and they lose a significant proportion of their volume in this way.

Sediment that fails to settle on the riverbed is carried all the way to the river mouth and into the sea. The soil particles are carried in freshwater. When the fresh river water starts to mix with seawater, negatively charged chlorine (Cl^-) and positively charged sodium (Na^+) ions form links between electrically charged soil particles, causing them to stick together in clumps (the technical term is flocculate). The clumps settle to the bottom as sediment that can form bars across the river mouth, obstructing the navigation channel used by ships entering the river, or raise the bed of harbors, necessitating periodic dredging to remove excess sediment in order to maintain the required depth of water.

Accumulating sediment also alters the shape and location of large deltas. In some places, the Mississippi delta is growing, extending the area of land into the sea, but where it is exposed to storms the adjacent coast is receding. The entire delta is also, very slowly, moving south.

Quite apart from their destruction of property and crops, floods damage both the land they cross and the rivers, reservoirs, and coasts where they deposit their loads of soil. As the example from Utah and the tradition of terracing vulnerable fields show, however, where the dangers are clearly identified, steps can be taken to reduce or eliminate them. Floods cannot be avoided altogether, but they need not be as destructive as many of them are.

Floods of the past

Major floods always cause extensive destruction and cost many lives. Even today, floods in the United States account for more than 40 percent of all dangerous-weather fatalities (averaged over 30 years). In monetary terms, floods account for almost 30 percent of all the damage to property caused by climatic disasters of all kinds—hurricanes, tornadoes, blizzards, droughts, lightning, hail, damage due to extremes of heat and cold, and floods. Floods are so destructive, in fact, that people remember them for a long time; some have even been immortalized in old myths and legends that refer to events that occurred long before people began recording events in writing.

Around 9,000 years ago, at the end of the last ice age, as the glaciers retreated and the weather grew warmer, many people settled near coasts. The shore was a good place to live, because catching fish and gathering shellfish was a lot easier than hunting animals, and seafood is highly nutritious. Drinkable water was available, from small streams flowing off the land, and edible plants could be found within a short distance inland. Unfortunately for some of the shore dwellers, however, the melting of the glaciers was causing a rise in sea level. This change was mostly gradual, but it did not happen at the same rate everywhere and on occasion was not gentle.

Suppose you lived back then, just a few hundred yards from the shore on ground that was at or even a little below sea level but protected by high ground between your dwelling and the shore. As the sea level rose, high tides would gradually reach further up the shore, and so would waves. Then there might be an unusually ferocious storm, following several days of onshore winds that pushed water against the coast. It would take only one huge storm wave that coincided with a high spring tide (see pages 73–77) to knock a passage through the high ground and allow the sea to flow inland. Your camp would be inundated in a matter of minutes. This disaster might well happen at night, when you and others are asleep. Floods like this must have occurred many times in many places. The few survivors from each disaster would have found their way to other communities and recounted their story in return for food and shelter, and no doubt the story improved with each telling.

In Asia, at about the time the sea level was rising due to the melting of ice sheets and glaciers, there may also have been a period during which the monsoons were much heavier than they are now (see pages 78–84). These would have caused the frequent and widespread flooding that gave rise to still more flood memories, in this case associated with rain rather than the rising sea.

Gilgamesh and Noah

There are many such stories of floods. Some of them may be older versions of the biblical Flood described in Genesis. The Sumerians, living at the northern end of the Persian Gulf about 5,000 years ago, for example, believed that the gods decided to send a flood to destroy all the people, but as their legend goes, a king, Ziusudra, was warned in advance and escaped death by riding out the flood in a boat.

The Babylonians, living further to the north, elaborated on this story, creating a myth with additional similarities to the flood of Noah. Their hero, King Atrahasis of Shuruppak, loaded his ship with his family, their goods, and birds and other animals, both wild and domesticated. The Assyrians also told a similar story, in which the hero, Utnapishtim, took workmen in his boat, as well as all his relatives and many animals. This is the tale recounted in the *Epic of Gilgamesh*.

In 1929, archaeologists excavating the site of the ancient city of Ur, in what is now Iraq, came across a layer of flood deposits that were 8 feet (2.4 m) thick. This was clear evidence of a major flood caused when the Euphrates River overflowed, and they dated the event to about 3200 B.C.E. There are also traces of floods between about 4000 B.C.E. and 2400 B.C.E. at the nearby sites of Kish and Nineveh. Although Iraq now has a very dry climate, that is where many flood stories originated. There was never a single flood that inundated the entire planet, but there were many smaller floods, affecting an area so large that the people experiencing them must have thought the whole world was flooded. These dramas happened repeatedly, especially in the lands between the Euphrates and Tigris Rivers, and they may well have influenced the way society developed (see pages 98–106).

Was there a real Noah's flood?

In 1996, two U.S. marine geologists, Professors William B. F. Ryan and Walter C. Pitman III, proposed that 7,600 years ago, a real and truly catastrophic flood inundated a Middle Eastern civilization. When the most recent ice age ended, about 9,000 years ago, the Black Sea was no more than a large freshwater lake. Where there is now the Bosporus Strait was a solid strip of land that formed a dam sealing the lake from the Sea of Marmara. The map shows the location of the Bosporus today. It is a channel 19 miles (30 km) long, between 787 yards and 2.25 miles (720–3,620 m) wide, and from 120 to 410 feet (37–125 m) deep. Istanbul lies on its southern end.

When the ice caps melted, the rising sea level breached the Bosporus. Ryan and Pitman found evidence that salt water burst over the strait at 200 times the force of Niagara Falls. The lake and the area around it was inundated with seawater that rose by 6 inches (15 cm) a day. In less than a year the water had covered an area of 60,000 square miles (155,400 km²). The shores of the lake had become populated as it provided a source of freshwater in an arid landscape. Many of these people perished, but the story told by the survivors eventually evolved into the stories of Ziusudra, Atrahasis, Gilgamesh, and Noah.

Intrigued by this suggestion from two distinguished scientists, the National Geographic Society financed a five-week submarine expedition

Bosporus Strait. The Bosporus links the Sea of Marmara and the Black Sea.

to seek archaeological evidence. On September 13, 2000, the society announced that the expedition, led by the oceanographer Robert Ballard, had found well-preserved items indicating human habitation at a depth of 311 feet (95 m) in the Black Sea, 12 miles (19 km) from the Turkish coast. Ballard's team found a collapsed structure, a building of some kind, with carved wooden beams and stone tools.

Histories and warnings

These old stories record memories of distant events, but they also provide warnings. In the Atrahasis epic, humans had become too numerous, so the gods who had created them sought to control their numbers. First they sent a plague, then a drought, and finally a famine, but each of these remedies provided only a temporary solution. Finally, they decided to destroy humans entirely. That was the purpose of the flood, but when the gods realized that they needed humans to produce food and manage Earth, they permitted them to survive, with lives punctuated by personal tragedies that would prevent their numbers from ever rising uncontrollably again. By the time the story was retold in Genesis in the Bible, the emphasis on population control had disappeared, although the flood ends with the imposition of laws on human behavior.

More immediately perhaps, these ancient stories also tell us to beware of living on low ground near coasts and on the floodplains of large rivers, where floods are most likely to occur. It was flooding due to a storm surge, for example, that in 1099 caused 100,000 deaths along the coasts of southern England and the Netherlands and that killed 2,000 people in England, Belgium, and the Netherlands on January 31 and February 1, 1953. The 1953 storm surge was one of the worst European natural disasters of modern times. On April 17, 1421, it was the sea breaking through dikes at Dort, in the Netherlands, that flooded polders (see pages 120–125) and drowned 100,000 people.

Many large rivers periodically overflow their banks. This kind of flooding is not confined to any particular region of the world. Just such a flood once devastated the important trading center of Timbuktu (Tombouctou), in Mali, although it is not a place where floods seem very likely. In Mali, an African country larger in size than Egypt and covered partly by the Sahara, the annual rainfall averages no more than 9 inches (229 mm). Timbuktu lies near a bend in the Niger River, to which it is linked by canals that supply the city's water. In December 1591, the river flooded because of very heavy rain near its source in Guinea, and Timbuktu's population, then of about 40,000, was forced to flee.

Floods in Tunisia, in October 1969, killed more than 300 people and left 150,000 homeless. Tunisia suffered again in the spring of 1973, when floods destroyed about 6,000 homes and 90 people died. In 1996, Khartoum, Sudan, was flooded following two hours of rain; thousands of homes were destroyed. In 2001, there was severe flooding in the Algerian capital of Algiers (see pages 125–131). Northeastern Iran has a dry climate. The city of Mashhad, for example, in the mountains not far from the border with Turkmenistan, has an average annual rainfall of 9.6 inches (243 mm), yet in August 2001, northeastern Iran suffered its worst flood in 200 years. About 10,000 people were driven from their homes, 181 died, and when the floods abated 168 were still missing.

Sometimes it is not even a river that overflows, but a dry creek or ravine. That is what happened when severe thunderstorms caused a flash flood at Farahzad, Iran, on August 17, 1954. A wall of water 90 feet (27 m) high crashed through a shrine where 3,000 people were worshiping. A mullah saw what was about to happen and shouted a warning, but more than 1,000 people lost their lives.

Australia also has a generally dry climate, but in 1955, nearly 40,000 people were made homeless when the Castlereagh, Namoi, and Gwydir Rivers overflowed in New South Wales. This was but a prelude to much more severe flooding the following year, when overflowing rivers created a temporary inland sea, 40 miles (64 km) wide, between the towns of Hay and Balranald.

The Arno River in Italy has flooded repeatedly. It drowned 300 people in 1333, but its most serious flood in terms of the damage it caused happened in November 1966 (see pages ix–xi). Florence was flooded, in places to a depth of 20 feet (6 m), and the water destroyed or damaged buildings of major historical importance and countless works of art.

U.S. floods

In 1955, the Quinebaug River destroyed one-quarter of all the buildings in Putnam, Connecticut. Two hurricanes, Connie and Diane, passed over southern New England within a few days of each other. Almost 8 inches (203 mm) of rain fell during the day and night of August 18 onto land drained by the river and already saturated by the 4 inches (102 mm) of rain that had fallen earlier. On the morning of August 19, a series of upstream dams failed, sending floodwater coursing through the town (see pages 37–42). Fortunately, everyone in Putnam survived the flood.

South Dakota was not so fortunate in June 1972. Rains in the Black Hills caused widespread flooding, and hundreds of people were killed. Melting snow can also cause floods. The Red and Minnesota Rivers burst their banks on April 17, 1997, when meltwater flooded down from high ground. Almost all of Grand Forks, North Dakota, was underwater, and 60,000 residents had to leave their homes. That flood caused damage costing around $3.7 billion, and 11 people died. In October 1973, heavy rain caused flash floods in the United States affecting a region extending from Nebraska to Texas.

The United States's greatest river, the Mississippi, has sometimes turned into something more closely resembling an inland sea. In August 1926, heavy rain increased the flow in the river. The water went on rising until the river finally overflowed its banks in April of the following year. The river level was so high that water was forced back into several tributaries, causing them to flood as well. Eventually the water covered more than 25,000 square miles (64,750 km^2) in seven states, the worst affected being Louisiana, Arkansas, and Mississippi. In some places the waters were 80 miles (129 km) wide and 18 feet (5.5 m) deep. It was July 1927 before they receded.

The Mississippi flooded again in January 1937, after heavy rains caused the Ohio River to flood and discharge a huge volume of water into the main river. At Cairo, Illinois, the Mississippi rose 63 feet (19 m) above its usual level, and 12,500 square miles (32,375 km^2) were inundated, destroying 13,000 homes and causing damage costing about $418 million. In April 1973, the river and its tributaries inundated nearly 1,000 square miles (2,590 km^2) around the junction of the Mississippi and Missouri Rivers, at St. Louis.

Floods in China

Not all river floods are natural events. In China, floods have been used as a weapon. For several centuries, as the power of Zhou dynasty declined, warlords fought one another for political control and land. During this period of upheaval, which finally came to an end in 222 B.C.E., canals, reservoirs, and dikes were built by one warlord to improve the productivity of the land and destroyed by another to flood the land of his enemy.

Much later, in 923 C.E., a general named Tuan Ning revived this custom during a war between forces of the Liang and Tang dynasties and flooded 1,000 square miles (2,590 km^2). Later, this time in 1642, the leader of a peasant revolt, Li Zicheng, ordered the breaking of Yellow River dikes to flood the city of Kaifeng, which he was besieging. The flood killed about 900,000 people. This devastating use of the Yellow River as a weapon occurred yet again in 1938, when Guomindang troops broke dikes to halt a Japanese advance, flooding about 9,000 square miles (23,310 km^2) and killing some 500,000 Chinese civilians.

Most Yellow River floods are natural catastrophes, of course, and sometimes their scale is immense. In September and October 1887, the failure of a dike near Zhengzhou sent floodwater from the river coursing through 1,500 or more towns and villages and covered 10,000 square miles (25,900 km^2). No one really knows how many lives were lost. Estimates range from 900,000 to 2.5 million. A flood that lasted from July through November 1931 was even more catastrophic. It covered about 34,000 square miles (88,060 km^2) and destroyed the homes of 80 million people. In the region, 1 million people drowned or died in the famine and disease epidemics that followed the flood.

China suffered doubly in 1931, as the Yangtze River also flooded when it rose 97 feet (30 m) after heavy rain. That flood, too, was followed by famine. More than 3.7 million people died by drowning or from starvation. Famine was the cause of most of the 30,000 deaths that followed another Yangtze flood, in 1954.

Southern China lies in the part of the world that experiences the summer monsoon, when the rains are concentrated in a short season of torrential downpours. A monsoon that brings more rain than usual can cause severe floods, as occurred in August 1973, for example. Rivers flowing south from the Himalayas inundated thousands of square miles of farmland in Pakistan, Bangladesh, and three Indian states. Entire towns were underwater, thousands of people died, and millions were left homeless.

European floods

Ice can also cause rivers to overflow. As the spring thaw begins and the ice starts to break, loose blocks of ice are carried downstream together with the meltwater pouring into the river and increasing its flow. If the ice blocks become trapped, however, they will form a dam. This happened in 1824 in the Neva River, which flows through St. Petersburg, Russia. Ten thousand people there and in the port of Kronshtadt, on an island in the Neva delta, were killed by the flood.

Britain, with its mild, wet, maritime climate, has suffered many floods. The Spey and Findhorn Rivers in Morayshire, Scotland, flooded in August 1829, and in September 1852 the Severn in central England flooded such a large area that its valley became a continuous freshwater sea. Flooding occurred in England again in the following year, and in November 1875 large parts of central London were inundated when the Thames rose, according to some accounts, by more than 28 feet (8.5 m). The worst English flood of modern times occurred in 1952, when the coastal village of Lynmouth was severely damaged in a flash flood (see pages 37–42).

Failure of the Vaiont Dam

It was in 1963 that the worst European flood disaster of modern times struck in the mountains of northeastern Italy, north of Venice and Padua. There, at the point where the Vaiont and Piave Rivers join, a dam 860 feet (262 m) high had been built to generate electric power. Completed in 1960, the dam was so well designed that it needed to be only 74 feet (22.6 m) thick at its base. In the shape of an arch, it was inherently strong, and despite the tragedy that followed, it did not fail. The reservoir behind the dam was designed to hold about 3 billion tons (2.7 billion metric tons) of water, but by 1963, the demand for power had increased, and the water level in the reservoir was allowed to rise until it was 76 feet (23 m) below the spillway.

Overlooking the reservoir is the northern slope of Mount Toc, about 1 square mile (2.6 km^2) of which was covered by loose rock, mainly limestone, and a layer of clay containing the remains of seashells, or marl. Although the slope was unstable, it was shallow near the base, and engineers believed that any rockslides from the steeper upper slope would be halted lower down before the sliding rock reached the water. As the reservoir filled, the entire rock mass began to creep down the slope, eventually at more than half an inch a day, but engineers still believed it would stabilize itself. In April 1963, however, heavy rains brought the water level to within about 40 feet (12 m) of the top of the dam wall.

On October 8, following 10 days of heavy rain, the loose rock started sliding faster, and two outlet tunnels were opened to release water from the reservoir rapidly. This proved difficult, however, because the heavy rains continued. The rain also saturated the surrounding land, raising the water table until it was very close to the surface and exerting an upward pressure on rocks on the lower slope. By then it was evident that the entire rock mass was on the move and that it covered a much bigger area than the engineers had supposed. Releasing water from the reservoir actually increased the instability. The weight of water pressing against the base of the rockslide had helped to restrain it, and lowering the level in the reservoir did not drain more water from the mountainside, because there it was held back by the layer of clay. The slide continued to accelerate through October 9.

At 10:40 P.M. on October 9, more than 314 million cubic yards (240 million m^3) of rock, moving at up to 70 miles per hour (113 km/h), fell into the reservoir. The sudden surge of rock, earth, and air sent waves high up the sides of the valley, some of them rising about 985 feet (300 m) above the level of water in the reservoir. One wave, rising higher than the top of the dam, overflowed the crest and swept down the valley. By the time it reached the town of Longarone, 1 mile (1.6 km) downstream from the dam, the water was advancing as a wave 230 feet (70 m) high. Nearly all the inhabitants of Longarone died. The wave swept on down the valley, inundating the villages of Pirago, Villonova, and Rivalta. The entire disaster lasted only 15 minutes, but it killed 2,600 people. The nearest eyewitness to survive lived in a house 850 feet (260 m) above the reservoir, on the side opposite to the landslide. He was awoken at 10:40 when the roof lifted off his house and a shower of water and rocks fell on him.

Every year brings more floods. More crops and homes are destroyed, and more people die. The stories on which the ancient legends are built are repeated endlessly. No doubt they will continue, but at least we may hope that in years to come floods will cause less damage and fewer deaths. Engineers and scientists now understand much better why floods happen and how they may be controlled, and meteorologists are better able to predict the weather conditions likely to cause floods.

PREVENTION, WARNING, AND SURVIVAL

Land drainage

Floods caused by water accumulating on what is ordinarily dry land can be forestalled simply by removing the water before it can flow across the surface. This is the purpose of drainage. Since flowing water removes soil, drainage can also help reduce soil erosion (see pages 131–137) and, through that, the transport of soil into rivers, as well as the problems of pollution and silting-up of estuaries and harbors.

Traditionally, farmers dug ditches to drain their fields, and you will still find many ditches in the countryside. They work by preventing water from entering a field, so they are made along the top of a field at right angles to the slope. Water draining from the ground above the field flows into the ditch, then along it, and eventually into a river or lake. How much water the ditch collects depends on its depth. The deeper the ditch is, the more water it will gather.

Water will accumulate naturally at the bottom of a slope. If it cannot escape, the ground is liable to become waterlogged. This greatly reduces its agricultural value and may even render it useless for farming. A series of ditches at intervals down a slope are very effective in preventing water-logging. Ditches need maintenance, however. This is labor intensive and therefore expensive, but unless ditches are cleared periodically, vegetation will choke and eventually clog them. Soil washed in from the field above gradually makes ditches shallower, reducing the amount of water they collect, and the sides of the ditch may erode. Without regular attention, in time a ditch will become useless. In areas where farming is very intensive and farmland is valuable, ditches also occupy land that could be cultivated and may interfere with the operation of modern farm machinery. The combination of high-maintenance cost, inconvenience, and loss of potentially cultivable land persuades some farmers to fill in their ditches and seek other ways of controlling the movement of water.

Pipes or ditches?

In some cases, it is possible to replace ditches with pipes that are perforated, allowing water to flow into them. These perform the same function as ditches, but they can be buried and once installed they are much cheaper and easier to maintain, although they are suitable for replacing only the smaller ditches. This is because the main ditches that are fed from the smaller ditches carry so much water it would be prohibitively expensive to substitute pipes.

Ditches have advantages, however. As well as providing drainage they can be used to store water, holding it until the tide or river level has fallen before discharging it. This is a useful service in some places, but it would be much more difficult with a system of piping.

Also, plants that are typical of riverbanks often line the banks on either side of large ditches. This can make such ditches valuable areas of wildlife habitat that should be preserved wherever possible.

Plants for land reclamation

Vegetation contributes to flood protection. All plants shift water from the ground into the air (see pages 91–97), and those that commonly grow along riverbanks are especially efficient at the task—after all, they grow there naturally because they thrive best in wet ground. Indeed, riverside species are often planted in the course of land reclamation projects precisely for this reason. They help dry out the land, and eventually, when the water table has fallen to below the level of their roots, they die out and other species arrive or are planted to take their place.

Plants, most commonly grasses, can also be used to reclaim eroded gullies. When water flows across the surface, its speed is proportional to the slope of the ground and the roughness of its surface. The rougher the ground, the more the flow is slowed. Grasses planted in gullies slow the flow of water, in effect by making the surface rougher. This reduces the energy of the flow, causing soil particles to be precipitated as sediment. Gradually, the gullies that have been turned into "green rivers" fill with soil carried into them from the ground to either side and trapped by the grass.

Field drains

Inside a field, drains buried below ground and feeding into ditches or larger pipes are used to lower the water table. Again, these are not a new idea. In the past, farmers who wished to drain a field in this way would dig a series of narrow trenches, parallel to one another and to the slope. They would line the trenches with gravel or larger stones, cover these with branches from shrubs and small trees laid along each trench, then return the soil they had removed, burying the drains. In time, of course, the plant material would decay and soil would fall in, filling the drains, which would have to be dug all over again. But drains of this type last for several years, and the materials cost the farmer nothing—except a lot of hard work.

Obviously, since the drains must carry water down the slope, they themselves must be inclined. This is no problem on a hillside, because if they are laid at a constant depth below the surface they will inevitably follow the natural slope of the hill. On shallower slopes they may need to exceed this and should have an incline of not less than about 1:1,000, meaning that the elevation of the pipe—usually measured with reference to sea level—decreases by one unit (feet or meters) for every 1,000 units measured horizontally down the slope. If the gradient is greater than 1:1,000, water will flow freely through the drains. Equally obvious, to be effective they must be able to carry as much water as is likely to drain during the heaviest rainstorm.

Mole drains and tile drains

Sandy soils, composed of relatively large particles with ample space between them (see pages 17–23), drain freely and need no help. It is the heavier soils that benefit from subsurface drainage, especially clay soils, where particles are so small and packed together so tightly that water can soak down from the surface only with difficulty. There is a tendency in clay soils for the soil just below the depth reached by plowing to be almost waterlogged in wet weather and to bake hard in dry weather. In both cases, this produces an impermeable layer that encourages the upper soil to waterlog, and when this happens, rainwater flows across the surface rather than soaking into it. The soil remains dry below the plowing depth, the uppermost layer dries out rapidly, and the valuable water is wasted.

The cheapest way for a farmer to deal with this situation is to install mole drains, using a mole plow, as illustrated in the drawings. The mole plow does not cut a furrow as made by an ordinary plow. Instead, it has a vertical blade with a cylinder, called the "mole," shaped rather like a bullet and mounted horizontally at the bottom, and behind the mole, there is a wider cylinder, the mole enlarger, to widen the hole cut by the mole. As this device is pulled through the soil, at a constant depth determined by an adjustable guide bar, it cuts a narrow slit with a tunnel at the bottom kept open by the packed soil lining it. Depending on the soil, the drains are cut at intervals of about 9 feet (2.7 m) and to a depth of 2 to 3 feet (0.6–0.9 m). This is deep enough to penetrate the subsoil.

As the mole plow is dragged along, it shatters the soil to either side, making fissures at an angle of about 45 degrees. Water drains down the fissures and into the mole drain, which carries it away to a ditch or pipe. Ordinary plowing causes little disturbance to the mole drain, because the plow shifts only the topmost foot or so of soil. On a heavy clay soil, a system of mole drains can last five or even 10 years before they start to collapse and must be cut again.

Tile drains provide a more permanent way to remove surplus water but are more expensive. Also, they can be used in soil that is too soft for mole drains and last longer. The drains are made from short sections of pipe laid end to end at the bottom of a trench. Traditionally, the pipes were made from porous clay; today, they are more often made from polyethylene or concrete and perforated with holes, because these materials are cheaper and more durable. The principle is the same as that of the mole drain, but the tile drains are bigger, with diameters of 3 to 12 inches (7.6–30 cm), and are laid much further apart. Again, it depends on the soil, but tile drains may be laid between 70 and 100 feet (21–30 m) apart. The system comprises lateral drains, approximately aligned with the contours

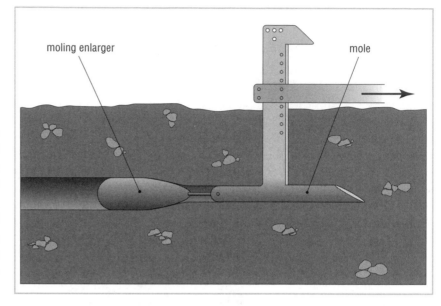

Mole plow. As the bullet-shaped mole is pulled through the soil, it cuts a hole that is widened by the moling enlarger. The two devices pack soil to the sides, creating a tunnel that acts as a drain and lasts for several years.

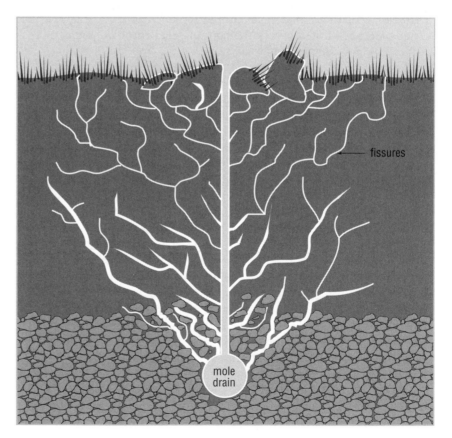

The effect of a mole drain.

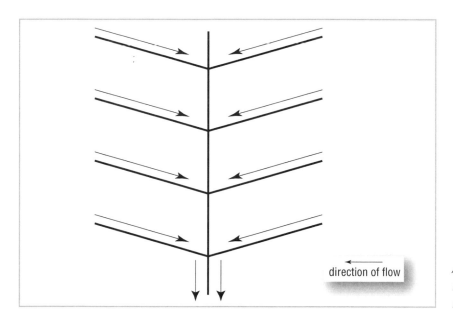

direction of flow

A herringbone pattern of lateral field drains feeding into a main drain.

of the field, that feed into main drains, often called "collectors," that carry the water away to a ditch or river. The drains form a pattern that varies according to the shape and slope of the ground. A herringbone pattern, shown in the diagram, is quite common.

The advantages

Field drains lower the water table by drawing water into them from either side. The water table falls first in the region closest to the pipes, then the effect spreads to the sides, and it may take several years for them to achieve their final drainage capacity. As the illustration on the following page suggests, it is the depth of the drains rather than their spacing that determines the extent to which the water table is lowered.

Drainage improves the quality of wet farmland and therefore crop yields, which is why it is popular with farmers. It also helps prevent flooding in low-lying areas by diverting water into rivers or into ponds where it can be held until river levels have fallen sufficiently for it to be released. This also reduces soil erosion and the raising of riverbeds by the deposition of sediment carried from fields (see pages 131–137).

The system that removes surplus water from fields is similar to the one that removes surplus water from the streets, buildings, and parking lots of our towns. There, the water flows through grills and into storm drains. Like field drains, these must be large enough to carry the maximum amount of water that is ever likely to flow into them. They must also discharge at a point that is lower than the area they drain. This presents difficulties in some cities, where there are areas below the level of the river receiving the discharge, and storm water must be pumped to the higher level.

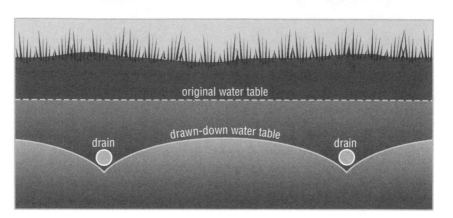

The effect of field drains on the water table.

Floodplains

Near coasts and on river floodplains, however, land drainage may increase the risk of floods (see pages 1–8). There, the only certain way to protect buildings is to locate them out of reach of the waters.

Floodplains are often defined as land that is vulnerable to 100-year floods. If a house is designed to last 70 years, there is a strong chance that it will be flooded at least once by a 100-year flood. The only way to avoid the risk is to set buildings back from the limit floodwaters are expected to reach. Much the same policy may be best for coastal areas where erosion is a problem (see pages 112–120) and in areas where hurricanes may cause storm surges. Some engineers who specialize in construction projects in coastal areas believe that erosion and flood risks should be calculated on the basis of a 100-year probability, similar to that used on floodplains, and that all buildings should be set an appropriate distance back from the shore.

Wetlands

Swamps, marshes, salt marshes, mudflats, and mangrove swamps may seem dull, useless places, but often they are in locations that could be made attractive. They can be drained and turned into dry land that is suitable for building homes or tourist hotels. Once that has been done, more people can move into what has then been converted into a desirable area.

At one time, wetland areas occupied nearly 350,000 square miles (906,500 km²) of the United States. Then, in 1849 and 1850, Congress passed the Swamp Land Acts to encourage their drainage, mainly to turn what were seen as "useless" areas into farmland. Presently, only about 155,000 square miles (401,450 km²) of wetlands remain—less than half.

About 90 percent of the surviving wetlands are inland; the rest lie along coasts where, in southernmost regions, they include mangrove swamps.

The Ramsar Convention

The loss of wetlands is not confined to the United States, of course. They are being lost throughout the world. As long ago as 1971 an international conference was held at Ramsar, Iran, to seek ways of protecting such areas, because they form chains of habitat for migrating water birds. The result was the Ramsar Convention on Wetlands of International Importance, under which especially valuable sites can be designated and protected from draining and development.

The convention has been signed by 131 countries, known as contracting parties, and a total of 1,150 sites have been identified and placed on the Ramsar list of wetlands of international importance. Together these Ramsar wetlands cover an area of about 372,000 square miles (963,000 km²)—more than the combined area of Texas, Louisiana, and Arkansas, or the combined area of France and Germany.

U.S. wetland conservation

In the United States, legislation governing the protection and restoration of wetlands is enshrined in the Coastal Zone Management Act of 1972 as amended by the Coastal Zone Management Act and the Coastal Zone Protection Act. These laws encourage states to regulate development in coastal areas generally, and an executive order issued by President Jimmy Carter in 1977 made it federal policy to conserve wetlands. The national Fish and Wildlife Service defines wetlands as places that are transitional between dry-land and aquatic areas, where saturation with water is the dominant factor determining the kind of soil and plants that are present, and where the water table is usually at or close to the surface.

Wetlands are of great importance to wildlife, but many of them serve a secondary purpose. They greatly reduce the risk of flooding and can recharge aquifers (see pages 1–8) by feeding water into them.

The Everglades

South of Lake Okeechobee, Florida, the Everglades is the most famous wetland area in the United States, now reduced to less than half of its original size. During the summer rainy season, the entire area used to become a slow-moving river about 80 miles (129 km) wide and just a foot or two (30–60 cm) deep, carrying water overflowing from Lake Okeechobee down to the sea. In winter, the flow ceased and the area dried into a vast meadow of a sedge called "saw grass," with clumps of trees on slightly higher ground, although no land rises more than 7 feet (2 m) above sea level. The saw grass readily caught fire and repeated fires prevented the establishment of woody plants on the low ground. The region maintained itself and was a haven for wildlife.

For humans, however, it was not a safe place to live. Hurricanes and heavy rains in 1926 caused serious flooding of land adjacent to the Everglades, and in 1928, a severe hurricane caused floods in which more than 1,800 people died. To make sure that such disasters would never happen again, the U.S. Army Corps of Engineers and the South Florida Water Management District set to work to control the flow of water.

Water entered Lake Okeechobee from the Kissimmee River to the north, a river that meandered for 100 miles (160 km). The river filtered the water passing along it so that by the time it reached the lake, the water was fairly pure. The Kissimmee was straightened under the flood control project, converting it into a 50-mile (80-km) canal. Dikes, pumps, channels, and spillways directed the water along prescribed routes. This increased the area available for farming, and channels linking Lake Okeechobee directly to the sea reduced the risk of flooding.

At the same time, however, the changes also prevented the seasonal floods from recharging the groundwater. This led to shortages of freshwater. Water running off farmland to the north and containing plant nutrients flowed through the Kissimmee channel, gathering more polluted water along the way, passed through the Everglades National Park, and was finally discharged into Florida Bay. There were large algal blooms in Lake Okeechobee in the 1980s and migratory birds ceased to arrive. More than 60 species of Everglades birds are now endangered. Pollution from the water discharging into the bay killed off the sea grass that had provided a breeding ground for fish.

Much of the Everglades area is now conserved and is being restored to something like its former condition. Early in 2001, the Army Corps of Engineers started shifting earth as part of the plan to restore the area. The task will take about 30 years and will cost an estimated $8 billion, shared between the federal government and the state of Florida. Many of the canals are to be filled, marshes will be established to filter water, and wells will be dug to store water.

Storing water and preventing floods

There are, or used to be, similar wetland areas along the lower reaches of many big rivers, including the Mississippi. These absorbed water overflowing from their rivers and so protected adjacent land from flooding.

Beside rivers are often low-lying fields where the ground is usually wet. Sedges grow there, as well as cattails, rushes, and other plants that look like grasses but are not. They grow in isolated clumps, and here and there you may find small pools of water with different plants growing in and around them. Part of the time, some of these areas are dry enough for cattle to graze and may have enough grass for the farmer to be able to cut it for hay. These areas are known as wet meadows, or in Britain as water meadows. Where the water lies deeper and is present for much more of the time they are called "marshes."

From time to time, after very heavy rain or when snow melts on the hills, the water level rises in the river and may overflow the banks. Then it inundates the adjacent wetland. The water may remain there until the level in the river falls again, then slowly drain back into the river, or water may flow across the wetland, effectively making the river that much wider, but at the same time slowing its rate of flow. Further downstream the water will drain back into the main river channel again.

Suppose the wetland is drained, however. During dry weather, when the river is low, drains are installed below ground (see pages 145–150) in order to lower the water table by moving water into the river. Then the riverbank is sealed so that water cannot seep back. Now the fields by the riverside can be farmed or houses can be built on them, with a fine view of the river. This kind of development has occurred many times. After a few years, as the ground below the houses dries out and shrinks, the weight of the houses depresses it, and the foundations crack. At the same time, septic tanks also crack and leak their contents into the river, polluting water that people living further downstream might need for irrigation and harming aquatic plants and animals.

Then the river level rises and overflows, as it had always done periodically, but there is no longer a belt of wetland to capture and control the movement of water. Instead, there are fields growing crops or homes with people living in them. The water inundates and destroys the crops and flows into and floods the houses, then continues downstream unchecked to cause flooding there as well. Land beside the river had often flooded in the past, but the flood had been limited and harmless. The plants growing beside the river thrived in the wet conditions and land-dwelling animals moved out of the way and returned later, when the water had subsided. Floods became harmful only after the wetland had been drained and put to other uses.

Coastal wetlands

Along low-lying coasts the effect is even more dramatic. There, the wetlands not only absorb water as the sea rises, but they also absorb the energy of waves. This reduces the likelihood of storm surges sweeping inland.

Water moves from the land into the sea, most of it through rivers, but some by draining directly from coastal lands or through small streams. Soil particles and sand grains, suspended in the freshwater, start to settle as they meet and mix with salt water (see pages 131–137). Sand banks and mudflats form, eventually growing to a height that leaves them exposed at low tide. Moving water cuts channels through them, so they come to resemble low ground with many small rivers flowing across it. Already the banks and flats are important for conservation. Mollusks, worms, and other invertebrate animals burrow into them in vast numbers and provide food for wading birds.

Salt marshes

When parts of the surface lie above the water all of the time except at spring tides and when big waves wash over them, plants can begin to grow. These trap more sediment, raising the surface still higher, and the sand bank or mudflat turns into a salt marsh, a place covered with plants that can tolerate both freshwater and salt water. At low tide, parts of the salt marsh are dry enough to walk on, and this is what encourages developers to exploit them; in their natural state, they often provide some grazing for livestock and opportunities for raising shellfish in the channels running across them.

The first step in reclaiming them is usually to shelter them behind a sea wall. Salt water can no longer cover them and rain gradually washes the salt from the soil, which is then very fertile. In fact, salt marshes are quite complex. As the drawing of a cross-section through one illustrates, channels intersect the high areas, some of them extending to below the average level of the low neap tides. Tidal water flows through these channels in both directions. Small hollows just above the average level of spring tides will catch water from waves and hold it long enough for much of the water to evaporate, increasing the salinity of the remaining water and producing a salt pan.

Salt marshes vary according to local conditions in size and in the range of plants they support. The more sheltered the coast, the bigger the salt marsh, but even on fairly exposed coasts plants may become established at the highest tide level. Waves are slowed as they pass over the sand, mud, and plants. They lose energy and strike the land behind the marsh with less force, protecting the adjacent inland area and the buildings standing on it. This is true even when the inland area is protected by its own sea wall, because the salt marsh protects the wall, reducing the amount of reinforcement it needs and the cost of its maintenance.

Cross-section through a salt marsh.

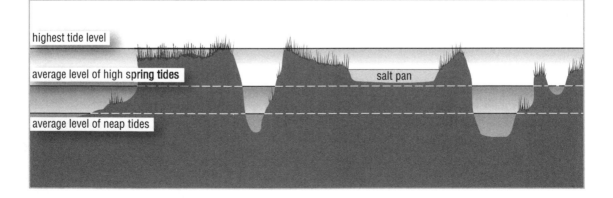

highest tide level

average level of high spring tides   salt pan

average level of neap tides

Mangrove swamps

Mangrove swamps are the tropical equivalent of salt marshes. They develop best on muddy, sheltered coasts, often behind barrier islands or coral reefs. At high tide, only the crowns of the trees project above the water, and some of the lower leaves may be immersed most of the time.

There are about 90 species of mangrove trees. All of them are broad-leaved evergreen trees or shrubs that grow poorly, if at all, away from salt water. Some have stilt roots that hold the main stem well clear of the water; others have pneumatophores, or "breathing roots," that project above the water from the main underground root and allow oxygen and carbon dioxide to pass into and out of the plant. Mangroves are even better at trapping sediment than salt-marsh plants. Indeed, they are so good at it that in many places, they gradually extend the coastline by moving further into the sea as the trapped sediment accumulates and the water becomes shallower.

Like the salt marshes and mudflats of temperate regions, mangrove swamps have been cleared extensively: mangrove wood is valuable for building and as fuel, land reclaimed from the swamps can be converted into fertile farmland that is especially good for growing sugarcane, and their location on sheltered coasts encourages tourist development. They have also been victims of war. During the Vietnam War, mangroves were sprayed repeatedly with defoliant herbicides to remove their leaves, and many died.

Wetlands in all their varieties, along coasts and beside rivers and lakes, absorb floodwater. They fill quickly, then release their water slowly, a little at a time as river or sea levels fall. Where they occur naturally they provide excellent flood protection. Removing them removes that protection and leaves the reclaimed land vulnerable. They also support a wide variety of wildlife, including many species that are adapted to the harsh conditions in habitats that are alternately dry and inundated, and in the case of coastal wetlands exposed to alternately fresh- and salt water. As the wetlands are drained, the habitat is destroyed and its plants and animals disappear. Wetlands should be conserved and, so far as is practicable, lost wetlands should be restored.

Levees

When a river overflows, the water is slowed down as it rises over the banks. As the water slows, it loses energy. This reduces its ability to transport soil particles; consequently, some of its load may be deposited on the top of the bank and remain there. After the flood has subsided, the sediment on the bank dries and, if it is made of clay particles, it becomes hard and solid. The bank has been raised a little, and each time the river floods, another layer of soil is deposited on top of the earlier layers and raises the bank further. At the same time, sediment deposited on the riverbed may be raising the river's level. Ordinarily this would make the river shallower, and more prone to flooding, but the raised embankments prevent this. Instead, the entire river rises, the bed and banks building upward together, until the river may flow at a higher level than the land to either side.

Embankments of this type can form naturally, so it is not surprising that long ago people who lived near rivers that now and then flooded their fields and homes realized that they could protect themselves by building similar embankments. Embankments were built along left (western) bank of the Nile in the time of the pharaohs. These extended for more than 600 miles (965 km) from Aswân in the south to the Mediterranean. Later, Arab engineers built embankments on the right (eastern) bank of the Nile. Embankments were also built along the Tigris and Euphrates Rivers in Mesopotamia, and along the great Chinese rivers. Some historians believe that organizing the vast amount of labor needed for these engineering projects encouraged the development of strong community life.

Louisiana and the Mississippi

Around 1718, this type of raised embankment was termed a *levee*, a French word that means "raised," but it was in America, not France, that it was given this name. What is now the U.S. state of Louisiana was then a French colony, and in 1718 the sieur de Bienville, its governor, decided that a town should be built on the east bank of the Mississippi at a point where there was access to several important waterways, in addition to the river itself. The town was named La Nouvelle Orléans in honor of the regent, the duc d'Orléans.

Although the chosen site was on relatively high ground, there was clearly a risk of flooding from the huge river and so an embankment, dubbed a levee, was built to protect it. At first the levee was quite small, but it was extended as the city grew, and by 1735, levees bordered the river for 30 miles (48 km) upstream of New Orleans and 12 miles (19 km) downstream. Their length was increased further as more farmers settled along the river. The levees were earth embankments, nearly 20 feet wide (6 m) at the top, but only about 3 feet (90 cm) high.

Eventually difficulties arose. Landowners built their own levees to protect their property, but this left gaps between one property and the next, and not all the levees were well maintained. The same problem arose in ancient China and has occurred everywhere else that embankments have been used to prevent flooding. If floodwater can flow through or over a levee in just one place it will inundate the land downstream, regardless of how big and robust the other embankments may be.

The need to supervise and enforce the building and maintenance of the levees led to a more organized community life, just as it has done wherever people have relied on them. By the 1830s, levee districts had been established along the Mississippi, and inspectors with powers of enforcement made regular examinations.

The U.S. Army Corps of Engineers also built some of the Mississippi embankments. At first this was in order to improve navigation, but severe flooding in 1849 and again in 1850 persuaded Congress to release funds for the corps to build levees for flood protection. Levees continued to be built, higher as well as longer, until by the 1960s there were more than 3,500 miles (5,632 km) of them along the Mississippi, with an average height of 24 feet (7.3 m).

Levees vulnerable to erosion

Other major rivers were also bordered by levees, but the construction cost was high, and the protection they afforded was far from complete. Embankments were constantly under attack from erosion and from animals that burrowed into and weakened them. Thousands of people had to be permanently employed to repair them, yet despite all this effort, they were breached repeatedly. Water would leak through holes, often made by animals, and other weak points, bubbling through the other side in what were called "boils." These were often the cause of breaks in embankments, called "crevasses."

Failure of a levee can lead to catastrophe. During heavy monsoon rains in the summer of 1998, a breach more than 130 feet (40 m) long appeared in a levee beside the Yangtze River in Guangdong Province, China (see map). The army and police used explosives to sink eight 1,000-ton (908–metric ton) boats in an unsuccessful attempt to close the breach. Water flooded the city of Jiujiang, to the southwest of Guangzhou (Canton), in places to a depth of more than 6 feet (1.8 m). Jiujiang has a population of about 40,000, and thousands lost their lives. Many more of the inhabitants were driven from their homes, and the authorities forcibly evacuated 330,000 people living along the river upstream of Jiujiang. This was part of their scheme to breach some of the upstream levees deliberately in order to reduce the pressure on the levees further downstream that protect several important industrial cities and had already started to leak.

All the same, regardless of the difficulties and the dreadful consequences of failure, levees do afford quite good protection and have prevented much flooding. It is only in this century, as scientists have learned more about the way river water flows, that better protection can be achieved if levees are only one of several methods employed.

Originally, only the speed of the water in a river was considered a factor in determining the amount of sediment the river carried. If the river was confined between reinforced banks or levees, it was believed that when the river had to carry more water, it would flow faster and cut a deeper channel for itself. This is broadly true, and large amounts of water are sometimes released into dammed rivers to clear excess sediment from them (see pages 161–168), but rivers are not all the same. Although levees usually protect against flooding, under certain conditions they can also

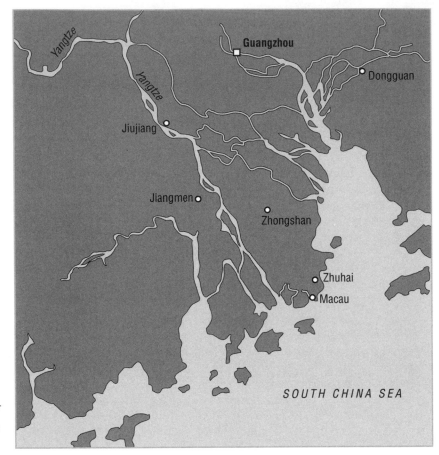

Region around Jiujiang, China. Upstream of Jiujiang, a levee broke in 1998.

contribute to their own erosion and failure and increase the risk of flooding downstream.

In some rivers, a faster flow may erode the banks rather than deepening the channel. In others, including parts of the lower Mississippi, sediment that once would have been deposited on the riverside land inundated by floods is now carried further downstream and deposited on the riverbed there, making the river shallower. This kind of downstream sedimentation contributed to six major Mississippi floods between 1881 and 1890. Where levees confine a river securely, at times of peak flow they make the water level rise higher than it would if the river had been able to overflow its banks. This means that the embankments must be built higher to compensate.

Luck also plays a part, and the catastrophic Mississippi flood of 1927 was the result of bad luck. That year more than 25,000 square miles (64,750 km²) were inundated, and the levees were breached in many places, but the circumstances were unusual. Eastern tributaries of the main river usually carry their maximum flow in late winter and spring, from January through

April. The Missouri and its tributaries, entering from the west, carry their peak flow in June. This allows the Mississippi to carry first one peak flow and then after an interval, the other. By pure chance, however, in 1927, the peaks occurred at the same time in all the tributaries, and the Mississippi and its levees were overwhelmed.

Ten years later, in January and February 1937, the Ohio overflowed to cause the biggest flood in its recorded history, and at Cairo, Illinois, the Mississippi rose 63 feet (19 m) above its usual level. Water flowed back into the smaller tributaries, which were not protected by levees, but that time, people living beside the lower Mississippi had better luck. On this occasion, the embankments held, even while 2 million cubic feet (56,600 m³) of water were flowing along the river every second. In fact, there have been no serious crevasses in levees in the lower Mississippi valley since 1928.

Augmenting the levees

Levee protection is now augmented in other ways. Setting the embankments further back from the riverbank helps. This allows some land bordering the river to flood harmlessly, and by absorbing some of the energy

Preventing floods by diverting river flow.

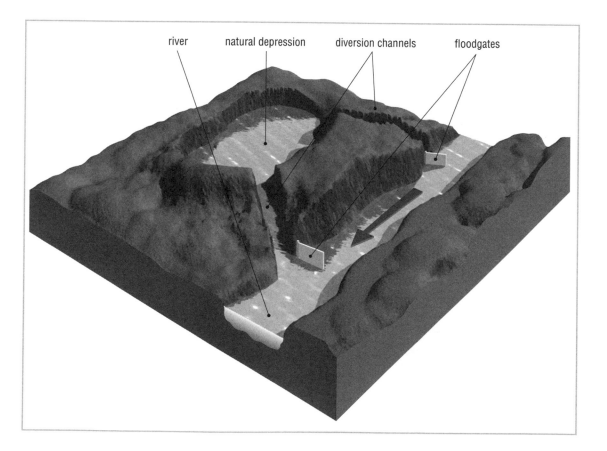

river   natural depression   diversion channels   floodgates

of the moving water, it reduces wear on the levees themselves. Above Baton Rouge, in Louisiana, for example, the distance between levees is less than a mile (1.6 km) in some places, and in others, as much as 15 miles (24 km).

Probably the most effective way of preventing floods is to remove the water before it can overwhelm the river system. Channels, controlled by floodgates, can be cut from the river to a natural depression in the land, as illustrated in the drawing. At times of peak flow, when flooding is likely, opening the floodgates diverts some of the water into the depression, from where it can be returned to the river when the flood risk has passed.

Obviously, this method is not possible everywhere. There may be no depression that is large and deep enough to be useful, or there may be houses in the only suitable depression. Where it can be used, however, it usually succeeds. The Tigris and Euphrates are prevented in this way from flooding Baghdad, the capital of Iraq, and the farmland around it. The Euphrates is linked to Lake Habbaniyah, and a channel 41 miles (66 km) long links the Tigris with the Tatar depression. Dams are often used to hold back peak flows in much the same way (see pages 161–168).

Making the river flow faster

Sometimes it is possible to help the river itself, by increasing its carrying capacity, measured as the rate at which water flows along it. This rate depends on the cross-sectional area of the river channel and its angle of slope. Widening and deepening channels to increase their capacity has some effect, but sometimes a river can also be made steeper.

Suppose, during part of its course, that the elevation of the river bed falls from 100 feet (30.5 m) to 50 feet (15.25 m) above sea level, but the river meanders, so its length over that part of its course is 20 miles (32 km). This is a fall of approximately 1 foot (or meter) in every 2,100 feet (or meters). Dig channels to join some of the meanders together, however, and the water will not have to travel so far. Suppose these channels halve the distance, from 20 to 10 miles (32 km to 16 km). This doubles the gradient, to 1 foot (or meter) in approximately every 1,050 feet (or meters), so the water will flow faster. If the water flows faster, more of it will be discharged from the river mouth each second, and this can be enough to prevent flooding. Rivers meander as they cross their almost level floodplains and it is there, on floodplains, that severe flooding is most likely. This makes the technique particularly useful. The faster flow will also reduce the deposition of sediment downstream, so the mouth of the river will silt up more slowly.

Where the river is meandering, the channels are usually cut as broad curves, to reduce erosion that can form new meanders, but when low-lying land is reclaimed from the sea, straight channels are often satisfactory. Channels for this purpose were constructed along the Mississippi in the 1930s. A total of 16 channels have reduced the length of the river between Memphis, Tennessee, and Baton Rouge, Louisiana, by 170 miles (274 km).

Whether they are called levees, dikes, or embankments, for thousands of years, people have been building walls to raise the height of riverbanks in order to prevent flooding. This method of protecting land and buildings has been discovered independently in many parts of the world and, by and large, it has succeeded. Today, engineers know more about the way rivers carry water, so they can compensate for the deficiencies of levees. Where alternative methods are used in conjunction with levees, even the biggest rivers can be tamed most of the time.

Dams

People have been building dams to control the flow of rivers almost since prehistoric times. The remains have been found of one that was built by the ancient Egyptians in about 4000 B.C.E. The Mesopotamians are also known to have built them, and the Romans built many. Dams were built for several reasons. Some were used to store water for irrigation or domestic use during the dry season. Others held water back when river levels were high and released it gradually during times of low flow. This regulated the flow of the river so that the amount of water downstream of the dam remained constant at all times. Dams were used to collect sediment in order to prevent the silting up of harbors and to form artificial lakes for the use of ships transporting cargoes.

In modern times, when the first factories were built, steam power had not yet been invented. At first, the large machines were driven by water power, provided by waterwheels. These required a reliable supply of flowing water, and more dams were built to provide it. When steam replaced water power, those dams were no longer needed, and most of them were abandoned, but more recently the technology of the waterwheel has been modernized to make turbines. These harness the kinetic energy of flowing water (see sidebar, page 28) to operate machinery much more efficiently than traditional waterwheels, and they are used to generate hydroelectric power. This has led to the building of still more dams. Today, about 19 percent of all the world's electricity is generated by water flowing through dams.

Dams can be huge

Many modern dams are very large. In 2001, there were more than 45,000 dams more than 50 feet (15.25 m) high functioning in more than 150 countries. Together, the reservoirs behind these dams hold back about 1,500 cubic miles (6,248 km³) of water. Some dams are much higher than 50 feet (15.25 m).

Technically, a dam 50 feet (15.25 m) high is not considered to be large. A large dam is defined as one that is more than 492 feet (150 m) high, or that holds back more than 19.6 million cubic yards (15 million m^3) of water, or that forms a reservoir capable of containing 12 million acre-feet of water. This is enough water to cover 12 million acres (4.9 million ha) to a depth of 1 foot (30 cm) and is equal to 3,910 billion gallons (14,802 billion liters).

When it is completed, the highest dam in the world will be the Rogun Dam, on the Vakhsh River, Tajikistan. It will measure 1,099 feet (335 m) from base to top. It is due to be completed in 2003 and will have a generating capacity of 3.6 gigawatts (1 GW = 10^9 watts). The distance along the crest of the Yacyretá-Apipe Dam on the Paraná River near the border between Argentina and Paraguay, is a little more than 43 miles (69 km). That dam was completed in 1998 and has a generating capacity of 12.6 gigawatts. The crest of the Birecik Dam, on the Euphrates River in Turkey, is 1.56 miles (2.5 km) long.

The first large dam to be built was the Hoover Dam on the Colorado River. It was completed in 1936 and stands 726 feet (221 m) high. The Mauvoisin Dam, on the Drance de Bagnes River, Switzerland, is 777 feet (237 m) high, and the Vaiont Dam, in northern Italy, is 860 feet (262 m) high (see pages 137–144). Several others are only slightly less high. The Aguamilpa Dam, on the Santiago River, Mexico, for example, is 613 feet (187 m) high, and the Lhakwar Dam, on the Yamuna River, India, is 670 feet (204 m) high.

Cascaded rivers

Size is only one measure of a dam. Obviously, no valley can accommodate a dam that is higher or wider than itself and so the dimensions of the valley impose a limitation on dam size. The limitation is not absolute, however, because it is sometimes possible to dam a river in more than one place, and two or three small dams may add up to the equivalent of one large dam.

Many rivers are dammed repeatedly along their courses. Such rivers are said to be "cascaded." In the United States, the Ohio, Tennessee, Missouri, upper Mississippi, and Columbia are among those that have been cascaded. The Columbia, in Washington State, has the longest cascade. Its series of 12 dams begins near the Canadian border and ends at the Pacific coast, about 640 miles (1,030 km) away. The cascade begins with the Grand Coulee Dam, 550 feet (168 m) high and more than 0.75 mile (1.2 km) long. The Grand Coulee is the most important member of the cascade in controlling river flow and preventing floods.

Dam construction

Most early dams were made from earth, rock, or a combination of the two. Building even a small dam is a major undertaking and uses a huge amount of material, so it was natural to use earth and rock, which were available locally. The first dams were probably made entirely from clay or other fine-grained soil that would be fairly impermeable when its particles were packed tightly together. A dam made from a single material is called "homogeneous."

One cubic foot of water weighs 62 pounds (1 m³ weighs 1,000 kg), so even a small reservoir exerts considerable pressure against a dam. This means that the dam wall must be substantial and usually much thicker at its base than at the top. The wall, therefore, is triangular in cross-section. The wall must not slope so steeply that the earth or rock is able to slump to the bottom. The slope must also distribute the weight of the wall, to prevent the ground beneath it from being depressed unevenly and causing the dam to collapse. On the upstream side, the wall must resist the action of waves and on the downstream side it must resist erosion by rain. Vegetation can be planted on the downstream side to bind the earth together. Rocks of varying sizes, called "riprap," are often piled against the upstream face to absorb the energy of waves. Alternatively, the upstream face can be protected by a surface of masonry, concrete, or asphalt.

Earth and rock are still widely used, but nowadays many dam walls also contain steel, concrete, and solid masonry. There are five basic types of construction, shown in the illustration. The one to be used is chosen according to its appropriateness to the site, and a cascade often includes dams of several types. In all the drawings, the steepness of the slopes has been exaggerated. In real dams, the base is much wider than it is shown here.

An earth dam may be homogeneous, but more commonly it consists of a core of impermeable clay with an outer layer of compacted earth and a riprap cladding to protect its upstream face. Earth dams can be built on soft ground, because they are so wide at the base that their weight is distributed over a large area. Rockfill dams are more substantial but are also heavier and need a solid foundation. As the name suggests, they are made from loose rocks of varying sizes and solid masonry or a skin of concrete or asphalt protects the upstream face. The facing must be impermeable to prevent water from penetrating the structure.

Earth and rockfill dams slope on both the upstream and downstream sides, but a gravity dam has a vertical face on the upstream side. It is made from rocks or concrete blocks that are held together with cement and faced with concrete. It is extremely heavy, and it is its weight that secures it to the foundation. It is held in place by gravity, hence the name. Its very wide base distributes the weight. Although the design looks modern, the first gravity dams were built in Spain in the 16th century; two of them are still in use.

The arch dam is a variant of the gravity dam. Its great weight secures it. The dam curves upstream, and this shape transmits the water pressure to the sides, pushing the dam into the banks and increasing its strength. The Hoover Dam is of this type, but some arch dams have more than one arch. The Bartlett Dam, on the Verde River in Arizona, is 800 feet (244 m) long and has 10 arches. In a buttress dam, it is the upstream face that slopes, often at about 45 degrees, and the downstream face that is vertical. Buttresses support the dam on the downstream side.

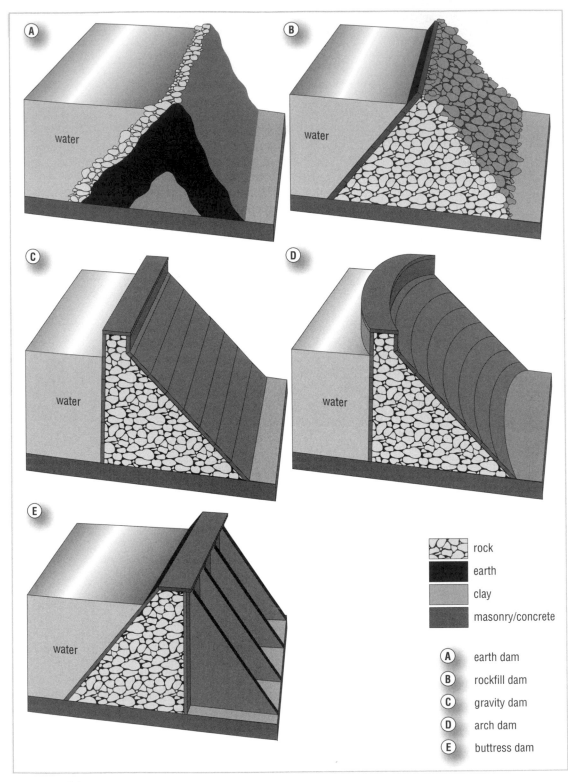

rock

earth

clay

masonry/concrete

A   earth dam
B   rockfill dam
C   gravity dam
D   arch dam
E   buttress dam

Five types of dam construction.

Preventing water overflowing

Once a dam has been built to block a river, water will accumulate behind the dam to form an artificial lake. Eventually, the water level in the lake will reach the top of the basin containing it. Dams are never as high as the valleys containing them, so water cannot spill over the sides of the lake onto the surrounding countryside. Unless water is also allowed to flow through or past the dam, however, there will be times when it overflows. In the case of an earth dam, this will wash away the top of the structure, and after a time it will destroy the dam. If the base of the dam is weak, water may flow through it and escape that way, washing away the wall until the dam collapses. Even dams made from solid masonry or concrete must allow excess water to escape in a controlled fashion.

All dams, therefore, have either spillways in the center or on one or both sides, or pipes at the base through which water can be discharged. Some have a combination of both. Regulating the outflow of water through the dam allows the water level behind the dam to be kept far enough below the crest to prevent waves from washing over the top. The distance between the crest and the maximum height the water is allowed to reach is called the "freeboard." If a dam is to be used for power generation, pipes carry water through the structure, allowing it to fall from a high to a low level and directing it to flow past turbines before being discharged on the downstream side.

Tennessee Valley Authority

Whatever their primary purpose, dams provide excellent flood protection. Probably the most famous of all dam-building and flood control projects was the one started in 1933 by the Tennessee Valley Authority (TVA). It was unique in that it brought together projects already being run by a number of government agencies and based them on the drainage basin of a river system that covers approximately 41,000 square miles (106,190 km²), mainly in Tennessee but extending into Kentucky, Virginia, North Carolina, Georgia, Alabama, and Mississippi. Aims of the TVA were to control floods on the Tennessee River and its tributaries, improve navigation, and generate electrical power. It was a spectacular success and much admired in other countries, not least for the social improvements it brought to the area under its administration. It has also prevented serious flooding.

Its dams are designed to maintain a navigable channel 9 feet (2.7 m) deep and to prevent floods throughout the 650 miles (1,046 km) from Paducah, Kentucky, to Knoxville, Tennessee. There are nine main dams, of which five are still under construction, but the smaller dams used for power generation bring the total to more than 50 dams. The reservoirs impounded behind them are known as the Great Lakes of the South. Together they hold about 12 million acre-feet, or about 3.55 cubic miles (14.79 km³), of water.

In February 1957, the Tennessee River would have inundated Chattanooga had the excess water not been held in reservoirs. Instead of rising to 54 feet (16.5 m), the river reached only a little over 32 feet (9.75 m). A year later, in May 1958, TVA reservoirs saved Cairo, Illinois, from flooding. Six dams built along the Missouri since 1944, combined with levees (see pages 155–161) to protect vulnerable farmland and towns, have also prevented flooding, and hydroelectric plants built into the dams generate enough power to meet all the needs of Nebraska. The dams hold back 105 reservoirs, spread along a chain 1,000 miles (1,600 km) long, with a total capacity of 75 million acre-feet, or 22.2 cubic miles (92.4 km^3).

Consequences of failure

This success has been repeated on many rivers, but there are risks. Should a dam fail, the result is catastrophic flooding of the valley downstream. Failures are rare but do happen. The Puentes Dam, a gravity dam on the Guadalentín River in Spain that was completed in 1791, failed in 1802 when unusually heavy rain delivered more water to the reservoir than the dam could hold.

Another gravity dam, the St. Francis in California, was constructed on geologically unstable foundations and collapsed in 1928, two years after it was completed. Concrete dams need solid foundations, on rock that is young and has not been eroded and cracked by weathering. When Clover Dam, a small buttress dam, was being built on the Kiewa River, Australia, weathering beneath some of the buttresses caused seepages that were difficult to repair. It was a small fault beneath the foundation that caused the collapse of the Malpasset Dam, an arch dam on the Reyran River in southern France, in November 1959.

Another arch dam, the Monte Jacques Dam in Spain, had to be abandoned completely, not because of cracks but due to caverns in the surrounding limestone rock. The dam was built and its reservoir filled, but water leaked into and through the caverns. Despite attempts to seal it, it proved impossible to make the reservoir watertight, so it has never held water. The Kentucky Dam, on the Tennessee River, suffered similar problems. In this case they were cured, using hay, bitumen, and cement to seal the reservoir, but the cost was very high.

On June 5, 1976, the Teton Dam, in Snake River Valley, Idaho, collapsed. It was an earth dam 305 feet (93 m) high and more than half a mile (0.8 km) long. It failed as its reservoir was filling and contained about 109 billion cubic feet (3 billion m^3) of water, 97 percent of its planned capacity. The resulting flood covered 25 square miles (64.75 km^2) and left 30,000 people homeless. The large Vaiont Dam did not fail, but the overflow that occurred when a mountainside collapsed into it nevertheless released a huge volume of water and caused many deaths (see pages 137–144).

Risk of earthquakes

Very occasionally, a large new reservoir may trigger an earthquake. This is a factor that engineers and designers must take into account when planning to dam a river. A major earthquake, measuring 6.2 on the Richter scale, occurred at Xinfengjiang, China, in 1962; one of magnitude 6.7 at Koyna, in Maharashtra State, India, in 1967; and there have been others in Australia. They all were linked to reservoirs.

The phenomenon came to be called "reservoir-induced seismicity" (RIS), but the term is slightly misleading, because dam reservoirs do not induce earthquakes directly. What usually happens is either that water penetrates the soil beneath the reservoir, or that the weight of the reservoir compresses the underlying soil. In either case, the water pressure increases in the pores between soil particles and this increases the likelihood that the rocks will fail. Less commonly, the weight of the reservoir alters the stresses in the surrounding rocks. This also increases the likelihood that the rocks will move. If there is an earthquake, the danger is that the dam will fail, catastrophically flooding the valley downstream.

Dams tend to be built in places at risk of earthquakes. Valleys develop where surface soil and rocks are being eroded rapidly. Geologically, this often means the rocks have risen upward in the recent past and that there is a fault in the rocks beneath the valley.

The risk of earthquakes due to RIS diminishes fairly quickly. If the reservoir is going to trigger the release of stored energy in the form of an earthquake, this will often happen as soon as the reservoir fills. If it takes some time for water to penetrate the soil beneath the reservoir there may be a delay of a few years before the earthquake happens. Once the stress in the rocks has been released, the dam will cause no further earthquakes. This does not mean there will never be another earthquake, of course, but only that if one should occur, the dam and its reservoir will not have been responsible. The earthquake hazard should not be exaggerated. It is present only in certain dam sites. Geological studies can recognize and measure it, and dams can be built to withstand earthquakes.

What happens to the river downstream?

Most major rivers experience a large seasonal variation in the amount of water they carry. A rainy season or melting snow increases the flow, and once all the snow has melted away, a dry season reduces it. Dams regulate the flow, so it remains constant through the year, but this alters the river downstream of the dam.

Seasonal floods along the Colorado River used to deposit sand along the banks, forming beaches, but the slower, regulated flow downstream from the Glen Canyon Dam caused the sand to settle along the bed. Wildlife habitats changed, and scientists realized this was because these habitats needed the periodic floods to maintain them, so they tried reinstating the spring flood. From March 26 to April 2, 1995, the dam released water as fast as it could through the Grand Canyon. When the ordinary flow was resumed, 55 new beaches had appeared and 75 percent of the existing ones had grown bigger. Bank-side vegetation that had grown into the slow-moving water was washed away, marshes and backwaters were revitalized, and habitats were improved for many species. The flood caused minor damage to some habitats, but overall it was judged a great success, and scientists began looking at other rivers that might benefit.

The Columbia was a prime candidate, but the next river to be treated was the Trinity, in Trinity County, northern California. It was dammed in 1963, and the slower flow allowed vegetation to grow out from the banks, reducing habitats for turtles, frogs, insects, and fish, and gravel beds used by salmon for spawning filled with sand. Since 1991, yearly floods lasting several days occur when water is rapidly released from the dam. Similar treatment is being considered for other rivers. The issue is controversial, especially in those parts of the West where water is in short supply, but it does help to maintain natural wildlife in and beside a river while retaining the advantages of the dam.

Dams are very successful at preventing flooding, but in the past they have caused problems by damaging habitats and altering patterns of downstream sedimentation, and occasional dam failures have caused appalling calamities. There is a well-established link between large, newly built dams and earthquakes. Scientists and engineers now understand much more than they did even a few years ago about the way rivers transport water, about identifying suitable sites for building dams and how to build them safely, and about the wildlife habitats that rivers provide and how to protect them. The risks are being reduced, while the advantages remain.

Canalization

Rivers cause flooding because now and again they are not big enough to carry all the water that is trying to flow through them. One remedy is to alter the river channel itself, in effect by rebuilding and rerouting it. Levees (see pages 155–161) raise the banks of a river and thus are a form of river rebuilding, but the process can go much further. The river can be widened or deepened, bends can be removed, the bed can be smoothed and leveled, and the gradient of the riverbed can be increased to make water flow faster. Such major engineering of rivers is called "canalization," or "channelization."

On a still larger scale, canals are sometimes built to link two adjacent drainage basins and move water from one to the other. One of the most ambitious schemes of this kind would have redirected two Siberian rivers so that instead of flowing northward into the Arctic Ocean, they carried water south to irrigate farmlands in the Kyzyl Kum Desert of Central

Asia. That plan was abandoned, but when, some years later, it became evident that so much water was being diverted from the rivers flowing into the Aral Sea for cotton and rice irrigation that the sea was drying up, Soviet planners proposed to replenish it by diverting the Ob River. That scheme was also abandoned.

There have been ambitious engineering projects of this sort in the United States. Following the floods caused by a hurricane in 1928, the Kissimmee River, in south Florida, was canalized, radically altering the Everglades (see pages 150–155). About 106 miles (170 km) of the Rio Grande, on the United States–Mexico border, was also canalized between 1939 and 1943. Similar projects are planned or being developed in other countries.

The Jonglei Canal

One of the biggest of these schemes is in the Sudan and is supported jointly by Egypt and Sudan, as both countries will benefit from it. Work commenced in 1980 but unfortunately came to a halt in 1983 because of the civil war in Sudan. It was reported that a missile had struck and destroyed the drill being used to dig the Jonglei Canal. By that time, 161 miles (260 km) of the canal had been dug, out of the total planned length of 224 miles (360 km). Jonglei is the name of a small village in the area where originally the canal was to commence; it now begins at Bor, further south, but the name has been retained.

At present, more than half the flow in the White Nile is lost by evaporation as it passes through the Sudd swamps, a complicated network of lakes, swamps, and small rivers in southern Sudan. When it is completed, the Jonglei Canal will divert about 25 percent of the water flowing through the White Nile so that it bypasses the Sudd. The water will be held behind dams, from where it can be released for irrigation as required. The diversion will drain an area of land that is permanently underwater, providing opportunities for cattle breeding; it will also offer opportunities for fishing. The canal will supply an estimated 0.9 cubic mile (3.8 km^3) of water for crop irrigation each year, to be shared between Egypt and Sudan.

In addition, the plan calls for a second canal that would double this amount. The amount of water that would be made available to farmers is approximately equal to the amount presently lost by evaporation in the Sudd. By regulating the flow in the river, the scheme would also reduce by almost 20 percent the area of low-lying grassland that is flooded every year. In some years, the flooding causes serious damage. In the 1960s, the land remained underwater for so long that many cattle died. Over a number of years, nearly 6.6 million animals were lost.

Local people grow crops on higher ground during the rainy season, when the grassland is underwater. During the dry season, they graze their animals on the grasslands. The flooding is crucial to the present economy of the 2 million people of the region, but the provision of modern irrigation and drainage should allow them to modernize their farming. Nevertheless, like all major schemes of this kind, the Jonglei Canal project is controversial, and its long-term effects are uncertain.

Turning a river into a canal

Canalization involves altering the character of a river. A canal is like a river, but one that is built by engineers in a place where no river flows naturally and, of course, the water in it is static. The more a natural river is altered by engineering, the more it comes to resemble a canal. If levees are considered a type of canalization, most of the great rivers of the world have been canalized along at least parts of their courses, and in years to come, many more miles of river will be modified. Floodwater is usually lost, but canalization can be used to redirect it to where it is needed, as is planned in the Jonglei Canal project. Channels cut from the river can convey water to farmland for irrigation.

Canalization is very effective. Provided the size and route of the channel is calculated accurately, it will divert water that would otherwise have caused flooding. Two channels, a little more than half a mile (0.8 km) apart and 19 miles (30 km) long, cross a low-lying part of eastern England and discharge their water into the sea. They were built two centuries ago, and the water they remove has converted nearly 50,000 acres (20,200 ha) of marsh and swamp into very fertile farmland. In England and Wales, more than 25,000 miles (40,200 km) of rivers have been canalized for flood prevention.

Effects on wildlife

Unfortunately, modifying rivers in this way also has disadvantages, especially for wildlife. Many of the rivers in the Northern Hemisphere were once bordered by swamp or forest, and these environments supported many native plants and animals. Now, the swamps have been drained, many of the riverside trees have disappeared, and the habitats are poorer. Otters, for example, rest and breed in dens along river banks, in some places preferring to make these among the roots of large trees. Many of the trees have been removed, because at high flow the river washes soil from around their roots, and eventually they fall into the water. In their unaltered habitat the otters were little affected because there were always more trees, but such sites are much less common now than they once were, although conservation groups have helped many sympathetic landowners to improve riverbank habitats.

Riverbank trees shade the water, and their leaves fall into the river. Without them, there is less food for aquatic animals, and water temperatures are more extreme. If the riverbed is leveled, the wildlife is directly affected. In a natural river, some parts are deeper than others, providing a variety of conditions suitable for different species. Furthermore, big rocks and overhanging stretches where the river has undercut its bank provide sheltered places. Engineering usually destroys these differences, so the riverbed is the same everywhere.

Careful planning of canalization can now minimize the harm to wildlife. Avoidable damage to habitats occurs when rivers are brought under more control than is necessary for flood prevention. Indeed, excessive canalization can cause water problems quite apart from the effect on natural habitats. It can even transfer the flood risk downstream.

Shifting the flood elsewhere

When a river is canalized along a stretch where it is prone to flood, the water is made to flow much faster instead of overflowing. At times of peak flow this can cause a rush of water from the canalized section into the unprotected channel downstream, greatly increasing the peak flow there. There are no more floods where they used to happen, but there may be floods further downstream in places that used to be safe. The increased rate of flow may also cause severe erosion of riverbanks downstream of the canalized stretch.

It is also possible for canalization to transform an excess of water into a deficit. This happens if the more rapid flow increases the rate at which water drains from surrounding land, lowering the water table. When this occurs, sluices must be installed to control the flow into the canalized stretch. Canalization, therefore, reduces the risk of floods, but there are risks in engineering the flow of water in a river. Without careful planning, river engineering can produce serious problems.

Flood prediction

Levees, dams, and the management of rivers and wetlands have done much to protect homes and farms from floods, but so far it has proved impossible to prevent floods altogether. They still happen, even if they are less frequent than they once were, and when they happen they are often as destructive as ever. Although there is no way to guarantee absolute protection to property from floods, it has been possible to reduce greatly the loss of life. Nowadays, many people escape harm because they have been warned in advance of likely flooding and because a well-prepared emergency plan has been implemented.

Weather monitoring and forecasting is now fairly accurate for several days ahead. Satellites observe the entire planet, sending a constant stream of pictures and measurements that allow meteorologists to watch weather systems as they develop and move. Hurricanes and typhoons can be watched and tracked and their behavior predicted, at least approximately. You might think, therefore, that there would be little problem in telling people living in low-lying areas near rivers or coasts to expect floods whenever unusually heavy rain was on its way. Unfortunately, it is not so simple. Predicting a flood is more difficult than it sounds.

In the first place, the cloud that produces a cloudburst (see pages 37–42) is always one among many clouds. Any one of them might cause torrential rain, but only some of them will do so, and the culprits are not easy to identify in advance. Nor does a cloudburst necessarily mean there will be floods. It depends on where the rain falls. If it falls on level ground, it may simply drain away without causing any problems, but if it falls over hills and the water drains into narrow valleys, these may flood. If the cloudburst cloud is difficult to identify, it is even harder to figure out precisely where it will be when it releases its water.

Prediction begins with weather forecasting

Obviously, flood prediction must begin with weather forecasting. Meteorologists at the National Meteorological Center track the movement of weather systems all over the world, using satellite images and measurements as well as regular reports from surface weather stations, ships, and aircraft. When they believe that a particular system might produce rain that will be sufficiently heavy or prolonged to cause flooding, they notify the river forecast center concerned.

In the United States, there are 13 river forecast centers, each covering a very large area and several drainage basins. Scientists at each center calculate the risk of floods should their area receive the amount of rain that has been forecast. This information is then sent to state and local weather forecasting offices to be used in conjunction with the information from the National Meteorological Center. If necessary, watches and warnings are issued. Most countries operate a similar system for flood prediction and warning.

Hydrologists, the scientists who study the way water moves through and over the ground, relate the weather forecast to what they know about the area in which the rain is expected to fall. Part of their investigation is historical. Many people measure the rainfall near their homes, and some send their records to their national meteorological service. Measuring rainfall is not difficult, but obviously, if rainfall (and snowfall) measurements are to be included in the official meteorological records, they must be made with standard equipment used under carefully stipulated conditions. A homemade rain gauge will not be suitable for this purpose, although you can compile a record of precipitation for your own use with such equipment.

Reliable records of rainfall have been kept for many years as have records of floods. By comparing past floods with the amount and duration of rainfall that preceded them, it is possible to make a rough estimate of the kind of weather that is most likely to cause flooding.

River gauging stations

Records of river levels do not go back many years, but these important figures are now being compiled. They are made at gauging stations along rivers. A gauging station comprises a small building containing a chamber that is connected by pipe running below ground to a borehole beside the riverbank but not in the riverbed. Water flows into the chamber and rises to the same height as the water in the river; waves or currents, however, do not disturb it, so the height can be read easily and accurately, and small changes are clearly visible. The principle underlying the technique is identical to that of the Nilometer, which has been used for centuries to monitor the water level in the Nile (see pages 98–106). The same device also provides information about the height of the water table.

These levels are monitored constantly by an automatic device. In older installations, they are recorded, often at 15-minute intervals, by holes punched in a roll of paper. The roll is collected later for examination. More modern stations transmit data directly to a central point. These data reveal almost immediately the slightest change in river level or water table.

Storm flow and base flow

Combined with information about rainfall, records of river levels and water tables gathered over a number of years can be used to calculate how long it takes for rain in a drainage basin to reach the river under different conditions of soil moisture. Two flows are involved. One is the storm flow of water running directly over the surface. Obviously, this flow will reach the river first. The other is the base flow of water that percolates downward through the soil and travels downhill as part of the groundwater. These give a value for the time-to-peak, which is the time that elapses between the onset of heavy rain and the maximum water level in rivers. Once these figures are known for drainage basins that are well monitored, the calculations can be applied to other drainage basins, where the rocks and soils are similar but there are few or no instruments to make actual measurements.

Even then, the data are usually insufficient to allow the prediction of rare floods (of the kind that can be expected only once in 50, 100 years, or longer), because accurate records have not been kept long enough. To make predictions of this kind, the available data must be used in the construction of models.

Modeling rivers

Some water-flow models known technically as analog models are physical. Miniature hills and rivers are built, and water is poured over and into them to see what conditions cause floods. Analog models are also used to test flood defenses before they are actually built. Small-scale models of dams, spillways (see pages 161–168), and river embankments are subjected to different volumes of water traveling at different speeds, with instruments measuring the currents and turbulence in the water and the force water exerts on various parts of the structures. In real rivers, colored dyes that are harmless to wildlife are used to track the speed and direction of water flow.

Computer models are also used. These display their results as pictures supported by long printouts of numbers. Despite the pictures, computer models are entirely mathematical and highly complex. Numerical values for the height of the water table, the amount of moisture held in the soil above the water table, the characteristics of the soil and underlying rock, the rate of groundwater flow, the amount of rain, the capacity of rivers, and many other factors are fed into the computer. These values are then related to one another by sets of equations. The model is run first to test whether it reproduces the conditions that are actually observed from the values that have been fed into it. Once any errors have been corrected so that the model describes accurately the situation in the real world, certain of the input data are altered to see how the model responds under different circumstances.

Physical models are limited to actual, present-day conditions and structures, but a computer model allows scientists more freedom. If they feed in actual data from weather that did and did not produce flooding in the past and the model correctly predicts the floods that actually occurred, the conditions can be hypothetically altered. Rainfall can be prolonged, for example, and made more intense to see what conditions would be necessary to trigger a very rare flood. Prolonged but moderate rainfall can be allowed to raise the water table for another scenario in the model, then an intense rainstorm can be added. It is only a calculation, of course, and no such flood has actually happened, but should those conditions occur in the real world, the model calculations will give ample warning of the scale of flooding that might result.

Once a reliable model has been compiled of the movement of water through a drainage basin, its state is kept up to date. The model allows for the rate at which rivers carry water out of the basin. Consequently, by feeding in the amount and distribution of rainfall as it happens, the experimenters can be confident that the model always represents the actual amount, location, and rate of movement of water. What the model tells the scientists can be checked against the situation in the real world outside, so corrections or adjustments can be made when necessary.

Warning the public

Everyone who might be affected by a flood needs to be warned, but some people may require more information than a simple flood warning. Farmers, for example, need to know not only whether their fields are likely to be flooded, but for how long they will remain underwater. Emergency services need to know the probable depth of the floodwater. Will they need boats to rescue people and, if so, what kind of boats? If temporary accommodation will be required for those evacuated from their homes, for how long? Such information as this can also be calculated from the state of the area as recorded by the model.

Along coasts, the risk of flooding comes from the sea as well as from rivers. Storm and tidal surges (see pages 73–77) can be predicted more simply than river overflows, because they do not involve the movement of water below ground. Storms are observed closely as they move across the ocean, and with the help of satellite images and measurements from specially equipped aircraft, forecasters are now able to measure their intensity long before they cross a coast. They can tell the size of waves that a storm will generate, and it is not difficult to relate their arrival at the coast to the state of the tide.

Predicting tsunamis

Tsunamis (see pages 58–65) can also be predicted. Most tsunamis are caused by earthquakes below the ocean floor, although less severe ones are also caused by seabed volcanic eruptions and the slumping of sediments down slopes. Earthquakes produce shock waves, called "seismic waves," that are detected within minutes by seismic stations all over the world. Information about them is then passed to the Pacific Tsunami Warning Center in Hawaii; the Alaska Tsunami Warning Center in Palmer, Alaska; the Yuzhno-Sakhalinsk Warning Center on Sakhalin Island, Russia; and other centers mainly around the Pacific Basin. Scientists at the warning centers process the data in order to predict where and when a tsunami may strike and its severity.

Flood prediction is not perfect, but it is sufficiently reliable for its warnings to be heeded. All flooding of farmland and urban areas causes damage, but at one time, it also caused many deaths. Prediction has greatly increased the chance of human survival and of protecting property.

Safety

If you live on low ground near a river or coast, your home could be at risk from flooding. Find out the height of your home above sea or river level and whether the area has been flooded in the past. If you live in a town, you will know its elevation. This is the height of the town center above sea level. You may, however, need to estimate the height of your home above or below the center of town. If a river runs through the town you can use large-scale contour maps to estimate the vertical distance between your home and the river. If you live in the country, you can calculate the elevation of your home from contour maps.

The history of your neighborhood will provide a useful guide to the extent of the risk. If your family has lived in the same place for many years, you will know whether there have been floods during that time. If you arrived recently, the local library and newspaper will have records of any past floods, and staff at your nearest office of the National Weather Service will know whether floods are likely. Local National Weather Service workers and staff at the local branch of the American Red Cross, emergency management, and civil defense offices will also be able to tell you what kind of weather emergencies occur in your area and what plans have been made for responding to them. During any emergency, events happen quickly, and you will have little time to act, so you must know what to do.

Be prepared

You may have to leave your home. Agree with everyone living with you on a safe place on high ground outside where all of you can meet in case you become dispersed. Also, arrange in advance with a friend or relative who lives beyond your emergency zone to act as a contact. If you are dispersed, telephone the contact, who will then keep track of where everyone is. Make sure that young children know how to use the telephone, can dial 911, and can give their name and home address clearly. If you are warned of an emergency, write down the contact number and make sure everyone carries a copy. Finally, teach everyone how to turn off the water, electricity, and gas supply.

Food and other supplies

Floodwater will contaminate any exposed food it touches. Keep a store of enough canned food to last everyone for three days, and a can opener. Your emergency supplies should also include a portable radio and flashlight, with spare batteries for both, a set of car keys, cash or a credit card, a first aid kit, and any items that will be needed for infants or people with special requirements.

Store these supplies in strong bags that you can grab quickly and carry easily. Nearby, keep rubber boots for everyone. When you receive a flood watch alert, add to these supplies a sleeping bag or blanket and one complete change of clothes for each person.

When the warning comes

When the warning comes, you are most likely to hear it first on the radio or television. The National Weather Service broadcasts local forecasts and warnings continuously. These can be received by NOAA weather radios, usually over a range of about 40 miles (64 km). You can buy a weather radio that runs on either electric power or batteries and has an alert tone that sounds automatically if a watch or warning is being broadcast.

Whether you use a weather radio or rely on ordinary radio or television, once a watch or warning has been issued leave the receiver on, so you will be kept up to date. The first message will be a flood watch or flash flood watch. This means a flood or flash flood is possible in your area within the next few hours. When you hear a watch announcement, check your emergency stores. If the power fails, gas station pumps may be no longer work, so also be sure your automobile has a full tank. Also, fill the bathtub and clean containers with water. You will need 3 gallons (11.5 liters) for each person. In the case of a flash flood watch, be ready to leave home at a moment's notice. If you plan to drive to safety, load your supplies in the car.

Next, you may hear an urban and small stream advisory. This means that small streams and rivers are already overflowing. Low-lying areas, including road and railroad underpasses and some streets are underwater, and water is flowing back from some storm drains. The problem is not serious, but you should avoid the places affected. If there are children in your household, make sure you know where they are. On no account let them play outdoors where they could be caught in the floodwater.

Alternatively, you may hear a flood warning. This means that serious flooding has already started or is imminent nearby. If you are on low ground, move to high ground. If you delay, floods may cut off your escape route. If the broadcasts advise you to evacuate your home, grab your emergency supplies and leave at once.

If you hear a flash flood warning, the danger is serious. It may not be raining where you are, but do not let this deceive you. The warning means that there has been very heavy rain, probably a cloudburst, in nearby hills, and the water is flowing across the surface in your direction. A flash flood can advance as a wall of muddy, turbulent water, trees, rocks, and other debris, up to 20 feet (6 m) high and traveling at the speed of a train. If you are on low ground, leave at once for high ground. Do not delay. You may have only seconds to escape.

Storm surges and tsunamis

Storm surges also cross coasts suddenly, and they can carry water for some distance inland, cutting off escape routes. Warnings of severe storms or hurricanes will also warn of the expected storm surge. Follow the instructions you are given, and if you are advised to evacuate your home, do so immediately.

Tsunamis are rare events, but if one approaches people in coastal areas will receive a tsunami warning. Treat this like a flash flood warning and leave at once, heading inland. Do not attempt to return home until you hear over the radio or from officials that it is safe to do so.

Safety outdoors

Once you are outdoors, remember that the key to survival is to keep away from the floodwater. Go to the highest spot you can find. Do not try to cross floodwater on foot or in a car. If the water reaches your ankles, turn back and find another route. The road may have been washed away beneath the water and may be much deeper than it looks. If you miss your footing and fall you could be swept away before anyone can do anything to save you.

If the car stalls in water, do not try to restart it. Leave it at once and head for high ground. The water does not need to rise very far before the car will float away, out of control. If you wait until the car is floating before trying to escape, you may find it difficult, or impossible, to fight against the currents. Be especially careful at night. Visibility may be poor in heavy rain, making flooded dips and hollows difficult to see.

Never pitch a tent or park a trailer or camper close to a river or along a stream, arroyo, or wash, especially if there are dark clouds in the sky. A cloudburst can turn a dry streambed into a raging torrent in a matter of seconds. When choosing a camping place, also remember that heavy rain can trigger mudslides and landslides. Avoid camping near the foot of a steep slope.

If you hear of floods but are not affected by them directly, keep away from the flooded area. You may have friends or relatives whom you would like to assist, but the emergency services will be on the scene already. They are trained and equipped to provide whatever assistance is needed, and you will either be in their way or get into difficulties yourself and need their help. If food, blankets, or other materials are needed, an appeal will be broadcast, and you will be told the location of collection points.

After the water recedes

When the floodwater recedes, you will be able to move downstairs if you have been trapped indoors. If you had to evacuate, you will be told when it is safe to return home.

Floodwater is filthy. It carries mud and debris everywhere, and you should assume that it is contaminated with raw sewage. If it has entered your home, it will have made a great deal of mess, but you will be able to see clearly the height it reached.

Destroy all food that has come into contact with the water. It will not be safe to eat. A refrigerator door should be watertight, and if you have been away for only a day or two, at least some of the food inside it may be fit to eat. When you open the door, it will be immediately obvious if water has penetrated. If it has, discard all the food, including food that is above the level the water reached.

Do not drink tap water or use it for cooking without boiling it first. If your water comes from a well, this must be pumped out, and as it refills, the water must be tested for bacterial or other contamination. You must not drink the water or use it for cooking until you know it is safe. If you are not sure how to check its safety, your local public health authority will advise you.

Do not turn on the electrical supply or try to use any electrical appliance until all the wiring has dried thoroughly and been checked for safety. Check gas pipes for breaks before reconnecting the supply. When entering any building, do not use naked flames to help you see. There could be flammable gases trapped inside, and a single spark could cause an explosion. Make a note of any power or telephone lines that are down, and report these to the appropriate authority.

If you need medical assistance, go to the nearest hospital. If you need first aid, food, clothing, or shelter, contact the Red Cross.

Provided you listen to and act on them, official watch and warning announcements can save your life, but you should be alert to the risk of floods at all times. Cloudbursts are associated with thunderstorms. If you hear thunder over the distant hills, turn on the radio. A flood could be on its way. If you live near a river, watch its level after heavy rain, and start preparing for a flood if you see it rising.

Warnings will be broadcast if a tsunami is heading for your stretch of coast. Next, watch the sea. Look for a wave that rises up the shore more than about 3 feet (90 cm) higher than the one preceding it. If the water level then remains high for a couple of minutes before the water flows back, and the sea retreats much further than usual, it is likely that a tsunami will arrive very soon. Move at once to high ground well away from the shore.

Of all the catastrophes that severe weather can cause, floods are by far the most devastating and dangerous. They can and do lead to loss of life, yet with adequate preparation and warning, people who carry out a sensible plan without panicking have a very good chance of surviving unharmed. It may be impossible to prevent a flood from destroying or damaging your property, but there is no need to let it take your life.

SI UNITS AND CONVERSIONS

Unit	Quantity	Symbol	Conversion
Base units			
Base units			
meter	length	m	1 m = 3.2808 inches
kilogram	mass	kg	1 kg = 2.205 pounds
second	time	s	
ampere	electric current	A	
kelvin	thermodynamic temperature	K	1 K = 1°C = 1.8°F
candela	luminous intensity	cd	
mole	amount of substance	mol	
Supplementary units			
radian	plane angle	rad	p/2 rad = 90°
steradian	solid angle	sr	
Derived units			
coulomb	quantity of electricity	C	
cubic meter	volume	m^3	1 m^3 = 1.308 $yards^3$
farad	capacitance	F	
henry	inductance	H	
hertz	frequency	H_z	
joule	energy	J	1 J = 0.2389 calories
kilogram per cubic meter	density	$kg\ m^{-3}$	1 $kg\ m^{-3}$ = 0.0624 lb. $ft.^{-3}$
lumen	luminous flux	lm	
lux	illuminance	lx	
meter per second	speed	$m\ s^{-1}$	1 $m\ s^{-1}$ = 3.281 ft. s^{-1}
meter per second squared	acceleration	$m\ s^{-2}$	
mole per cubic meter	concentration	$mol\ m^{-3}$	
newton	force	N	1 N = 7.218 lb. force
ohm	electric resistance	W	

SI UNITS AND CONVERSIONS (*continued*)

Unit	Quantity	Symbol	Conversion
Derived units			
pascal	pressure	Pa	1 Pa = 0.145 lb. in.$^{-2}$
radian per second	angular velocity	rad s^{-1}	
radian per second squared	angular acceleration	rad s^{-2}	
square meter	area	m^2	1 m^2 = 1.196 yards^2
tesla	magnetic flux density	T	
volt	electromotive force	V	
watt	power	W	1 W = 3.412 Btu h^{-1}
weber	magnetic flux	Wb	

PREFIXES USED WITH SI UNITS

Prefixes attached to SI units alter their value.

Prefix	Symbol	Value
atto	a	× 10^{-18}
femto	f	× 10^{-15}
pico	p	× 10^{-12}
nano	n	× 10^{-9}
micro	m	× 10^{-6}
milli	m	× 10^{-3}
centi	c	× 10^{-2}
deci	d	× 10^{-1}
deca	da	× 10
hecto	h	× 10^2
kilo	k	× 10^3
mega	M	× 10^6
giga	G	× 10^9
tera	T	× 10^{12}

Bibliography and further reading

"Agriculture Goes International." Egypt State Information Service. Available on-line. URL: http://www.sis.gov.eg/egyptinf/economy/html/eep/html/text25.htm. Accessed November 5, 2002.

Allaby, Michael. *Basics of Environmental Science, Second Edition.* New York: Routledge, 2000.

———. *Deserts.* New York: Facts On File, 2001.

———. *Elements: Earth.* New York: Facts On File, 1993.

———. *Encyclopedia of Weather and Climate.* 2 vols. New York: Facts On File, 2001.

———. *The Facts On File Weather and Climate Handbook.* New York: Facts On File, 2002.

———. *Plants and Plant Life: Plants Used by People.* Vol. 5. Danbury, Conn.: Grolier Educational, 2001.

———. *Temperate Forests.* New York: Facts On File, 1999.

American Red Cross. "Flood and Flash Flood." Available on-line. URL: http://www.redcross.org/services/disaster/keepsafe/readyflood.html. Accessed November 7, 2002.

Arnett, Bill. "Europa." Available on-line. URL: http://www.seds.org/nineplanets/nineplanets/europa.html. Updated February 26, 2001.

———. "Ganymede." Available on-line. URL: http://www.seds.org/nineplanets/nineplanets/ganymede.html. Updated October 31, 1997.

———. "Io." Available on-line. URL: http://www.seds.org/nineplanets/nineplanets/io.html. Updated January 10, 2001.

———. "Titan." Available on-line. URL: http://www.seds.org/nineplanets/nineplanets/titan.html. Updated October 20, 2000.

———. "Triton." Available on-line. URL: http://www.seds.org/nineplanets/nineplanets/triton.html. Updated October 13, 1998.

Arnold, J. B., et al. "Soil Erosion—Causes and Effects." Ministry of Agriculture and Food, Government of Ontario. Available on-line. URL: http://www.gov.on.ca/OMAFRA/english/engineer/facts/87-040.htm. Accessed November 6, 2002.

Asmal, Kader. "Dams and Development Harnessing Collective Energies." *United Nations Chronicle.* Available on-line. URL: http://www.un.org/Pubs/chronicle/2001/issue3/0103p50.html. Accessed November 6, 2002.

Bapat, Arun. "Dams and Earthquakes." *Frontline,* vol. 16, no. 27 (1999–2000). Available on-line. URL: http://www.flonnet.com/fl1627/16270870.htm. Accessed November 6, 2002.

Barry, Roger G., and Richard J. Chorley. *Atmosphere, Weather and Climate.* 7th ed. New York: Routledge, 1998.

Baumann, Paul. "Flood Analysis." Available on-line. URL: http://www.oneonta.edu/faculty/baumanpr/geosat2/Flood_Management/FLOOD_MANAGEMENT.htm. Accessed November 3, 2002.

Baur, Jörg, and Jochen Rudolph. "Water Facts and Findings on Large Dams as Pulled from the Report of the World Commission on Dams". *D+C Development and Cooperation* (March/April 2001), no. 2. Available on-line. URL: http://www.dse.de/zeitschr/de201-4.htm. Accessed November 6, 2002.

Best, Robert M. "The First Book About Noah's Flood That Makes Sense." Available on-line. URL: http://www.flood-myth.com/homecont.htm. Accessed November 6, 2002.

Bijlsma, Floris, Herman Harperink, and Bernard Hulshof. "About Lightning." Dutch Storm Chase Team. Available on-line. URL: http://www.stormchasing.nl/lightning.html. Accessed November 4, 2002.

Bueno, Juan Antonio, et al. "The Canalization of South Florida." Available on-line. URL: http://www.eng.fiu.edu/cegrad/case2.htm. Accessed November 6, 2002.

Central Intelligence Agency. "Nepal." *The World Factbook 2002.* Available on-line. URL: http://www.cia.gov/cia/publications/factbook/geos.np.html. Updated January 1, 2002.

"China Floods Kill 1,532 People Through Aug." Muzi.com. Available on-line. URL: http://latelinenews.com/cc/english/23743/shtml. Posted September 15, 2002.

CISRG Database. "History of Rogun Dam." Available on-line. URL: http://www.cadvision.com/retom/rogun.htm. Accessed November 6, 2002.

"Coastal Zone Management Act of 1972." Office of Ocean and Coastal Resource Management. Available on-line. URL: http://www.ocrm.nos.noaa.gov/czm/czm_act.html. Revised March 12, 2001.

Collins, Jocelyn. "Soil Erosion." Department of Botany, University of the Western Cape. Available on-line. URL: http://www.botany.uwc.ac.za/EnvFacts/facts/erosion.htm. Last updated February 1, 2001.

"The Comprehensive Everglades Restoration Plan." Available on-line. URL: http://www.evergladesplan.org/about/rest_plan.cfm. Updated June 2002.

CO_2 & Climate Resource Center. Available on-line. URL: http://www.greening earthsociety.org/index2.html. Updated November 5, 2002.

Daly, John L. "The 'Isle of the Dead': Zero Point of the Sea?" Available on-line. URL: http://www.vision.net.au/~daly/ross1841.htm. Accessed November 5, 2002.

"Earthforce in the Water." The Franklin Institute Online. Available on-line. URL: http://www.fi.edu/earth/water.html. Accessed November 6, 2002.

Emiliani, Cesare. *Planet Earth: Cosmology, Geology, and the Evolution of Life and Environment.* Cambridge, U.K.: Cambridge University Press, 1992.

———. *The Scientific Companion: Exploring the Physical World with Facts, Figures, and Formulas.* 2d ed. New York: John Wiley & Sons, 1995.

Federal Writers' Project of the Work Projects Administration for the State of Tennessee. "Tennessee Valley Authority." *Tennessee: A Guide to the State.* Available on-line. URL: http://newdeal.feri.org/guides/tnguide/ch09.htm. Accessed November 6, 2002.

"The Flood of '97." Available on-line. URL: http://www.canoe.ca/Flood/home.html. Posted May 23, 1997.

Florida Department of Environmental Protection. "Everglades Restoration." Available on-line. URL: http://www.dep.state.fl.us/secretary/everglades/default.htm. Updated August 8, 2002.

Food and Agriculture Organization of the United Nations. "Nepal Forestry." Available on-line. URL: http://www.fao.org/forestry/fo/country/index.jsp?geo_id=35&lang_id=1. Updated December 31, 2000.

Foth, H. D. *Fundamentals of Soil Science.* 8th ed. New York: John Wiley & Sons, 1991.

Frymer-Kensky, Tikva. "The Atrahasis Epic and Its Significance for Our Understanding of Genesis 1–9." *Biblical Archeologist* (December 1977), pp. 147–55. Available on-line. URL: http://home.apu.edu/~geraldwilson/atrahasis.html. Accessed November 6, 2002.

Geoscience Australia. "Tsunamis." Available on-line. URL: http://www.agso.gov.au/factsheets/urban/20010821_7.jsp. Updated September 15, 2002.

Glantz, Michael. "Diverting Russian Rivers: An Idea That Won't Die." Fragilecologies. Available on-line. URL: http://www.fragilecologies.com/oct09_95.html. Posted October 9, 1995.

"Hazards: Storm Surge." National Oceanic and Atmospheric Administration. Available on-line. URL: http://hurricanes.noaa.gov/prepare/surge.htm. Accessed November 5, 2002.

"Heavy Rains, Flooding and Landslides Hit Vast Areas of China." Geneva: ACT Alert. Available on-line. URL: http://act-intl.org/alerts/AlChFl-2-02.html. Posted June 13, 2002.

"Historical Events—the Vaiont Disaster, Northern Italy, 1963." Natural Environment Research Council, Coventry University, and University College London. Available on-line. URL: http://www.nerc-bas.ac.uk/tsunami-risks/html/Hvaiont.htm. Accessed November 6, 2002.

Hydrologic Information Center. "Locations Above Flood Stage." Available on-line URL: http://www.nws.noaa.gov/oh/hic/current/river_flooding/floodtable.shtml. Updated November 5, 2002.

IPCC Working Group II. "Summary for Policymakers: Climate Change 2001: Impacts, Adaptation, and Vulnerability." Intergovernmental Panel on Climate Change (IPCC). Available on-line. URL: http://www.ipcc.ch/pub/wg2SPMfinal.pdf. Accessed November 5, 2002.

International Boundary and Water Commission, United States Section. "Rio Grande Canalization Project: Environmental Impact Statement and River Management Plan." Available on-line. URL: http://www.ibwc.state.gov/ENVIRONM/body_canalization.htm. Accessed November 6, 2002.

International Rice Research Institute. "Rice Facts." Available on-line. URL: http://www.irri.org/Facts.htm. Accessed November 5, 2002.

Kent, Michael. *Advanced Biology.* New York: Oxford University Press, 2000.

Kidd, David. "Maryborough City Life." Available on-line. URL: http://dkd.net/maryboro/flood99.html. Accessed November 3, 2002.

Kriner, Stephanie. "Flood Disaster Averted Again in Siberian City." DisasterRelief.org. Available on-line. URL: http://www.disasterrelief.org/Disasters/010523Siberiafloods4/. Posted May 23, 2001.

Leung, George. "Yellow River: Geographic and Historical Settings." In "Reclamation and Sediment Control in the Middle Yellow River Valley." *Water International*, vol. 21, no. 1 (March 1996), pp. 12–19. Available on-line. URL: http://www.cis.umassd.edu/~gleung/geofo/geogren.html.

———. Yellow River Home Page. Available on-line. URL: http://www.cis.umass.edu/~gleung/. Modified April 26, 1996.

Long, Cynthia. "China Floods Displace 5.5 Million People, Create Poverty Trap." Available on-line. URL: http://www.disasterrelief.org/Disasters/990908chinaflood/. Posted September 6, 1999.

Lutgens, Frederick K., and Edward J. Tarbuck. *The Atmosphere.* 7th ed. Upper Saddle River, N.J.: Prentice Hall, 1998.

McCully, Patrick. "About Reservoir-Induced Seismicity." *World Rivers Review*, vol. 12, no. 3 (June 1997). Available on-line. URL: http://www.irn.org/pubs/wrr/9706/ris/html. Accessed November 6, 2002.

Marsh, T. J. "The Risk of Tidal Flooding in London." *Climate, Hydrology, Sea Level and Air Pollution.* Available on-line. URL: http://www.nbu.ac.uk/iccuk/indicators/10.htm. Accessed November 5, 2002.

Marshall, Jacques. "Population and Wealth, More Than Climate, Drive Soaring Costs of U.S. Flood Damage." University Corporation for Atmospheric Research (UCAR), National Center for Atmospheric Research (NCAR). Available on-line. URL: http://www.ucar.edu/communications/newsreleases/2000/floods.html. Last revised October 19, 2000.

Metz, Helen Chapin, ed. *Egypt—a Country Study.* Federal Research Division, Library of Congress. Available on-line. URL: http://memory.loc.gov/frd/cs/egtoc.html. Accessed November 5, 2002.

"Mississippi River Flood: 1993." University of Akron. Available on-line. URL: http://lists.uakron.edu/geology/natscigeo/lectures/streams/miss_flood.htm. Updated February 24, 1998.

Moore, Peter D. *Wetlands.* New York: Facts On File, 2000.

National Weather Service. "Flood Forecasting." Available on-line. URL: http://www.wrh.noaa.gov/cnrfc/flood_forecasting.html. Modified July 16, 2002.

———. "IWIN National Warnings Area: Warning Categories." Available on-line. URL: http://iwin.nws.noaa.gov/iwin/nationalwarnings.html. Accessed November 7, 2002.

———. "National Hydrologic Summary." Available on-line. URL: http://iwin.nws.noaa/gov/iwin/us/nationalflood.html. Accessed November 4, 2002.

———. Office of Hydrologic Development. Available on-line. URL: http://www.nws.noaa.gov/oh/. Modified August 29, 2002.

———. Pacific Tsunami Warning Center. Available on-line. URL: http://www.prh.noaa.gov/pr/ptwc/. Accessed November 7, 2002.

———. "River Forecast Centers." Available on-line. URL: http://www.srh.noaa.gov/rfc/html.srrfc.html. Modified March 19, 2002.

———. "Watch, Warning and Advisory Display." Available on-line. URL: http://www.spc.noaa.gov/products/wwa/. Updated every 5 minutes.

———. West Coast and Alaska Tsunami Warning Center. Available on-line. URL: http://wcatwc.arh.noaa.gov/. Updated July 10, 2002.

National Wetlands Conservation Alliance. Available on-line. URL: http://users.erols.com/wetlandg/. Accessed November 6, 2002.

Nelson, Stephen A. "Hazards Associated with Flooding." *Flooding Hazards, Prediction and Human Intervention.* Tulane University. Available on-line. URL: http://www.tulane.edu/~sanelson/geol204/floodhaz.htm. Updated July 29, 2002.

Nepal Home Page. Available on-line. URL: http://www.info-nepal.com/firstpage/. Accessed November 5, 2002.

"The Netherlands: Tulips and Windmills." Available on-line. URL: http://www2.wizards.net/ccraig/holland/pieterStory.htm. Updated April 26, 2000.

"1903 Heppner Flood." Available on-line. URL: http://www.rootsweb.com/~ormorrow/HeppnerFlood.htm. Posted January 19, 2002.

Oke, T.R. *Boundary Layer Climates.* 2d ed. New York: Routledge, 1987.

Oliver, John E., and John J. Hidore. *Climatology: An Atmospheric Science.* 2d ed. Upper Saddle River, N.J.: Prentice Hall, 2002.

Plotnikova, Rita. "Siberian Flood Waters Wreak Havoc." International Federation of Red Cross and Red Crescent Societies. Available on-line. URL: http://www.ifrc.org/docs/news/01/052301/. Posted May 23, 2001.

The Ramsar Convention on Wetlands. Available on-line. URL: http://www.ramsar.org/. Updated November 6, 2002.

Rekenthaler, Doug. "Thousands Missing After Major Levee Collapses Along Yangtze in China." DisasterRelief.org. Available on-line. URL: http://www.disasterrelief.org/Disasters/980808China7/. Posted August 8, 1998.

Rosenberg, Matt. "Polders and Dykes of the Netherlands." About. Available on-line. URL: http://geography.about.com/library/weekly/aa03300a.htm. Accessed November 5, 2002.

Sa'oudi, Mohammed Abdel-Ghani. "An Overview of the Egyptian-Sudanese Jonglei Canal Project." *International Politics Journal.* Available on-line. URL: http://www.siyassa.org.eg/ESiyassa/ahram/2001/1/1/STUD4.htm. Posted January 2001.

Seismology Research Centre. "Dams and Earthquakes." Available on-line. URL: http://www.seis.com.au/Basics/Dams.html. Modified October 30, 2002.

Sevada, Andrea Matles, ed. *Nepal—a Country Study.* Federal Research Division, Library of Congress. Available on-line. URL: http://memory.loc.gov/frd/cs/nptoc.html. Accessed November 5, 2002.

Tennessee Valley Authority. Available on-line. URL: http://www.tva.gov/. Accessed November 6, 2002.

Thieler, E. Robert, and Erika S. Hammer-Klose. "National Assessment of Coastal Vulnerability to Sea-Level Rise." U.S. Geological Survey. Available on-line. URL: http://pubs.usgs.gov/openfile/of99-593/pages.res.html. Accessed November 2002.

Trimel, Suzanne. "Discovery of Human Artifacts Below Surface of Black Sea Backs Theory by Columbia University Faculty of Ancient Flood." *Earth Institute News.* Available on-line. URL: http://www.earthinstitute.columbia.edu/news/story9_1.html. Posted September 13, 2000.

"The Tsunami Warning System." Available on-line. URL: http://www.geophys.washington.edu/tsunami/general/warning/warning.html. Accessed November 7,2002.

UN Office for the Coordination of Humanitarian Affairs (OCHA). "Algeria—Floods." OCHA Situation Report 7. Available on-line. URL: http://www.reliefweb.int/w/rwb.nsf/6686f45896fl5dbc852567ae00530132/003696al4bb6c65585256b100061d469?OpenDocument. Posted November 26, 2001.

US Agency for International Development (USAID). "Algeria—Floods Fact Sheet #1 (FY02)." Available on-line. URL: http://www.reliefweb.int/w/rwb.nsf/6686f45896fl5dbc852567ae00530132/de4697b6727de8e049256b170007a50e?OpenDocument. Posted November 30, 2001.

USC Tsunami Research Group. University of Southern California. Available on-line. URL: http://www.usc.edu/dept/tsunamis/index.html. Accessed November 4, 2002.

———. "Papua New Guinea July 31–August 8, 1998." Available on-line. URL: http://www.usc.edu/dept/tsunamis/PNG/. Accessed November 4, 2002.

U.S. Fish and Wildlife Service. "National Coastal Wetlands Conservation Grant Program." Available on-line. URL: http://www.fws.gov/cep.cwgcover.html. Updated July 30, 2002.

U.S. Geological Survey. Available on-line. URL: http://www.usgs.gov/. Last modified November 1, 2002.

———. "Flash Flood Laboratory." Available on-line. URL: http://www.cira.colostate.edu/fflab/international.htm. Accessed November 7, 2002.

———. "National Assessment of Coastal Vulnerability to Sea-Level Rise." Available on-line. URL: http://pubs.usgs.gov/openfile/of00-179/pages/data.html. Modified September 6, 2001.

————. "Prediction." Available on-line. URL: http://www.cira.colostate.edu/fflab/prediction.htm. Accessed November 7, 2002.

————. "Tsunamis and Earthquakes." Available on-line. URL: http://walrus.wr.usgs.gov/tsunami/. Modified August 3, 2001.

U.S. Global Change Research Information Office. "Soil and Sediment Erosion." Available on-line. URL: http://www.gcrio.org/geo/soil.html. Accessed November 6, 2002.

"VVV Noord-Holland: About the Province." North Holland Tourist Board. Available on-line. URL: http://www.noord-holland-tourist.nl/uk/emolens.htm. Accessed November 5, 2002.

The Weather Channel. "Forecasting Floods." *Storm Encyclopedia*. Available on-line. URL: http://www.weather.com/encyclopedia/flood./forecast.html. Accessed November 7, 2002.

World Bank. "World Bank Lending for Large Dams: A Preliminary Review of Impacts." Available on-line. URL: http://wbln0018.worldbank.org/oed/oeddoclib.nsf/3ff836dc39b23cef85256885007b956b/bb68e3aeed5d12a4852567f5005d8d95?OpenDocument. Posted January 9, 1996.

Wright, Jerry, and Gary Sands. "Planning an Agricultural Subsurface Drainage System." *Agricultural Drainage*. Available on-line. URL: http://www.extension.umn.edu/distribution/cropsystems/DC7685.html. Accessed November 6, 2002.

Yazoo-Mississippi Delta Levee District. Available on-line. URL: http://www.leveeboard.org/. Modified July 17, 2002.

Yuzhno-Sakhalinsk Tsunami Warning Center. Available on-line. URL: http://www.science.sakhalin.ru/Tsunami/. Accessed November 7, 2002.

Zavisa, John. "How Lightning Works." Howstuffworks. Available on-line. URL: http://www.howstuffworks.com/lightning.htm. Accessed November 4, 2002.

Index

Page numbers in *italic* refer to illustrations.

A

absolute humidity 16
absolute instability 44, *45*
absolute stability 44, *45*
adhesion water 20, *20*
African monsoons 84
Afsluitdijk Dam (Netherlands)
   121
agriculture
   crop losses to floods 130
   field drainage 145–150
   Nile floods and Aswân
     Dams 98–106
   polders 4–5, 120–124
   and soil erosion 134–135
   terracing 135, *135*
   wet rice farming 106–111
Aguamilpa Dam (Mexico) 162
air pressure 74–76
Algiers (Algeria) 40, 129
alluvium 34, 99
Amazon River basin 26
amphidromic points 71, 72, 77
anticyclones 79, 81
anvil cloud 47, *48*
Apennine Mountains (Italy) 93
aquifers 84–85, 87–91
aquifuges 85
aquitards (aquicludes) 85
arch dams 163, *164*
Archimedes 126–127
Arizona 163
Arkansas 142
Arkansas river basin 24, *27*
Arno River vii–viii, 93, 126,
   141
artesian wells (overflowing
   wells) *88*, 90
Arunachal Pradesh (India) 83
Assam (India) 83, 129
Aswân Dam (Egypt) 101

Aswân High Dam (Egypt)
   101–106, *102*
Atbara River 98
atmospheric pressure 13, 14,
   74–76
Atrahasis, king of Shuruppak
   138, 140
Australia 1, 3, 62, 141, 166
automobiles 128, 178

B

Baghdad (Iraq) 160
Ballard, Robert 140
Baltimore (Maryland) 114
Banggai Island (Indonesia) 58
Bangladesh 7, 29, 36, 83, 129
bankfull stage 40
barrier islands 119
Bartlett Dam (Arizona) 163
base flow 173
beach berms 3
beach erosion. *See* coastal
   erosion
Belgium 4–5
bench marks 114
Bengal, Bay of ix
Bernoulli, Daniel 34, 35
Bernoulli effect 34, 35, *35*
Biescas (Spain) 41
Big Thompson Canyon
   (Colorado) 49
Birecik Dam (Turkey) 162
Blue Nile 98
boiling point of water 13
Bolivia 126
Bombay (India) 78
Bosporus Strait 138–139, *139*
Bourke (Australia) 1
Brahmaputra River (Jamuna) 7,
   29, 129
Brazil 42

British Columbia 64
bulges, tidal 67, *67*–70
buoyancy 126–128
burst of monsoon 82–83
Burundi 98, *99*
buttress dams 163, *164*
Büyük Menderes River (Turkey)
   32, *33*

C

Cairo (Illinois) 142, 166
California
   monsoon climate 84
   St. Francis Dam 166
   San Gabriel Mountains
     drainage basin 133
   Trinity River 168
   tsunamis 59
calm before the storm 41
Camaná (Peru) 58
Cambodia 29, 83
Canada
   Bay of Fundy tidal
     movement 65
   British Columbia tsunami
     legend 64
   cost of floods 131
   glacioisostasy 113
   Manitoba evacuation 129
   Saguenay River 31, 42
canalization 168–171
Cape Fear (North Carolina) 73
capillarity 22–23, *23*, 85
capillary fringe 22, *22*
Caracas (Venezuela) 96
CCN (cloud condensation
   nuclei) 15
Celebes Island (Indonesia) 58
Changane River viii
channels 160
charge separation 53

Charleston (South Carolina) 3, 114
Cherrapunji (India) 78–79
Chiang Mai (Thailand) 29
Chile 58, 59
China
　deforestation 92
　floods as weapons 142
　monsoon 29, 129, 142–143
　mudslides 83
　tropical cyclones
　　(hurricanes) 73
　winter temperatures 81
　Yangtze (Chang) River
　　viii–ix, 5, 6, 157, 158
　Yellow (Huang) River 5, 6,
　　93, 142
Choqueapu River 126
cities, flood damage to 125–126
cliff erosion 115
cloudbursts 41, 49, 172
cloud condensation nuclei
　(CCN) 15
clouds 16–17, 41, 43–49
Clover Dam (Australia) 166
coastal erosion
barrier islands and 119
　glacioisostasy and 112–114,
　　113
　littoral drift and 73,
　　116–117, 117, 118
　longshore currents and
　　71–73, 116
　rivers and 119–120
　sea walls and 115
　waves and 115–119
coastal plains 3–4, 4
coastal wetlands 124–125,
　153–155
Coastal Zone Management Act
　(1972) 151
coastlines
　buildup 115–116
　erosion of. See coastal
　　erosion
　high- and low-energy 115
　shore zones 2
cohesion water 20, 20
cold lightning 51
Colombia 42

Colorado 42, 49
Colorado River 162, 167–168
Colorado River basin 24, 27
Columbia River 162
Columbia River basin 24, 27
computer models, flood
　prediction 174
condensation 14–15
conditional instability 44, 45
confined aquifers 90
Congo River basin 26
Connecticut 42
continental climates 28
convergence 79–80, 80
Corinne (West Virginia) 40
Coriolis effect (CorF) 71, 75
cost of floods 130–131
crevasses 157
cumulonimbus clouds 43, 45,
　50, 53
Cyclone Eline viii
cyclones (depressions) 73–74.
　See also tropical cyclones

D

DALR (dry adiabatic lapse rate)
　44, 45
Daly, John L. 114
dams 161–168
　Afsluitdijk Dam 121
　arch dams 163, 164
　Aswân Dams 101–106
　buttress dams 163, 164
　cascades 162
　consequences of 167–168
　construction 162–163, 164
　earth dams 163, 164
　earthquakes and reservoirs
　　167
　failures 166
　gravity dams 163, 164
　height of 161–162
　history of 161
　rockfill dams 163, 164
　spillways 165
　Vaiont Dam 143–144, 162
dart leaders 52, 54
Delhi (India) 81
deltas 6–7

deposition 15
depressions (cyclones) 73–74
desert floods 40–41, 133–134
Devon (England) 115
dew point 46–47, 47
dikes. See levees
diseases 106, 130
ditches, drainage 145–146
divides 24
Dort (Netherlands) 129, 140
downdrafts 48, 48, 49
drainage
　deforestation and flooding
　　91–93
　and flood prevention
　　145–150
　rivers and 24–28
　water movement through
　　soil 17–23, 85–87, 173
drainage basins 24–26, 133,
　173
Drance de Bagnes River 162
dry adiabatic lapse rate (DALR)
　44, 45

E

earth dams 163, 164
earthquakes 62, 167, 175
Egypt
　Aswân High Dam
　　101–103, 102, 105–106
　crop production 103–105
　Jonglei Canal 169–170
　Nile River floods 1,
　　98–101, 156
El Niño 7–8, 8
ELR (environmental lapse rate)
　44, 45
embankments. See levees
emergency supplies 176
England
　Bude storm 3
　canalized rivers 170
　Devon cliff erosion 115
　Folkestone flash flood 42
　Lynmouth-Lynton flood
　　(1952) 3, 37–39, 38, 143
　Severn River 143
　storm surges 77, 140

Thames Barrier 76–77, 112
Thames River 65, 143
entrainment 48
environmental lapse rate (ELR) 44, *45*
Epic of Gilgamesh 138
Equatorial Current 8
erosion. *See* soil erosion
Ethiopia 99, *99*
Euphrates River 98, 138, 156, 160, 162
Europa (Jupiter II) 12, 66
Europe. *See also specific countries*
    cost of floods 131
    floods 4–5, 143
    glacioisostasy 113
evacuation 129, 176
evaporation 13–14
evapotranspiration 16
Everest, Mount 92
Everglades (Florida) 151–152

F

farming. *See* agriculture
field capacity 21
field drainage 145–150
Finhorn River 143
flash floods 37–42
    in dry climates 40–41
    landslides and mudslides 41–42
    predicting 39–40
    warnings 177
flood barriers 76–77
flood damage
    to cities 125–126
    crops, destruction of 130
    diseases 130
    erosion. *See* soil erosion
    fatalities 128, 129
    to homes 128–129
    measuring 130–131
    salt water infiltration of groundwater 120–125
    to vehicles 128
flood legends and myths 64, 137–140
floodplains 5, 31–37
    formation of 31–34, *33*

land drainage and 150
living and building on 34, 37, 150
Nile River 99–100
types of 34–37, *36*
flood prediction 171–175
flood prevention 145–171
    canalization 168–171
    dams. *See* dams
    drainage 145–146
    levees (dikes, embankments) 155–161
    wetlands 150–155
flood ratings 1–3
floods, cost of 130–131
flood stage 40
flood survival 175–179
    after the flood 178–179
    during floods 176–178
    preparation 175–176
    in vehicles 128, 178
flood warnings 129, 174–175, 176–177
flood watches 177
Florence (Italy) vii–viii, 93, 126, 141
Florida 114, 124, 151–152
Folkestone (England) 42
forests 91–93, 95
France 59, 166
freezing 15, 46, *47*
Fundy, Bay of 65

G

Galveston (Texas) 73
Ganges River (Padma) 7, 29, 129
Ganymede (Jupiter III) 12, 66
gauging stations 173
al-Geili (Sudan) 40
Genesis flood 138, 139, 140
geostrophic winds 75
Gilgamesh flood 138, 139
glacioisostasy 112–114, *113*
Glen Canyon Dam (Arizona) 167–168
gradient winds 75
Grand Canyon 168
Grand Coulee Dam (Washington) 162

Grand Forks (North Dakota) 141
gravity dams 163, *164*
Greece 92
Greenland 113
groins 116–117, *118*
groundwater 84–91
    aquifers 84–85, 87–91
    definition 21
    irrigation and 105
    saltwater infiltration of 122–125
    seeps *88*, 89
    springs *88*, 89
    wells *88*, 89–90
Guadalentín River 166
Guadeloupe (West Indies) 49
Guyandotte River 40

H

Hachijo Island (Japan) 59
hailstones 53
Hanoi River 129
Han River 7
harbor waves. *See* tsunamis
Hawaii 59
heat lightning 51
Heppner (Oregon) 129–130
high-energy coastlines 115
highs (high pressure) 74–76
homes, loss of 128–129
Honduras 74
Honshu (Japan) 59
Hoover Dam (Arizona, Nevada) 162, 163
hot lightning 51
Hudson River 124
humidity 16
Hurricane Connie 141
Hurricane Diane 141
Hurricane Fran 73, 74
Hurricane Mitch 74–76
Hurricane Opal 73
hurricanes (tropical cyclones) ix, 3–4, 73–74, 76, 141
Hyderabad (India) 81
hydraulic head 31
hydrogen bonds *19*, 19–20
hydrologic cycle 9–11, *10*
hydrologists 1, 172

I

ice 46
ice dams 30–31
Idaho 166
Illinois 5, 142, 166
India 29, 78, 81, 83, 129, 162
Indonesia 58, 83
inertia 66, 68
instability, absolute 44, *45*
intertropical convergence zone
    (ITCZ) *79*, 79–80, *80*, 81, 82,
    82
intertropical front (ITF) 79
Io 66
Iowa 5
Iran 140–141
Iraq 138, 160
Isle of the Dead (Tasmania) 114
isobars 75
Italy
    Apennine Mountains
        deforestation 93
    Florence (Arno River) flood
        vii–viii, 126, 141
    Lake Maggiore flash flood
        and landslides 31, 41–42,
        126
    mudslides 42
    Vaiont Dam 143–144, 162
ITCZ (intertropical
    convergence zone) *79*, 79–80,
    80, 81, 82, *82*

J

Jacobabad (Pakistan) 78
Japan 59, 64
Java (Indonesia) 58
jet streams 81, 82
Jhagraku (Nepal) 41, 91–92
Jiujiang (China) 157, *158*
Jonglei Canal (Sudan) 169–170
Jupiter 66

K

Kaifeng (China) 142
Kentucky 39–40, 165, 166
Kentucky Dam 166

Khartoum (Sudan) 140
Kiewa River 166
Kimball (West Virginia) 40
kinetic energy 28, 31
Korea. *See* North Korea; South
    Korea

L

laminar flow 32
landslides and mudslides 41–42,
    83, 91–92, 96–97, 143–144
Laos 83
La Paz (Bolivia) 126
lapse rates 44, *45*
latent heat 46–47, *47*
laws of motion 66
Lempriere, Thomas 114
Lena River (Siberia) *30*, 30–31
levees (dikes, embankments)
    155–161
    augmenting 159–161
    failure 157–159
    Mississippi River 156–157
    and polders 121
Lhakwar Dam (India) 162
Lhasa (Tibet) 81
lifting condensation level 25,
    44, *45*
lightning 50–57
    damage from 50
    definition 51
    negative flashes 54
    people struck by 50
    stages of 51–54, *52*
    thunder 54–56
    types of 51, 56–57
Limpopo River viii
littoral drift 73, 116–117, *117*,
    118
loess 93
London (England) 65, 76–77,
    112, 143
Longarone (Italy) 144
longshore currents 71–73, 116
Los Angeles (California) 84
Louisiana 142, 156–157
low-energy coastlines 115
lows (low pressure) 74–76, *75*

Lynmouth-Lynton flood
    (England) 3, 37–39, *38*, 143
Lyn River (England) 37–39, *38*

M

Maggiore, Lake 31, 41–42, 126
Malaysia 83
Mali 140
Malpasset Dam (France) 166
Maracaibo (Venezuela) 96
maritime climates 28
Mars 13
marshes. *See* wetlands
Maryborough (Australia) 3
Mashhad (Iran) 141
Mauvoisin Dam (Switzerland)
    162
meanders 32–34, *33*, *36*, 36–37,
    160
Mediterranean sardine fishing
    106
Mediterranean tidal movements
    65
Mekong River 83
melting 46, *47*
Mesopotamia 98
Mexico 162
Miami (Florida) 3, 114
microclimates 94
millibars 75
Minnesota 5
Minnesota River 141
Mississippi (state) 142
Mississippi-Missouri River basin
    24, 26, *27*
Mississippi River
    channels 160
    floods 2–3, 5, 141–142
    levees 156–157, 158–159
    sediment in 136–137
    soil erosion reduction 119
Missouri River 28, 131, 142,
    166
mixing ratio 16
models, flood prediction
    173–174
mole drains 147, *148*
mole plow 147, *148*
Mongolia 1, 79

monsoons 78–84
    African 84
    arrival of 78–79, 82–83
    flooding from 29, 83, 129
    and rice cultivation 111
    summer 81–83, *82*
    winter 79–81, *82*
Monte Jacques Dam (Spain)
    166
Moon and tides 66, *67*, 67–68
motion, laws of 66
mountains 24, 25, *25*, 91–93
Mozambique viii
mudslides. *See* landslides and
    mudslides
Mullen (West Virginia) 40

N

Nasser, Lake 103, 105
National Geographic Society
    139
National Meteorological Center
    172
National Oceanic an
    Atmospheric Administration
    (NOAA) 65
National Weather Service 176
neap tides 67–70, *69*
Nebraska 166
negative flashes 54
Nepal 29, 41, *91*, 91–92
Netherlands
    Afsluitdijk Dam 121
    Dort flood 129, 140
    polders 4–5, 120–124
    storm surge 77
Neva River 143
New Orleans (Louisiana) 156
New York 124
Nicaragua 59
Niger River 140
Nile River
    Aswân High Dam
        101–106, *102*
    embankments 156
    floods 1, 98–101
Nile River basin 26
Nilometers 100, *100*, 173
nimbostratus clouds 50

NOAA (National Oceanic an
    Atmospheric Administration)
    65
Noah's flood 138, 139, 140
Norfolk (Virginia) 3, 114
North Carolina 73, 74, 119,
    165
North Dakota 141
North Korea 7, 29, 41, 130
North Sea 70–71, 72, 77, 112,
    121

O

Ob River 168–169
Ohio River 159
Ohio River basin 24, *27*
Oregon 64, 129–130
orographic lifting 25
Oryza spp. (rice) 109
osmosis 120
otters 170
overflowing wells (artesian wells)
    88, 90

P

Pacific Ocean, tsunamis and 62
Pakistan 78
Papua New Guinea 58–59
Paraná River 162
partially permeable membranes
    120
partial pressure 14
pascals 75
Pecos River basin 24, *27*
Peleng Island (Indonesia) 58
Pennsylvania 49
permeability, soil 87
permeable membranes 120
Peru 8, 58
Philippines ix, 29
Pitman, Walter C., III 138–139
plants
    and flooding 91–93, 95–96,
        146
    microclimates produced by
        94
    roots systems 94–95
    and salt 120

and soil erosion 18, 96–97
    transpiration 15–16, 93–94
Platte River basin 24, *27*
polders 4–5, 120–124
pore spaces 85–86
porosity 85–86
potential energy 31
precipitation, definition 11. *See
    also* rain; snow
predicting floods 171–175
pressure gradient 75, 76
preventing floods. *See* flood
    prevention
Puentes Dam (Spain) 166
Putnam (Connecticut) 42, 141

Q

Quinebaug River 42, 141

R

rain. *See also* rainstorms
    erosivity of 134
    on mountains 25, *25*
    records of 172
    and soil 17–23
    summer monsoon 81–83,
        82
    surface flow 17–18
rainstorms. *See also* lightning
    calm before the storm 41
    cloudbursts 41, 49, 172
    cloud formation 43–45
    precipitation from 49
    and river flooding 31, 38,
        39, 40
    storm cloud development
        45–49
rainy seasons. *See* summer
    monsoons
Ramsar Convention 151
Red River (United States) 141
Red River (Vietnam) 129
Red River Basin 24, *27*
relative humidity (RH) 15, 16, 47
reservoir-induced seismicity
    (RIS) 167
reservoirs 165. *See also* dams
    earthquakes and 167

reservoirs (*continued*)
    Lake Nasser 103, 105
    Vaiont Dam 143–144, 162
    Washington Mills Reservoir
      136
residence time 9–10
return strokes *52*, 54
Réunion 49
Reyran River 166
rice 106–111
    cultivation 107, 109–110
    description of 107, 109, *109*
    harvest 110
    parboiling 110–111
    production by country 108
    species and varieties 109
ring of fire 62
Rio Grande River 169
Rio Grande River basin 24, 27
river forecast centers 172
rivers 24–42. *See also specific*
    rivers
    aquifers and 87, *88*, 89,
      90–91
    canalization 168–171
    and coastal erosion
      119–120
    deltas 6–7
    drainage basins 24–26
    flash floods 37–42, 177
    floodplains 5, 31–37
    flood stage (bankfull stage)
      40
    gradients 32
    levees 155–161
    meanders 32–34, 33, *36*,
      36–37, 160
    seasonal flow 27–29
    soil erosion and 131–137
    soil transported by
      (alluvium) 34
    in spate 17
    speed and force (energy) of
      26–27, 31–32, 126
    wetlands and 152–153
rockfill dams 163, *164*
Rogun Dam (Tajikistan) 162
Ross, James Clark 114
Russia *30*, 30–31, 131, 143,
    168–169
Ryan, William B. F. 138–139

S

safety. *See* flood survival
Saffir-Simpson Hurricane Scale
    73
Saguenay River 31, 42
St. Francis Dam (California) 166
St. Louis (Missouri) 142
St. Petersburg (Russia) 143
SALR (saturated adiabatic lapse
    rate) 44, *45*
Salt Lake City (Utah) 133–134
salt marshes 154, *154*
salt water infiltration of
    groundwater 102–125
sand barriers 3
San Gabriel Mountains
    (California) 133
Sanibel Island (Florida) 124
Sanriku (Japan) 59
saturated adiabatic lapse rate
    (SALR) 44, *45*
saturated layer 23
schistosomiasis 106
Scotland 112, 113, 143
sea level 75
sea walls 112, 115
sediment and sedimentation
    119, 131, 136–137
seeps *88*, 89
Severn River 143
Shaanxi Province (China) 83
sheet lightning 51
shock waves 62–63
shore zones 2
Siberia *30*, 30–31, 168–169
silent lightning 51, 56–57
Smethport (Pennsylvania) 49
Snake River 166
snow 27–28, 49
soil. *See also* soil erosion
    alluvial 34, 99
    field capacity 21
    loess 93
    movement of water through
      and over 17–23, 85–87,
      173
    particles 85–86, *86*, 132
    and plant roots and 94–96
    pore spaces 94–95

soil erosion 18, 131–137
    coastal. *See* coastal erosion
    in deserts 133–134
    detachment of particles
      132
    and increased flooding 136
    length of slope and
      132–133
    plants and 96–97
    rate of, *vs.* rate of formation
      134–135
    sedimentation 119, 131,
      136–137
    speed of flow and 132
    terracing and 135, *135*
soil particles 85–86, *86*, 132
sound waves 54–56, *55*
South Carolina 3, 74, 114
South Dakota 141
Southend (England) 77
Southern Oscillation 8
South Korea 7, 29, 41, 131
South Platte River 42
Spain 41, 166
specific humidity 16
Spey River 143
spillways 165
springs *88*, 89
spring tides 67–70, *69*
stability 44, *45*
stepped leaders 52, *52*
storm clouds (thunderheads) 41,
    43–49
storm flow 173
storms. *See* rainstorms;
    thunderstorms
storm surges 73–77, 175, 177
sublimation 15
Sudan 98, 99, *99*
    al-Geili flash flood 40
    Jonglei Canal 169–170
    Khartoum flood 140
Sudd swamps 169
Sumatra (Indonesia) 58
summer monsoons 81–83, *82*
Sun, tides and 66, 67, 70
supercooled water 15
supersaturation 15
surface tension 23
surges 73–77, 175, 177

Swamp Land Acts (1849,1850) 150
Switzerland 162

T

Tajikistan 162
Talcahuano (Chile) 58
Tanzania 42
Tasmania 114
Tennessee 165
Tennessee River 131, 165–166, 166
Tennessee Valley Authority (TVA) 165–166
terracing 135, *135*
Teton Dam (Idaho) 166
Texas 73, 119
Thailand 29, 83
Thames Barrier 76–77, 112
Thames River 65, 143
thunder 54–56
thunderstorms 50
Tianjin (China) 73
Tibet 13, 81
Tibetan Plateau 81
tidal surges 73–77, 175, 177
tidal waves ix, 70–73. *See also* tsunamis
tide gauges 114
tides 3–4, 65–72
    bulges 67, 67–70
    coasts and islands and 70–73
    described 65
    Earth's rotation and 66–67
    measuring 114
    Moon's influence on 66, 67, 67–68
    neap 67–70, *69*
    spring 67–70, *69*
    Sun's influence on 66, 67, 70
Tigris River 98, 156, 160
tile drains 147, 149
Timbuktu (Mali) 140
Titan (Saturn VI) 12
trade winds 8, 79–81
transpiration 15–16, 93–94
trees 91–95. *See also* plants
Trinity River 168
Triton (Neptune I) 13

tropical cyclones (hurricanes) ix, 3–4, 73–74, 76
Tropical Storm Polly 73
tsunamis (harbor waves) ix, 58–65
    arrival on shore 63–64
    causes of 61–62
    legends of 64
    of the past 58–59
    prediction 175
    shock waves 62–63
    surviving 64, 177, 179
    warnings 65
    wave behavior and 59–62
Tsunami Warning System 65
Tunisia 140
turbulent flow 32
Turkey 32, *33*, 162
TVA (Tennessee Valley Authority) 165–166
typhoons. *See* tropical cyclones

U

Ulaanbaatar (Mongolia) 1
unconfined aquifers 90
United States. *See also specific states*
    cost of floods 131
    eastern coastal plain 3–4, *4*, 112, 113, 114, 119, 124
    flood fatalities 137
    floods 141–142. *See also specific states*
    lightning flashes, number of 50
    monsoon climate 84
    polders 121
    rice cultivation 107, 110
    river basins 24, 26, *27*
    saltwater infiltration 124
    soil erosion 133–135
    storms, cause of 45
    weather forecasting 172
    wetlands 150–152
updrafts 46–48, *48*, 49
upward discharges 52, *52*
Ürümqi (China) 81
U.S. Army Corps of Engineers 152, 157
Utah 133–134

V

Vaiont Dam (Italy) 143–144, 162
Vakhsh River 162
Vanuatu 59
vapor pressure 14
vehicles 128, 178
Venezuela 96
Verde River 163
Vietnam 29, 83, 129
Virginia 3, 74, 114, 136, 165

W

Walker, Gilbert 8
Walker circulation 8
Washington (state) 64, 162
Washington Mills Reservoir (Virginia) 136
water. *See also* groundwater
    adhesion 20, *20*
    boiling point and atmospheric pressure 13
    buoyancy 126–128
    capillarity 22–23, *23*
    cloud droplets 16–17
    cohesion 20, *20*
    force of 126
    hydrologic cycle 9–11, *10*
    and life on Earth 11–13
    molecule residence time 9–10
    movement through and over soil 17–23, 85–87, 173
    phases of 12–15, 46–47, *47*
    potential energy of 31
    transpiration 15–16
watersheds 24
water table 21, 105, 149, *150*
water vapor 13–15, 16, 46–47, *47*
waves
    and coastal erosion 115–119
    properties (behavior) of 59–62
weather forecasting 171, 172–173

weathering 132
wells *88*, 89–90
West Indies 49
West Timor (Indonesia) 83
West Virginia 39–40, 74
wetlands
    coastal 124–125, 153–155
    and flood prevention
      152–153
    loss of 150–151
    mangrove swamps 155
    Ramsar Convention 151
    salt marshes 154, *154*
wet meadows (water meadows)
  153

White Nile 98, 169–170
wildlife 167–168, 170–171
wild rice 109
windmills 121–122
winds
    geostrophic *75*
    gradient *75*
    jet streams 81, 82
    trade winds 8, 79–81
winter monsoons 79–81, *82*
Wisconsin 5

X

Xinfengjiang (China) 167

Y

Yacyretá-Apipe Dam 162
Yamuna River 162
Yangtze (Chang) River viii–ix, 5,
  6, 142, 157, *158*
Yellow (Huang) River 5, 6, 93,
  142

Z

Zambezi River viii
Zhengzhou (China) 142
Ziusudra, King 138